ROOTS & REFLECTIONS

ROOTS & REFLECTIONS

South Asians in the Pacific Northwest

AMY BHATT AND NALINI IYER

Foreword by Deepa Banerjee

UNIVERSITY *of* WASHINGTON PRESS
Seattle & London

in association with

THE SOUTH ASIAN ORAL HISTORY PROJECT *and*
THE UNIVERSITY *of* WASHINGTON LIBRARIES

UNIVERSITY OF WASHINGTON PRESS
PO Box 50096, Seattle, WA 98145, USA
www.washington.edu/uwpress

SOUTH ASIAN ORAL HISTORY PROJECT
UNIVERSITY OF WASHINGTON LIBRARIES
http:// libwashingtonedu/saoh

LIBRARY OF CONGRESS CATALOGING-IN-PUBLICATION DATA
Bhatt, Amy Pradip.
Roots and reflections : South Asians in the Pacific Northwest / Amy Bhatt and Nalini
Iyer ; foreword by Deepa Banerjee. — First edition.
    pages cm
    Includes bibliographical references and index.
    ISBN 978-0-295-99244-0 (cloth : alkaline paper)
1. South Asian Americans—Northwest, Pacific—Social conditions. 2. Immigrants—
Northwest, Pacific—Social conditions. 3. South Asian Americans—Northwest,
Pacific—Interviews. 4. Immigrants—Northwest, Pacific—Interviews. 5. Northwest,
Pacific—Biography. 6. Oral history—Northwest, Pacific. 7. Community life—North-
west, Pacific. 8. Northwest, Pacific—Ethnic relations.
I. Iyer, Nalini. II. South Asian Oral History Project. III. University of Washington.
Libraries. IV. Title.
F855.2.S69B47 2013
305.8009795—dc23   2012032694

Amy Bhatt dedicates this book to her parents, Pradip and Ranjana Bhatt, whose departures and arrivals made her own journey possible.

Nalini Iyer dedicates this book to her daughters, Mallika and Geetanjali. These are the stories of their community.

Together, we dedicate this book to the memory of Irene Joshi, whose vision and belief in the power of community guides this project.

CONTENTS

ILLUSTRATIONS

FOREWORD

G ROUNDED in the South Asian Oral History Project (SAOHP) sponsored by the University of Washington Libraries, *Roots and Reflections: South Asians in the Pacific Northwest* is a pioneering study of the
establishment and growth of the vibrant South Asian communities in the
Pacific Northwest. Unlike other histories of the region, this book unfolds
through the voices of individuals who were an integral part of building local
communities historically and who continue to shape them today. Their stories shed light on the complexities of pre– and post–World War Two immigration to the United States, the important role played by South Asians in
the development of the region's industries and businesses, and the South
Asian diaspora's rich diversity of culture. An example of community-based
scholarship, this book provides insight into the often undisclosed stories of
immigrant life. It represents one of the first attempts in the United States
to record pan–South Asian immigrant experiences using the method of
oral history. With more than 100 years of immigration to the region, these
communities continue to build a significant legacy in Pacific Northwest.

FOUNDING LEGACIES: THE DEVELOPMENT OF
THE SOUTH ASIAN STUDIES COLLECTION

The South Asian Oral History Project was initiated at the University of
Washington in order to preserve the memories and experiences of South
Asians who immigrated to the Pacific Northwest in an era when such migration was relatively rare. This project started with the vision of Irene Joshi,
former University of Washington South Asian studies librarian. Mrs. Joshi
worked for the University Libraries from 1970 until she retired in 2000.
A dedicated librarian and preservationist, Mrs. Joshi was the first person
to hold the position of South Asian studies librarian at the University of

Washington and she helped develop the university collection. Married to Rajnikant (Raj) Joshi, an immigrant from India, Mrs. Joshi had an interest in South Asian diasporas that was both professional and deeply personal. Under her leadership, the South Asian Collection at the University of Washington has achieved national and world renown. After identifying gaps in the collection built prior to World War Two, she worked to expand the collection with an emphasis on the social sciences and the humanities. She led the University of Washington Libraries' participation in the South Asian Cooperative Acquisitions Program, which brought together the Library of Congress and major American libraries to acquire publications from Bangladesh, China, Tibet, India, the Maldives, Nepal, and Sri Lanka. In addition, Mrs. Joshi compiled several bibliographies and databases pertaining to the field of South Asian studies more broadly. Her bibliography "South Asian Diaspora Literature Written in English" demonstrated her commitment to all forms of South Asian public culture and expression and is often referenced by scholars.

The South Asian Collection at the University of Washington has also grown under the leadership of several other committed librarians and faculty members. For example, a partnership between the University of Washington Libraries and the British Library led to the acquisition of the Gandharan scrolls as part of the Early Buddhist Manuscript Project. Former interim South Asian studies librarian Linda Di Biase also produced an online resource entitled "New, Thinking, Agile and Patriotic: 'Hindu' Students at the University of Washington, 1908–1915," based on primary sources housed at the University of Washington. Her research has been instrumental to scholars interested in piecing together histories and life stories of early South Asian immigrants to the Pacific Northwest. Starting in the mid-2000s, there was a significant expansion in the collection as the research needs of the Henry M. Jackson School of International Studies grew in scope and size. This expansion required a more strategic approach to the development of the South Asian Collection; at the same time, one immediate challenge has been to reconcile the needs of burgeoning interdisciplinary fields of research and South Asian specialization with the realities of declining university budgets. Thus, new community collaborations and partnerships are becoming even more vital to maintaining and continually enhancing the South Asian Collection with the right blend of contemporary resources and more traditional texts.

COLLABORATIONS: THE EVOLUTION OF
THE SOUTH ASIAN ORAL HISTORY PROJECT

The establishment of the SAOHP is one example of a community-based and collaborative project that brought together stakeholders in the university, regional donors and granting institutions, and wider community members. The SAOHP has helped to address a large gap in the historical record where there is little or no information about contemporary South Asian immigrants in the Pacific Northwest. This project has brought the library closer to its mission of promoting "respect for all human diversity" and its goal of serving increasingly diverse communities more effectively. It has opened many doors for future collaborations with other partner organizations to enhance the South Asian Collection and its visibility.

The SAOHP was initially funded through a generous grant made by Irene Joshi in 2005 after her retirement and was conceived as an effort to capture the life histories of a handful of South Asian immigrants who had immigrated to the Pacific Northwest in the 1940s and 1950s. Irene's interest in preserving these community memories was triggered by the death of an Indian friend who had migrated in that time period. Under the direction of interim South Asian studies librarian Linda Di Biase, the Museum of History and Industry (MOHAI) in Seattle was contracted to collect and archive the first set of interviews in order to make them readily available to scholars through the University of Washington Libraries Special Collections division. Julie Kerssen, a community historian at MOHAI, conducted these interviews and Amy Bhatt, then a doctoral student at the University of Washington, worked along with her as the transcriber for the project. The first set of seven narrators came from India and Pakistan and shared their amazing experiences, such as working on the early Apollo space missions, joining the Peace Corps, and studying at the University of Washington and other regional universities. They tell stories about overcoming cultural and economic challenges to get to the United States, establishing networks of family and friendship in a time when few South Asians lived in the region, and breaking new ground for future generations.

Soon after the completion of the first round of oral history interviews, I joined the University of Washington Libraries as the South Asian studies librarian. Amy and I revived the project. After securing an internal University of Washington Libraries grant, we launched the second phase of oral history collection. At this time, we established an advisory committee made up of community, faculty, and library staff members who nominated potential narrators and proffered suggestions and guidelines for the project. The advisory committee consisted of Prem Kumar, Bharti Kirchner, Nalini Iyer, Debadutta Dash, Keith Snodgrass, Joyce Agee, Amy Bhatt, and me, Deepa Banerjee. Not only did the advisory committee shape the selection of narrators but it also played a major role in securing funding from local South Asian organizations and individual donors. Amy transitioned from transcriber to oral historian and worked over the next five years collecting oral histories, editing and archiving materials, and acting as a liaison between the narrators and the University of Washington Libraries.

Since the initial set of interviews covered the experiences of South Asians migrating in the 1940s and 1950s, the second phase of the project sought to capture the stories of immigrants who came from the mid-1960s through the end of the 1970s. The mid-1960s marked a turning point for South Asian immigration nationwide. The passage of the landmark Immigration and Nationality Act of 1965, which created new opportunities for migration from South Asia, had the effect of substantially increasing South Asian populations in the Pacific Northwest. Thus, the next set of interviews captures the stories of immigrants coming in this critical period of changing national immigration policies. Ten narrators were nominated by the advisory committee, which strove for regional, linguistic, and religious diversity. Working as engineers, business owners, real estate agents, educators, administrators, doctors, and homemakers, the men and women interviewed represent a wide range of backgrounds. They include Indians, Pakistanis, and Bangladeshis, as well as Hindus, Muslims, Zoroastrians, and atheists. Their stories take a close look at what it means to be part of South Asian diasporas and document the challenges and struggles associated with integrating into American society. Discussing topics like developing their careers, adjusting to western food, practicing religious and cultural customs, keeping in touch with news from home, raising children, and responding to geopolitical events, narrators' stories enrich how South Asians are represented and represent themselves.

The third phase of the project covered immigrants who came to the United States between 1980 and the early 1990s. This phase records the experience of South Asians who were integral to the booming technology sectors of the Pacific Northwest, including businesses such as Microsoft, as well as many others who came to work in various regional industries. This phase is also characterized by the passage of new immigration legislation in the 1980s allowing for greater family reunification. Some of our narrators came through these new avenues, while others continued to arrive as students, workers, and refugees. Our archive ends in the 1990s because we see the 2000s as the beginning of a new phase of immigration from South Asia spurred by the dot-com boom and rapidly expanding technology industries—we hope these new histories will continue to be documented as the SAOHP unfolds. Currently, the SAOHP consists of an archive of nearly thirty recorded and transcribed interviews and photographs and is housed at the University of Washington Libraries Special Collections. The Digital Initiatives Department at the University of Washington has established an online database to make electronic versions of the transcripts and audio and video recordings widely available for public use. This database can be accessed at http://content.lib.washington.edu/saohcweb/index.html.

As the powerful and poignant stories of the interviewees were recorded, Amy Bhatt and Nalini Iyer realized that these histories could form the basis for a compelling book that situates narrators' stories against the larger social, economic, and geopolitical histories of the Pacific Northwest, the United States, and South Asia. Such a text broadens and deepens the SAOHP's impact and complements the oral history database. The book also marks another unique milestone: this is one of the very first collaborations between academics, the University of Washington Press, and the University of Washington Libraries Special Collections to create scholarship grounded in regional histories and South Asian communities.

◆ ◆ ◆

On behalf of the SAOHP and all of the people involved in crafting *Roots and Reflections: South Asians in the Pacific Northwest*, I would like to first thank Irene Joshi for her initial grant and vision, the Friends of the University of Washington Libraries, and the University of Washington Library administration and staff who have been essential to the completion of this project: Dean Lizabeth (Betsy) Wilson, Nancy Huling, Linda Di Biase, Nicole Bouche, Helice Koffler, and A. C. Peterson. The University of Washington Libraries Digital Initiatives has made the online database of the project possible and we thank Ann Lally, Anne Graham, Angie Rossette Tavares, and Theo Gerantakos for their innovative work.

Many thanks to our community supporters, including the members of the SAOHP advisory board, the UW South Asia Center, the Indian American Education Foundation under the leadership of Prem Kumar, the India Association of Western Washington under the leadership of Debadutta Dash and Nalini Niranjan, 4Culture of King County, the Microsoft Corporation, the Microsoft Corporation Matching Gifts Program, and the Boeing Company Gift Matching Program.

We would also like to acknowledge the generous gifts made by individual donors, including Joyce Agee, Akhtar Badshah, Lakshmi Gaur, Ganesh and Nalini Iyer, Rajnikant (Raj) Joshi, Bharti Kirchner, Prem Kumar, Zakir Parpia, Rao Remala and the Remala Family Foundation, Indu Sundaresan, and Vijay and Sita Vashee. Special thanks goes out to the University of Washington students and employees whose labor made this project possible, including Michiko Urita, Vasudha Swaminathan, Cara Nicholls, Rahul Mode, Nishant Sharad Satanekar, and many others. My deepest appreciation also goes to Joyce Agee, associate director of development for the University of Washington Libraries, who has been a tireless champion of the SAOHP and my personal supporter. I would not have come so far without her encouragement and guidance. I would also like to thank my husband and two daughters, Piya and Joyita, for their love and support—they are also very much a part of the community profiled in this book.

Finally, and most importantly, I thank all of the narrators of the SAOHP (whose biographies appear in the appendix). They have shared their time, homes, and life stories so that future generations might continue to learn from and admire the legacy they have worked so hard to achieve.

DEEPA BANERJEE
South Asian Studies Librarian
University of Washington, Seattle

PREFACE

THIS book is the result of many levels of collaboration; by its very design, the South Asian Oral History Project (SAOHP) has been a collaborative endeavor among the narrators, the University of Washington Libraries, members of the SAOHP advisory board, and the larger University of Washington community, including the University of Washington Press. As in any enterprise with multiple stakeholders, the content, parameters, and products of the project have been subject to rigorous debate. The transition from the SAOHP archive to a book has resulted in new collaborations and considerations, namely between Amy Bhatt and Nalini Iyer as co-authors. As scholars interested in feminist praxis and community studies, we drew inspiration from Amanda Lock Swarr and Richa Nagar, who write:

> Collaboration is not merely a set of concrete strategies or models with ethical dilemmas and conceptual difficulties that must be addressed and attended to. On the contrary, collaboration itself posed a theoretical challenge to and potential for rethinking transnational feminist frameworks beyond disciplinary borders, academic/artistic/activist divides, and North/South dichotomies (2009).[1]

Collaboration is by no means an easy task, as working together has meant undoing years of disciplinary training to produce a publication that examines community-generated texts alongside academic and popular culture materials. The work chronicled in this book is truly the product of countless hours of conversations, brainstorming, joint writing, revisions, and much more. We have deliberately chosen to cross humanities and social science methodologies to enliven and present these stories through various frames, even though neither of us identifies primarily as a historian.

Together, however, we have attempted to situate these oral histories within larger narratives of migration, and our own stories as South Asian academics and community members are inextricably woven into those same narrative tapestries.

Amy Bhatt: I found that my own experience of growing up between cultures, so to speak, as an Indian-American daughter of immigrants living on the East Coast piqued my interest in how the Pacific Northwest has proved to be fertile ground for a deeply rooted, and decidedly unique, South Asian community. My family's immigration history to the United States starts in the 1950s, though both of my parents were part of Gujarati diasporic communities living in Maharashtra, India. My paternal grandfather, who earned his Ph.D. from the University of London in chemistry and taught at universities in Mumbai, visited the United States in 1954 as part of international conversations aimed at bolstering nascent energy industries in India. He came to Chicago to participate in a technical exchange program developed between the newly independent Indian government and American scientists soon after World War Two. Impressed by what he saw, my grandfather encouraged his youngest son, my father, to imagine a life abroad. Nearly two decades after that visit, my father left Mumbai and arrived at John F. Kennedy International Airport in New York City as an aspiring engineering student in 1972. Coming to join his two sisters who were already living in the Philadelphia area, my father began studying and working odd-jobs to pay for school, ranging from gas station attendant to taxi driver.

Four years later, my father returned to India to marry and bring over his new bride (my mother)—a story that has been echoed in popular culture representations of Indian immigration as well as in many of the stories related by SAOHP narrators. Although he was hoping to complete his electrical engineering degree, he soon found that the cost of schooling was prohibitive and decided to find work on electronics assembly lines to support his new family. His entry into this work occurred just as companies were beginning to phase out such jobs in the United States after discerning that they could get the same work overseas for much less. Just as the electronics industry began to boom and silicon microchips became used in nearly every device, it also became more profitable to hire workers in India, China, Taiwan, Thailand, and the Philippines to produce them. Those very countries that once supplied a cheap pool of labor to the West to fill engineering, medical, and other technical positions had begun to offer even cheaper local populations

of semi-skilled and technically-educated workers, which helped shift manu-
facturing toward the global south. After a cycle of temporary positions and
what seemed like an endless tickertape of pink slips, my father decided to
take work as an exterminator with a small business to make ends meet. A
year into his moonlighting job, he joined the ranks of countless other Indian
small business owners and bought out the owner of his company. Built on
the unpaid labor of our family (and especially that of my mother) Filcco Pest
Control, as the company was named, became the buttress against which
my family's livelihood was built. It was not exactly the fulfillment of the
"American Dream," as our family actually experienced downward mobility
in the move to the United States with my father's transition from engineer
to exterminator. Nonetheless, my family began its complicated process of
settling into the landscape of suburban Philadelphia while attempting to
preserve the customs, traditions, and stories of life in India. Over time, and
in ways probably not even recognized by themselves, my parents made the
shift from sojourners to settlers. This was particularly the case as the family
grew to include children in the early 1980s. I am the oldest of three, and my
siblings—Rekha and Ajay—and I were all born in Pennsylvania.

Over the years, much of my extended family has moved to the United
States. After helping subsequent migrants through the process, my parents developed a nuanced understanding of the intricacies of ever-changing
American immigration laws. It is difficult to say if it occurred by choice or
necessity, but over time and particularly as they put deeper roots down in
the United States, my parents began the laborious process of reuniting their
family across the ocean. They have sponsored my maternal grandparents
and uncle's family to join us in the United States, while four out of five of my
father's siblings also settled on the East Coast. Countless other friends and
families continue to call on them for advice on how to gain entry into the
American immigration and naturalization systems, as well as in other more
mundane matters like enrolling children in school, applying for a driver's
license and car insurance, or where to shop for the best produce and spices.

I stepped out of this dense familial network on the East Coast to settle
temporarily in Seattle when I decided to pursue my doctoral degree at the
University of Washington. This decision to take on the PhD was not the
only break that I have made; more recently, I began the process of creating
a new life with my partner Kevin Bromer, who, having been brought up in a
mixed Jewish and Catholic household, is not at all the match my parents had

predicted for me. Nonetheless, with their support, as well as the blessing of his parents, Denise and Craig, and our community of friends and families, we embarked on the journey of building a life together that blends multiple cultures and backgrounds while continuing to honor each other's differences. While we had known one another for many years prior to making the formal commitment of marriage, the coming together of our families through a ritual like a wedding has certainly brought home the struggles and joys that arise from living your life as part of multiple communities—those that you are born into, those that you choose, and those that claim you. In making this choice to build a life with someone outside of my South Asian community, my own location within it has shifted in many ways.

Thus, as a result of growing up in a similar but geographically and culturally distinct South Asian community located on the East Coast, I do not easily fall into the category of a community insider. I am, however, trained in methods based in the social sciences through my interdisciplinary degree in feminist studies at the University of Washington. My research experience has given me the tools needed to serve as the SAOHP's primary oral historian. As a qualitative researcher working at the intersection of immigration and diaspora studies, feminist studies, and South Asian studies, I have been well positioned to act as an interlocutor of the life stories narrated. But on a personal level, my own history and position in the Pacific Northwest community helped build trust among the project participants. Therefore, there are significant differences between the stories elicited by the oral historian from the first phase of the project, who was not of South Asian descent, and those that I gathered. Narrators assumed that I was familiar with specific histories, customs, foods, or rituals since my parents had been born and raised in India. As a second-generation South Asian brought up in the United States, but living far from my parents, and as someone who was close in age to the children or grandchildren of many of the narrators, I also experienced the warm generosity of many cups of tea and plates of food, as well as plenty of invitations for dinner in the future. Several narrators assumed a tone of familiarity in the interviews that provide rich insight into everyday matters of immigrant life, forgoing much of the background information that is normally assumed for an audience less familiar with South Asian diasporic experiences. Moreover, while the SAOHP transcripts primarily capture the responses to questions posed by me, what is *not* fully visible is the "reverse" interview that happened after each encounter. Every interview was nearly always followed by a second interview of me in which narrators asked about my family background, educational trajectory, marital status, and future plans. At moments, these questions do creep into the oral history transcripts, alluding to the dialectical nature of the interview process.

At the same time, my position in the liminal space between researcher and community member also created some barriers to eliciting certain types of reflections from narrators. Since I have been involved in specific South Asian community-based organizations with progressive agendas in Seattle, it is also possible that narrators may have been more guarded about particular political views or perspectives. On one hand, I was viewed as a younger community member engaged in a noble project of discovering and preserving heritage. On the other hand, as a second-generation person, I also represented the difficulties of defining a community, even one bound by geographic, cultural, or political markers. Furthermore, even though I am undeniably part of specific South Asian communities, my class, caste, linguistic, and cultural background were mediating factors in each interview and point to the deep complexities of understanding any community as a presumed whole.

Nalini Iyer: I became involved in the South Asian Oral History Project when I joined its advisory board in 2006. As a literary scholar who focuses on South Asian American culture and as an immigrant from India, I was particularly interested in how these oral histories could be read as narratives that individuals use to fashion their identities within the shifting terrain of migration. In many ways, my experiences resemble those of the profiled narrators. My history is intertwined with that of diaspora, first within India and then to the United States. Family lore on my maternal side locates the origins of our clan in the heart of Thanjavur district in Tamil Nadu, though a great-great-grandfather migrated west to Palghat in Kerala for presumably economic reasons. In the early twentieth century, my maternal grandfather migrated from Palghat along with other relatives to work for the Tata Iron and Steel Company in Jamshedpur. He became a community leader in the small Tamil community there. Though he was well-established, family narratives resonate with stories about cultural loss, the alienation of children from their "native land," and tensions between subsequent generations around retaining Tamil culture at home while repudiating a negative "madrassi" identity. My mother left Jamshedpur in 1957 after she married my father, who came from a Tamil diasporic family in Trivandrum. He had moved to Mumbai (then Bombay) in the wake of Indian independence. Compelled to get a job to support himself right after high school, my father went to night school and completed his college education in electrical engineering. He eventually became an officer in the Western Railway system. As Tamilians in Mumbai, my parents found themselves within another diasporic community which experienced various forms of discrimination because of the shifting tides of nationalism and ethnocentric politics in Maharashtra.

I was born in Mumbai in 1966, eight years after my brother Ravi, and the cosmopolitan setting of the Railway community became my cultural milieu. At the same time, my brother and I grew up with the persistent sense of never being able to put out roots in a community because of the constant threat of job transfers for my father. When I was four, my father was posted in Madras, now Chennai, and, ironically, that was the first time in many generations that my family had lived in the land of Tamils that we considered our homeland. By some odd quirk of fate, my father's subsequent transfers were within Southern Railway and I completed all my schooling in Madras. In 1982, my brother, an alumnus of the Indian Institutes of Technology, Madras, left India for Purdue University to pursue a doctoral degree in computer science. Two years later, his wife, Chaya, joined him immediately after their wedding. My brother's first return visit to India was a critical moment of transformation for me. Never having imagined that I would be able to have a career, given that most of the women in my family married right after graduation and were primarily housewives, I was pleasantly surprised when my brother and sister-in-law suggested that I pursue higher education in the United States. Not only was I not trained in the scientific field like many of the young men (and some women) of my community, but I was also the first in my extended social circle to pursue a degree in the United States as a single woman. My conservative Tamil Brahmin community was both shocked and somewhat intrigued by my family's choice to support this decision.

As a graduate student, my research interests moved toward the then nascent field of postcolonial studies. My work was also highly influenced by feminist theory and women's studies. Consequently, I began my study of migration and diasporas and the ways in which writers like Salman Rushdie, Amitav Ghosh, Hanif Kureshi, Bharati Mukherjee, and others conceptualized and narrated diasporic experiences. In 1991 while completing my doctoral work, I met and married a fellow graduate student, Ganesh, who also came from the Tamil diasporic community in Mumbai. We moved to Seattle to pursue our careers in 1993 when the South Asian community was experiencing a population boom fueled by the success of Microsoft. As an academic interested in diasporas, I have since then been a keen observer of the Indian diaspora in the Seattle area. In informal social gatherings, events sponsored by the music society Ragamala and the India Association of Western Washington, and the academic circles of Seattle (notably through the University of Washington's South Asia Studies Center), I live the diasporic experience to which I now bring my analytic lens. I was drawn to the SAOHP for two major reasons: first, I am the mother of two daughters, Geetanjali and Mallika, and recognized that though they have a critical mass of South Asian friends and acquaintances in their schools, soccer teams, and other social arenas, few of these children have a sense of the history of this community in the region. It was important to me that such narratives archive the plurality of the South Asian diasporic community's experiences so that the next generation does not feel that it lives and operates either in a vacuum or in a world of irreconcilable binaries of "home" and "abroad" or "here" and "there." Secondly, I feel that the vibrant communities grown amidst the emerald green of the Pacific Northwest are distinct from other South Asian diasporic communities across the United States because of the histories of migration and settlement in the region and that they deserve to have their stories archived for future scholars.

※　　※　　※

Our desire not just to gather the stories of the community and archive them but also to analyze them drew us to consider co-authoring this book. As the oral histories unfolded, we realized that even though these stories were recorded and made easily available to the general public and scholars alike, these stories also needed to be contextualized within the larger history of the Pacific Northwest. Such a cultural history had yet to be written by members of South Asian communities who knew these stories intimately. Thus, the result is a collaborative project between community organizations, academics, educational institutions, local industries, and the many people who make up the region's South Asian diasporas. It is a narrative of transnational migration and community formation told through the myriad experiences of the men and women who undertook these journeys, experienced the exhilaration and adventure of creating homes in a new country, learned to cope with the losses and heartbreaks that such displacement inevitably provokes, and ultimately shaped the vibrant cultural, social, and economic life of the Pacific Northwest.

As authors of this book, we have many people and institutions to thank for their roles in seeing this project to fruition. First, we thank the narrators for their generosity: it is their stories, time, photographs, and resources that are reflected in the pages that follow. We are also deeply indebted to the University of Washington Libraries, particularly Deepa Banerjee and Joyce Agee, whose dedication and efforts made this book a reality. We are thankful for financial support from the many institutions and donors that contributed to the SAOHP and the book, as well as for the hard work of the University of Washington Libraries' staff and student employees involved in this project. At the University of Washington Press, we are grateful for the careful reading and feedback of Marianne Keddington-Lang, Marilyn Trueblood, Beth Fuget, and other staff members who helped with producing the manuscript, as well as the comments of two anonymous reviewers. We would also like to thank the following sources for giving us permission to reprint their photographs in this text: The University of Washington Libraries Special Collections; the Whatcom Museum; the Wing Luke Museum; the Vedanta Society of Western Washington; and Kris Gupta, Raj Joshi and the Joshi family, Bharti Kirchner, Prem Kumar, Amy Laly, Rizwan Nasar, Jeff Siddiqui, and the family of Asgar Ahmedi.

Amy Bhatt: I thank Nalini Iyer for her collaboration and friendship. As a scholar, mentor, and friend, Nalini has taught me so much as I have transitioned from graduate student to assistant professor in the course of this project. Our work together has spanned many years and has been a source of joy and invigoration to me. I count myself lucky to have met her when I did and look forward to future opportunities to work together. At the University of Washington, many thanks go to the South Asia Center and the Department of Gender, Women and Sexuality Studies. These rich communities have provided support and feedback throughout the project. At the University of Maryland, Baltimore County, I would like to thank the Gender and Women's Studies Program, the Dresher Center for the Humanities, the Asian Studies Program, and the Office of the Dean of Arts, Humanities, and Social Sciences for their support in the completion of this manuscript.

Finally, I want to express my deepest gratitude to my mentors, friends, and family, who have been sources of invaluable encouragement, Priti Ramamurthy and David Allen from the University of Washington, Shiwani Srivastava, for her close reading and keen editorial eye, Teresa Mares, Madhavi Murty, Juned Shaikh, Sarah Childers, our Seattle family of Phelps Feeley, Neha Chawla, Tim Jones, Greg Reaume, and the Games Group. Special thanks goes to my mother, Ranjana, who is the strongest woman I know; my amazing sister, Rekha; brother Ajay; and my grandparents, Niranjana Raval and the late Prabhuram Raval, who became immigrants in their sixties and provided our family with a foundation of love and support. More than anything, I am grateful for my wonderful father, Pradip Bhatt, who was taken from us suddenly before the publication of this book but whose legacy of generosity and love motivate and inspire me every day. Thanks also goes to the Bromer family, who have welcomed me as one of their own. Last and never least, my best friend and partner, Kevin: thank you for all that you do to make my life great.

Nalini Iyer: I thank Amy Bhatt for collaborating on this project. This serendipitous connection through the SAOHP has become one of the most valued intellectual and personal experiences of my life. Amy's vast knowledge, high aspirations, extraordinary editing skills, and sense of humor have all made this project a joy. I would also like to thank Seattle University, particularly Provost Isiaah Crawford, for support of my scholarship. I extend my deepest thanks to Femi Taiwo, Connie Anthony, Gabriella Gutierrez y Muhs, Jeanette Rodriguez, Sharon Suh, Tayyab Mahmud, Ki Gottberg, Mary-Antoinette Smith, Christina Roberts, Jacquelyn Miller, Vicky Minderhout, Greg Prussia, and Jeff Philpott for their friendship and support. Many thanks to my students at Seattle University, who have helped shape a lot of my thinking on diasporas and culture with their insights. Special thanks to Bonnie Sue Zare, my first collaborator, for her continued support and friendship. My "intentional desi family" in the Seattle area—Gauri and Ravindra Deo, Vinay and Kshama Datar, Meena Rishi and Niranjan Chipalkatti, Madhu Rao, Sonora Jha, Vidya and Punita Awasthi—I thank you for the many gatherings, meals, conversations, and advice, and for all the joy you bring. I hope this book will inspire the children in this group—Ishani and Sneha Deo, Neil Datar, Aseem and Devika Chipalkatti, Adi Rao, Sahir Jha Nambiar, and Isha and Varun Awasthi.

Finally, many thanks to my family—Ravi, Chaya, Sanyu, Deepak, and my parents, Seetha Narayanan and the late J. N. Iyer—you inspired and supported my transcontinental journey. Thanks also to my extended Jamshedpur clan in India and to my Bombay family, particularly R. Mahadevan and Rama. Such a project is never possible without the unwavering support of one's partner and children. My husband, Ganesh, has shared with me many life adventures these last twenty years, and my daughters, Geetanjali and Mallika, inspire me every day.

ROOTS & REFLECTIONS

INTRODUCTION: SITUATING STORIES

AN INTRODUCTION TO SOUTH ASIAN COMMUNITIES IN THE PACIFIC NORTHWEST

THE Pacific Northwest,[1] with its snowcapped mountains, bountiful waterways, and emerald forests, has long occupied a place in the American imagination as a site of exploration, discovery, and the conclusion of a nation's "manifest destiny." With a rich and storied history, the region has played host to old and new cultures coexisting in a sometimes tenuous, but always vibrant, balance. At the beginning of the twentieth century, it became the home of South Asian[2] immigrants who joined early Chinese and Japanese settlers to work in local timber, fishing, railroad, and agricultural industries. Since the time of that initial settlement, South Asian immigrants have made an indelible mark on the region: they have made basmati rice, Bollywood cinema, and Urdu poetry as much a part of the cultural landscape of the Pacific Northwest as fresh-caught salmon and summertime hiking. As the region's aerospace, technology, agricultural, and biomedical industries have expanded, so too have the populations of South Asians coming to work within them; these immigrants and descendents of previous settlers make up the communities that exist today.

South Asians' experiences of departing from beloved homes, arriving on strange shores, and adjusting to life in a new land are at the heart of the stories that define these communities. Stories, whether they are informal family lore, the backbone of literary imaginings, or the basis for nonfiction narratives, are the medium through which immigrants organize, interpret, and make sense of the realities produced by dislocation, migration, and cross-cultural encounters. Each immigrant, whether he or she migrated for education or employment, family or fortune, has a unique story about this journey. At the same time, these stories resonate with others who have traveled similar paths. These tales of going, coming, and adjusting circulate in living rooms, at potluck dinners, and at community gatherings. People tell these ordinary stories to make and preserve memories, to entertain others, to pass on a sense of cultural heritage to children and grandchildren, to educate outsiders about the uniqueness of their community, and to keep the connections between "back home" and "over here" alive. Though deeply personal, their retelling and interpretation offer insight into local, national, and transnational histories.

In the Pacific Northwest, stories are an integral part of how South Asian communities imagine themselves and relate to others. Though the region has long been home to South Asian immigrants who came in the late nineteenth century, new waves of migration have changed the character of the communities established locally. While some of these histories have been recorded, many of the experiences of early immigrants exist only in the stories shared by individuals. The unique yet universal nature of these stories aroused the interest of Irene and Rajnikant (Raj) Joshi. Raj Joshi migrated from India in the 1940s as a teenager. After attending school on the East Coast, he made a cross-country trip to attend the University of Washington, where he met, dated, and, eventually, married Irene. Irene went on to become the South Asian studies librarian at the University of Washington and developed a personal and professional interest in the history of South Asian migration. When an Indian friend who was another mid-century immigrant to the Pacific Northwest passed away, the Joshis realized that the stories of this early generation would dissipate unless someone acted to preserve them. Upon Irene's retirement, they made the donation to the University of Washington Libraries that laid the foundation for the South Asian Oral History Project (SAOHP).

With the Joshis' help, seven narrators[3] were identified and interviewed for the project. These narrators had arrived in the Seattle area between 1945 and 1960. Among those interviewed were Asgar Ahmedi, a Madagascar-born entrepreneur and businessman who once ran a booth at the 1962 World's Fair in Seattle; Padmini Vasishth, an Indian scientist who put her education on hold to migrate with her husband, but eventually earned her doctoral degree when she was in her sixties; and Sat Kapahi, one of the first South Asian engineers at the Boeing Company. The project was expanded to include narrators who came between 1965 and 1980 such as Amy Laly, a documentary filmmaker; Dev Manhas, a cardiac surgeon and founding

FIG. I.1 Irene Joshi, Seattle, Washington, 2004. Mrs. Joshi launched the SAOHP. Photo courtesy of Raj Joshi.

member of a Hindu temple in Bothell, Washington; Jamal Rahman, an interfaith imam and peace activist from Bangladesh; and Rajinder Manhas, a former Seattle Public School District superintendent. Additional stories were collected from narrators who came to the United States between 1980 and 2000, such as Rao Remala, the first Indian to be hired by Microsoft; Rizwan Nassar, a leader in the Pakistani American community; and Nirmala Gnanapragasam, a Sri Lankan Tamil professor of civil engineering. These narrators built local organizations, established their careers, raised children, and helped grow the various South Asian communities in the region. Now, their stories make up the backbone of a living archive of immigrant experience in the Pacific Northwest and are the basis for this study.

TELLING STORIES: ORAL HISTORIES AND COMMUNITY FORMATIONS

Though this book and the SAOHP cover several decades of immigration history, the individual experiences reflected in narrators' stories resonate across community lines and historical moments. They point to the importance of examining both large-scale and personal events in order to form nuanced understandings of how new communities develop and of the changes in the local landscape and culture wrought by their formation. At the same time, stories reveal the complications that arise when individuals must reframe their identities and national affiliations in order to fit into a new society. Former superintendent of the Seattle Public School District Rajinder Manhas reflects on how he sees himself today after spending decades living and working in the Pacific Northwest. Though he and his family are firmly established in the region, he relates, "I am an American. I have spent almost thirty-four years here. . . . But, I am Indian. I am Asian. . . . Yes, it will always be written on my face: I'm from India. You know, my accent, my language, my culture."

For Manhas, his path to becoming an American was not at all predetermined: several seemingly small decisions and twists of fate took him thousands of miles away from his natal Saroya, a small village in India, to the Pacific Northwest. Following an older brother who came before him to study in New York, Manhas arrived in Seattle in 1974. He came in order to pursue his master's degree in engineering and was drawn to the waterfront city because of the sizable aeronautics industry located in the greater metropolitan area. He had initially planned to spend a few years working after finishing his degree and then return to India, but ended up building a career in banking and public administration. Today he is a long way from the engineering degree that took him across states, nations, and oceans, but nonetheless, he is firmly established in the region through his career and family. While still not considering himself fully American, Manhas is no longer only Indian. He and the other narrators in this book reflect how South Asians have come to understand themselves differently as a result of living in the Pacific Northwest and how the region, too, has been changed by their settlement.

South Asian communities in the Pacific Northwest have roots in the early voyages made by young Sikhs across the *kala pani* (black waters) to the New World in the 1890s.[4] Seeking adventure and fortune, these men came as sailors and soldiers and made the journey from the fertile farmlands of the Punjab, then under British colonial rule, to the western shores of another English colony, Canada. Enticed by economic opportunities across the border and seeking refuge from oppressive immigration policies in Canada intended to stem the tide of new immigrants, Sikhs ventured further south into the United States and found work in burgeoning farming and timber industries. Over time, the population of South Asians waxed and waned due to American restrictions on Asian migration, particularly on the West Coast. However, by the early twenty-first century, the Pacific Northwest has become home to some of the fastest-growing South Asian communities in the nation and is recognized globally as an important site where South Asians are making an impact in various fields.

Today, South Asians in the Pacific Northwest come from all regions across the Indian subcontinent and represent a wide variety of linguistic, religious, and cultural groups. Many are polyglots who claim languages such as Urdu, Hindi, Gujarati, Panjabi, Tamil, or Bengali as their "mother tongues," in addition to fluency in English.[5] In the SAOHP, most of the narrators identify as Hindus or Muslims, though Christians, Buddhists, Sikhs, Jains, and Zoroastrians are also represented. Many narrators claim strong national affiliations to their countries of origin, though others identify with the regions in which they were raised or with transnational cultural or religious communities. While some grew up in small towns or in rural settings, most are urbanites who have lived in cosmopolitan cities like Mumbai, Karachi, Delhi, Colombo, or Dhaka. However, the terrains left behind by South Asian immigrants range from the arid deserts of Pakistan's northwest provinces, to snowy villages nestled in the foothills of the Himalayas, to the humid congestion of Sri Lanka's capital city. These homelands and ethnic connections continue to evoke deep emotions in those who have learned to appreciate the very different cloud-covered and multicultural environment of the Pacific Northwest.

Despite the long history and increasing numbers of South Asians settling in the region, there has been little scholarly or public attention given to why the Pacific Northwest attracted these South Asian immigrants and how the communities here have evolved differently than those in other parts of the United States. The SAOHP is one of the first attempts in the United States to record pan-South Asian immigrant experiences to augment the histories that do exist. Local institutions and community museums, such as The Wing Luke Asian American Museum in Seattle, and the Japanese American National Museum and the Chinese American Museum in Los Angeles, collect personal papers, oral histories, art, and other memorabilia and have been invaluable resources for preserving and propagating Asian American histories. Online archives hosted by Densho: The Japanese American Legacy Project, California State University, Fullerton, and the University

of California, Berkeley, have gone far in promoting digitally accessible arti-
facts relevant to Asian Americans and there is a growing body of academic
work that uses oral histories to capture specific community experiences in
Asian American studies.[6] However, South Asians are underrepresented in
these forums and the SAOHP at the University of Washington was partly
conceived as a way to add to these efforts.

This book is therefore grounded in the SAOHP and yet offers a broader
examination of how a transnational phenomenon like migration becomes
intertwined with the formation of local communities. In the last decade,
an increasing number of ethnographic and journalistic accounts have
focused on South Asian communities in particular states or cities, such as
New Jersey, Chicago, or New York. Many of these studies have used local
narratives and expressions of culture to generalize about the experience
of South Asians in North America more broadly.[7] This study joins those
works in further documenting the experiences of South Asian diasporas in
the United States, but also differs by emphasizing how the Pacific Northwest has become an important location to consider in the longer history
of South Asian migration. The book focuses on the experience of migrants
who have lived in Washington, Oregon, and Idaho, with special emphasis
on the Seattle metro area. The Seattle-centeredness of this project is largely
because of the connections made through the University of Washington
(which is located in the heart of Seattle) to create this pool of project participants. It is also partly reflective of the larger demographic patterns in the
region whereby many South Asians have come to settle in the greater Seattle
area, even if they began their journeys elsewhere in the country or the world.

While documenting how South Asians have dealt with education, work,
family relationships, gender roles, and community institutions as they settled in the Pacific Northwest, there is a central question that runs through
this project: how do these individuals represent themselves as South Asian
immigrants and as part of larger communities in the region? These questions are important, particularly in an era of globalization, when cultural
lines are increasingly blurred and the idea of who is considered a citizen is
changing with the expansion and rootedness of cross-border communities.
Too often, the term South Asian is used to refer back to the region from
which immigrants have come; as a result, this emphasis on the nation or
region of origin ignores how people from that part of the world have shaped
representations of South Asia and made an impact on local communities. It

also creates a false division between "locals," that is, authentic Northwest-erners, and "immigrants" who are not fully linked to the places in which they live. Because of the colonial and contemporary histories that bind dif-ferent South Asian nations together, however, we still use the term South Asian, but are more interested in not only how narrators connect to their countries of origin, but also the ways in which South Asian communities have affected the educational, cultural, business, and political terrain of the Pacific Northwest. In other words, the different facets of South Asian com-munity life in the Pacific Northwest, while sometimes seemingly similar to those in other parts of the United States, are shaped by a specific set of cir-cumstances that cannot be generalized. These stories also add to narratives about life in the Pacific Northwest by contributing perspectives from com-munities that are not often considered to be vital to the history of the region.

We turn to oral history sources as the primary data through which to tell these community histories. As a form of storytelling, oral history pro-vides insight into the everyday and even mundane matters that give texture to lives. Often community histories focus on large cultural displays, such as the building of mosques and temples or participation in public events like parades and marches. While those are important spaces of community expression, oral history allows for a more nuanced understanding of how communities are formed and how individuals situate themselves within larger cultural phenomena. It focuses on aspects of immigrant life such as creating friendships, starting families, raising children, and passing culture and traditions onto next generations.

In particular, oral histories are a useful way to highlight the stories of immigrant women, who are not always part of the visible representations of immigrant life because of their occupation as homemakers or because their work is less visible in the public sphere. However, oral histories bring women's voices to the forefront alongside men's because the focus of oral history is not only on public accomplishments, but on the meanings behind those accomplishments. At first glance, tales of learning how to cook in an American-style kitchen or figuring out how to be a good mother or daughter in a foreign land might seem stereotypical or perhaps less important than the stories of men building businesses, developing inventions, or holding public office. However, the experiences of those who went through intimate transformations, such as learning how to work an oven for the first time or raising children who straddle cultural norms and traditions, are the backdrop of immigrant life in America. In that way, oral history allows room for multiple voices to contribute to diverse representations about South Asians.

Oral histories also complement and reflect stories told or imagined through fictional or third-person accounts. Popular culture, media accounts, academic studies, film, and literature are often the basis for mainstream understandings about South Asian communities. *The Namesake*, by Pulitzer Prize–winner Jhumpa Lahiri, is a prime example of a widely read novel that reflects the challenges and joys that South Asian immigrants experience as they create lives in North America. *The Namesake* has become a paradigmatic text about South Asian American experiences and was turned into a popularly acclaimed film. As just one example of its impact, the Seattle Public Libraries featured the novel in its 2007 Seattle Reads program, which annually highlights a contemporary literary work and organizes year-long community events and readings around it. *The Namesake* follows the immigration and settlement of one couple, Ashok and Ashima, who migrate to the Boston area in the 1960s. Despite facing intense cultural alienation and the challenge of balancing the values of two very different cultures, the protagonists build a life and a community that is very familiar to South Asian audiences. As a young bride, Ashima is transported thousands of miles away from India and left to navigate the considerably foreign territory in New England on her own. In contrast, her husband moves more easily through the academic worlds that brought him to the United States.

Ashima's feelings of isolation and frustration are echoed in the stories told by narrator Shanta Gangolli about her adjustment when she first came to the United States in 1950. Like Ashima, who left her friends and family in India when she moved to follow her husband, who was a student in America, Gangolli remembers, "After we came, we were in Boston and I was very homesick the first few months. Because my husband got involved with studying at the university, and I was not sure what I wanted to do." She spent her early days trying to fight the loneliness of living away from the home that she loved and knew so well and to adapt to her new role as a wife and soon, mother. Her story shows the relationship between literary narratives and lived experiences, where life is often the inspiration for art. While there are uncanny resemblances between immigrants' life experiences and those that are recounted in South Asian fiction, stories—real and imagined—are important vehicles that capture the nuances and contours of everyday life.

Although Lahiri's work is firmly rooted in the landscape and culture of Bengali Indians in New England in the 1970s and 1980s, it has come to represent all South Asians in the United States. Similarly, the growing body of literary works by South Asian Americans like Bharati Mukherjee, Tahira Naqvi, Chitra Divakaruni, and Bapsi Sidhwa and films by Mira Nair and Nisha Ganatra, among others, create a canon of works that seem both ethnographic and autobiographic. Oral history is not simply a counterpoint to this body of narratives; as a form of storytelling, oral history employs similar strategies to a novel or film. In fact, oral history traditions prefer the term "narrator" to "interviewee" because of the ways in which oral history highlights the importance of stories as a form of knowledge production. In an oral history, the narrator is the protagonist who sees patterns, connections, and causality amongst occurrences and weaves the events of his or her life into a discernible plot with drama and emotion that draw the audience into the story. The narrator constructs these correlations when looking back on his or her life, even as the interviews are shaped by the questions and prompts from the oral historian. When the narrator is a prominent member of the community who has told her or his story frequently in public contexts, the narrative that emerges is sometimes intended to preserve a self-consciously constructed public image. In other words, oral histories are crafted narratives and should be read as such, particularly because narrators are constantly constructing their stories in light of their audience, the public nature of such stories, and their relationship to people, places, and events from the past. They are also personal histories that reflect how real (not fictional) people experienced major historical events as well as local and personal ones.

At the same time, any history that relies on oral sources has its gaps and silences. Narrators weigh the risks of revealing details about themselves to be publically immortalized. They worry about offending others or what their friends or family might think of their version of events. When narrators choose *not* to share a particular story, decide to recast an experience in a more positive light, or even just refuse to participate in the project at all, the public nature of the project is often at the forefront of their minds. Narrators are constantly determining how much to reveal, how much to embellish, and how much to reframe. Issues of veracity and accuracy abound in oral history projects as well; one's account of an event or experience may well differ from "official" accounts or even those of other individuals.

What is important, however, is that the story, the perspective, and the insight of each person are taken seriously and contextualized in broader accounts and histories. For that reason, we use oral histories as sources of information that are essential to consider when mapping a cultural history of South Asians in the Pacific Northwest. At the same time, we also examine these oral histories as narratives that reveal individual and community self-fashioning, and, where appropriate, we draw parallels between these oral histories and other types of narratives such as literary works, film, popular culture, or stories from the media to demonstrate how these narratives frame and interpret individual, communal, regional, and national identities. We therefore read these oral histories alongside other forms of representation in order to examine important themes that are central to immigration studies: work, education, gender, family, friendship, and community building.

CONTOURS OF THE BOOK: SOUTH ASIAN COMMUNITIES IN THE PACIFIC NORTHWEST

So, who are the South Asians that populate the Pacific Northwest? The individuals who make up these communities are overwhelmingly middle class and are concentrated in cities like Seattle, Washington; Portland, Oregon; Vancouver, British Columbia; and their suburbs. Census data from 2000[8] reveal that Asian Indians (or Indian Americans as we refer to them here) make up the vast majority of the South Asian American population and are estimated to number 1,600,000. In 2007, the U.S. Census estimated that the number of Indians living in America was closer to 2,570,000 and this number is expected to be higher still in the next ten years. In Washington State, the proportion of Indians to immigrants from other South Asian nations is decidedly high and follows national trends. The U.S. Census reported 25,651 South Asians living in Washington; of that number, 23,992 were from India. Another community survey from 2005 found the number of Indian Americans to be close to 41,583.[9] Many of these Indians live in metropolitan areas of Washington State. Comparatively, in 2000, 9,575 Indians were reported to live in Oregon and 1,289 in Idaho.[10] Moreover, roughly 65 percent of the South Asians living in Washington State live in King County alone, which includes the cities of Seattle, Bellevue, Bothell, Kent, Redmond, and Renton. Numerical estimates of communities alone do not explain the various factors that pull people to settle in a particular place, such as the presence of job and educational opportunities: the triumvirate of the University of Washington, the Boeing Company, and, more recently, the Microsoft Corporation has been essential in influencing South Asian migration to the Pacific Northwest more generally.

Today, South Asians in the Pacific Northwest come from all regions across the Indian subcontinent and represent a wide variety of linguistic, religious, and cultural groups. Despite this diversity, there are still limitations in representation: most materials available to researchers, including the SAOHP transcripts, are written in English and thus there is a dearth of narratives in South Asian languages. Also notably absent are the stories of immigrants from South Asian nations like Nepal that have distinct and rich histories of migration within and outside of South Asia or twice- or thrice-transplanted South Asian immigrants coming to the United States via former plantation colonies like Fiji or Trinidad and Tobago. National, class, and caste diversity are also likewise skewed in this study, as most narrators and publically available information are from Indian, middle-class, and upper-caste populations. Our hope is that the project and its methodology will open up these areas for other scholars to pursue. As authors, our own relationship to the SAOHP and commitment to the community-driven nature of the project also implicate us in this omission. At the same time, as oral historian and advisory board member respectively, we hope to highlight not only the very important stories of narrators, but also the silences.

There is much to be learned from a cultural and community history of South Asians, despite the limitations posed by our sources. These life histories reflect continuities across time periods that shape immigrant experiences, no matter when people arrived. In many cases, the taken-for-granted way of life that narrators experienced in their home countries no longer fit the new social, economic, and political environments that they encountered in the United States. At the same time, changes in telecommunications, the availability of cultural, entertainment, and religious institutions, and just the sheer increase in the numbers of South Asians have created a different landscape for more recently arrived immigrants. Considering the differences and similarities across the narrators' stories, it is clear that these oral histories cannot be viewed as some sort of definitive archive, but rather as a living database of stories that, taken together, create a lively and expansive quilt of experience.

In addition, the similarities that cut across the narrators' stories despite country of origin are also striking. For instance, Prasanna Samarawickrama's arrival in Oregon from Sri Lanka as an exchange student while in high school and his experience of adapting to American ways of schooling resonate with Rizwan Nasar's stories of coming from Pakistan to Michigan as a young college student. Both young men found themselves far from their families and home, but threw themselves into student life. Samarawickrama, who came from Colombo, and Nasar, who came from Karachi, both found the pace of life in Oregon and Michigan to be very slow and even slightly dull compared to the fast-paced cities of their birth. Nonetheless, each made the most of his student-centered environment and was influenced enough to decide to make the United States his permanent home. Even though these stories appear similar from the onset, the political, social, and economic conditions from which Samarawickrama and Nasar came cannot be easily equated; yet, they both shed light on the experiences of young South Asian students arriving to pursue their dreams of higher education.

While the narrators who participated in the project are far from a representative sample of the geographic, linguistic, or national diversity of South Asia, the stories that have been collected do offer a rare personal glimpse into the political and economic forces that cut across national borders. For example, stories about the effects of the collapse of the British Indian Empire that led to the independent nations of India, Pakistan, Sri Lanka, and eventually Bangladesh echo through nearly all of the oral histories recounted here. As survivors of the mass violence and relocation resulting from Partition or as "midnight's children,"[11] narrators show how political upheaval in South Asia has impacted the trajectory of individuals and their families. In that vein, the war of independence in Bangladesh in the late 1960s and the eruption of civil war in Sri Lanka in the 1980s also left indelible marks on narrators and in some cases influenced their decisions to leave home and move abroad. Such stories show how important specific geopolitical histories are to the conceptualization of South Asia as a region and how the histories of individual nations are intertwined across the region and reconstituted abroad.[12] In many ways, the long history of colonial influences and contemporary political and economic interactions between South Asian nations binds the region together, while common cultural elements also create a sense of shared values and traditions.

Considering that South Asian history is rich and well-documented, oral histories of South Asians in America must also be carefully situated against larger historical backdrops. In some cases, oral histories can reinforce conventional ideas about historical events because they are told from a first-person perspective and may reflect well-known and rehearsed renditions of events. At the same time, histories of war and trauma also have material consequences for both memory and recollection of experiences. For example, narrators who lived through various forms of civil war were sometimes reluctant to directly comment on the politics that were in motion during times of upheaval. Still, through their accounts of daily traumas in those periods, we are offered a glimpse into the ways that people negotiated such disruptions and how those ruptures connected to and, in some cases, ensured their migration. Najma Rizvi first came to the United States from Bangladesh in the 1960s as a young wife and graduate student. She recounts the early days of the Bengali Language Movement in Bangladesh and its lingering effects on university life in Dhaka before she left the country.[13] Her late husband was then a professor at Dhaka University, but as a non-Bengali speaker, he began to fear for his safety and that of his family. Rizvi recalls:

> So the trouble had started and the Bangladeshi, that movement for autonomy. . . . And see, the central government was based in West Pakistan and was Urdu-speaking. And even though my husband [was Urdu speaking], I think he didn't discuss that much, but he used to probably fear that if somebody came and attacked because he was not a Bengali, you know, [what could happen?] Not for his life, but he said [to our daughter], "If something happened to me, take your mom to the U.S." I mean, it happened during the Bangladesh Civil War.

Through a set of tragic circumstances, Rizvi found herself a young widow with two children and ended up moving to the United States permanently in 1969, partly to escape the escalation of violence and death in the buildup to the Bangladesh Liberation War. Looking to personal narratives like Rizvi's adds a vital human element when considering how events like war are understood historically. It also reveals the various reasons—the political and economic, as well as the personal—that move individuals and families across oceans and national borders. While Rizvi's decision to migrate was prompted by a complicated set of factors, her story shows how personal choice is not the only arbiter for migration: in her case, the confluence of historical conditions and life crises fundamentally shaped her path.

In addition to South Asian regional histories, American social and political forces have strongly shaped the experience and formation of South Asian communities in the Pacific Northwest. Carefully crafted immigration, education, and labor policies in the United States that have ensured the migration of highly educated and middle-class individuals must also be considered vital factors. While the period between 1882 and World War Two was considered a "dead zone" for Asian immigration because of the passage of a series of Asian Exclusion Acts that barred or severely restricted immigration from many parts of the world, the Immigration and Nationality Act (also known as the Hart-Cellar Act) was passed in 1965, opening the door for new waves of migrants from Asia, Africa, and Latin America. As a result, while narrators who came in the 1940s and 1950s tell stories of experiencing redlining when seeking to rent or buy homes in the Pacific Northwest in an era when segregation and Jim Crow laws were still in effect, those who came in the later waves of migration found a country eager for their educational and occupational talents. The civil rights movement, the women's movement, and the anti–Vietnam War movement all deeply affected narrators who came to the United States to study and work at the height of social upheaval in the late 1960s and 1970s.

In recent days, South Asian communities have been seen as potential allies for the United States' interests locally and globally. Take, for instance, the attention given by U.S. presidents to increasing South Asian and American business collaborations and official State Department visits to countries like India aimed at increasing ties between the two nations. At the same time, American involvement in Pakistan as part of the "war on terror" following the attacks of September 11, 2001, and the discovery of terrorist Osama bin Laden within Pakistani borders have created tensions for Pakistanis living in the United States. American involvement in the wars in Iraq and Afghanistan through the 2000s has also created a new political consciousness for South Asians, particularly for Muslim and Sikh communities which have suffered backlash on account of their religion, even though they have lived in the same communities for decades.

CONCLUSIONS

Considering the increasingly frequent interaction between those immigrants living in the United States and people in South Asia, as well as in other parts of the world, this book offers a glimpse into a living archive where historical events are still open to interpretation. In the pages that follow, we combine the stories of narrators, historical documents, and various representations of South Asians in fiction, film, and the media to demonstrate the mosaic of experiences of South Asian communities. In doing so, we critically consider how individuals navigate the worlds that they encounter, how they become acculturated, reject assimilation, reinvent their connections to their homelands and national identity—and ultimately show how, despite the various routes that led them here, South Asians are very much rooted in the Pacific Northwest.

1

"FINDING TRACES OF OUR EXISTENCE HERE"

PRE-WORLD WAR TWO SOUTH ASIAN MIGRATIONS

> We earnestly wish that the leaders of our country, especially of the
> Punjab, will do their duty to the cause of the oppressed people with a
> united effort, like men, not cowards and slaves.
> —Taraknath Das in *Free Hindusthan*, April 1908.[1]

> I try to envision my mother's life before I arrived. I marvel at her
> survival as the family trekked around California and Oregon, living as
> they could wherever my father found work.
> —Kartar Dhillon, "The Parrot's Beak"[2]

O N the evening of September 4, 1907, several Indian[3] men were settling in for the night after putting in a long day at the local lumber mills in Bellingham, Washington. Close to the Canadian border in the northwestern corner of Washington State, Bellingham was then a bustling mill town and seaport and the county seat of Whatcom County. Although the sky was clear, a feeling of uneasiness was palpable in the evening air. The mostly Sikh workers had been living and working in the community for some time now, but they kept to themselves socially. Nonetheless, their presence was the source of mounting tension between white workers also employed in the mills and the mill owners, who were paying the Indian workers lower wages.[4]

At the city's Labor Day parade a few days before, several white workers used the town festivities to voice their disapproval of the foreign newcomers. Informal leaders levied an ultimatum to the mill owners: fire the "Hindoos,"[5] as the Indian men were commonly known, after the Labor Day holiday passed or trouble would ensue. While there had been small skir-

FIG. 1.1   Whatcom Museum of Art, Bellingham, Washington, 2011. This building was the Bellingham City Hall in 1907 and housed South Asian immigrants in its basement after the Labor Day Riots. Photo courtesy of the Iyer family.

mishes since the town's parade, nothing could prepare the Indian workers for the sight of nearly five hundred seething white men gathered outside of their ramshackle homesteads perched precariously near the city's waterfront. The mob pulsed with an angry energy as Indian workers were dragged out to the street to watch as their meager belongings were destroyed and their bunkhouses lit on fire. Some of the men in the mob turned violent and began to beat the shocked Indian men shivering in the streets. In an attempt to restore order and provide a semblance of safety to the Indian workers, the beleaguered Bellingham chief of police herded some two hundred of them into the basement of City Hall for the night, while others were rounded up and locked in the city's jail, purportedly for their protection.

The next morning, three of the men, Nand Singh, Attar Singh, and Sergent Singh, appeared before the city council to register their grievances. The council recognized that the Indians had a right to stay in the town, as long as they did not break any laws. But many of the Bellingham residents did not want the Indians to remain and the anger began to foment anew. No longer welcome by their neighbors, acquaintances, or employers and fearful of a reprisal of the previous evening's atrocities, the Indians gathered their belongings and boarded trains heading south to California.[6] As the men peered out of the train windows at the town that had been their home and place of livelihood since arriving in America, the white residents of the town gathered at the station to cheer and celebrate their departure.

Today the memory of the Bellingham riots has long faded in the Pacific Northwest, and yet they represent an important moment in the history of South Asian migration to the region. As deplorable as the riots were, the anti-immigrant racism faced by South Asians was far from an anomaly in that period. In the 1880s, the denizens of the same city had driven out all the Chinese immigrants following the passage of the Chinese Exclusion Act of 1882. After the 1907 riots, South Asians stayed away from Whatcom County for most of the twentieth century. Even as late as 1986, only about ten South Asian families lived in Whatcom County and most of them were farmers. Though there are traces of these early South Asian workers in archives housed at county museums and regional historical societies, there are several questions that remain about the lives of these pioneers: How did these early immigrants conceive of their place in American society? Did they maintain cultural and religious practices? Did men and women experience and negotiate immigrant life differently? In some cases, we stretch our imaginations to visualize what their lives were like as we view photographs of unnamed individuals pursuing the most ordinary of tasks, or read newspaper reports that document the horrors of racist violence. Otherwise, we are left to piece together answers to these questions by examining fragments of memoirs, reading between the lines of publicly recorded statements, or combing narratives created by their descendants.

The paucity of information on early South Asian immigrant life is in part a problem of historiography. Records from the 1880s and early 1900s in the Pacific Northwest are scarce and incomplete; minority populations are even less likely to appear as subjects of official histories. Although the substantive immigration reforms in the latter half of the twentieth century dramatically increased the numbers of South Asians entering the United States, the history of early South Asian immigrants to the Pacific coast is often overshadowed by the stories of immigrants who were more widely recognized and welcomed to the area. While some ethnographies and histories of South

Asian American immigration do discuss this region, these studies tend to see the Pacific Northwest as a port of entry, rather than as an important site of settlement. Instead, the experiences of the communities residing in California or other places around the United States are profiled.[7] However, when looking more closely at historical and contemporary archives, it is clear that immigrants in the Pacific Northwest have played a very significant role in South Asian community building regionally and nationally, sparked revolutionary political activity in the United States and across the Indian subcontinent, and helped shape the discourse on immigration spanning from the early twentieth century through the contemporary moment.

The period between the 1880s and the 1960s is often considered by immigration historians to be a period of restriction and dormancy.[8] The passage of several laws including the Chinese Exclusion Act of 1882 (which was subsequently renewed until its repeal in 1943) and the Immigration Acts of 1914, 1917, and 1924 created what was known as the "Asiatic Barred Zone" and effectively prevented migration from Asian countries. Although these measures were intended to curb the so-called "yellow tide" or the increasing numbers of immigrants coming from China, Japan, South Asia, and the Pacific Rim to work on the West Coast, populations of Asians grew as the rapidly expanding railroad, timber, fishing, and farming industries demanded large numbers of cheap laborers. It was not until the Chinese Exclusion Repeal Act of 1943 was sponsored by Senator Warren G. Magnuson of Washington State that the period prohibiting Chinese migration ended and citizenship was offered to some Chinese who were already residing in the United States. The Luce-Cellar Act of 1946 was a further step toward full recognition of Asian communities, stating that South Asians and Filipinos were also eligible to become citizens. Still, race-based country of origin quotas in place during that period meant that only one hundred immigrants from the Indian subcontinent were eligible to enter the United States in any given year. The Immigration and Nationality Act of 1952, also known as the McCarran-Walter Act, formally recognized citizenship rights of Japanese, Koreans, and other Asians, but it was the passage of the 1965 Immigration and Nationality Act, or the Hart-Cellar Act, that finally repealed the country of origin quotas and established new criteria for immigration that prioritized education and training, American labor needs, and family reunification.

Because of the long interlude of restriction that characterized American immigration policy in the early to middle part of the twentieth century, studies of South Asians in the United States tend to presume that community formation stagnated before 1965. In the Pacific Northwest, however, events such as the riots in Bellingham demonstrate that while immigration may have been curtailed, South Asians were very much part of a tense and xenophobic environment in which anxiety about wages and job security translated into the demonization of minority races and foreign nationals. At the same time, they were also instrumental in laying the groundwork for the thriving communities that populate the Pacific Northwest today.

FROM SOJOURNERS TO SETTLERS: EARLY SOUTH ASIAN IMMIGRATION

So how are early South Asian immigrants and contemporary communities connected? While small in number, early immigrants left an indelible mark on the communities already existing in the Pacific Northwest. Local events had national repercussions, as newspaper coverage of the Bellingham riots in 1907 and other anti-Asian demonstrations were instrumental in shaping anti-immigrant discourse in the region and reflected sentiments brewing around the country.[9] Ironically, while there were far fewer South Asians residing in the area than there were Chinese or Japanese immigrants at the time, they were nonetheless central to the debate over Asian immigration in the early twentieth century.[10]

These migrants were young men primarily from the Punjab region, which spans the border of modern-day India and Pakistan. The Punjab is home to ancient civilizations and boasts some of the most fertile farmland in the world. Although many Punjabi families flourished as agriculturalists, the growing unrest caused by British rule over the Indian subcontinent created dismal economic conditions and younger sons of large families began to migrate out of the area to seek their fortunes elsewhere. Many of these men joined the British military and took postings that brought them all over the globe as subjects of the Empire. Many Sikh veterans who could not find agricultural work in their villages, and young men in search of adventure, migrated to British Columbia, Canada. As another British colony, Canada was an easier port of entry than the United States or Europe, and many Sikhs came initially to North America via Vancouver. New opportunities and proximity to the expanding American western territories drew these Sikh

FIG. 1.2 Sikhs at a Canadian Pacific Railroad station, British Columbia, date unknown. Photo courtesy of the University of Washington Libraries, Special Collections, UW 18745.

pioneers south toward Washington, Oregon, and California. In 1903, only twenty Indians entered the United States; however, by 1906, this number had jumped to six hundred.[11] By the fall of 1907, several hundred immigrants had arrived in Bellingham, Washington, and began working in the lumber mills. Companies such as Bellingham Bay Company, Whatcom Falls Mill, and the Larson Lumber Company employed many of these men.

As photographs from this period show, the lumber mills were nestled in the bucolic landscape provided by the Cascade Mountains to the east and the lush forests to the west of Bellingham. Amid the serene snow-capped mountains and placid lakes, darker currents were coursing through the town. While these photographs document the growing industrialization of the region, they do not reveal the tensions seething among the people of the region.[12] The South Asians were hard workers and eager for employment and the mill owners turned a blind eye to the men's national origin as they hired them at cut-rate wages. In return, the mill owners got cheap, reliable, and steady labor. However, organizations such as the Asiatic Exclusion League began to target the new immigrants. The Asiatic Exclusion League was formed in San Francisco in 1905 and traveled north in 1907 under the

FIG. 1.3   Sikh at a Canadian
Pacific Railroad station, Brit-
ish Columbia, date unknown.
Photo courtesy of University of
Washington Libraries, Special
Collections, UW 15673

FIG. 1.4   Larson's Lumber Mill, Bellingham, Washington, 1909.
Photo courtesy of Whatcom Museum, 5313.

leadership of A. E. Fowler. Initially called the Japanese-Korean Exclusion League, the organization quickly expanded to target the religious and cultural traditions of the Sikhs. The physical differences between the South Asians and the local populations of mostly white workers were pronounced: a photograph in the Whatcom Museum depicts three unnamed Sikh men in a typical studio shot. These men were likely workers at the lumber mills and the photograph was perhaps intended to be sent back to family in India. Each man is sharply dressed in a suit and tie, wears an elaborate turban, and projects a proud and dignified gaze into the camera. Their clothing marks both their acculturation (the suits and ties) and their adherence to their cultural customs, as they also sport the turban and facial hair mandated by the Sikh religion. A South Asian viewer of this photo would have likely interpreted the photograph as signifying economic advancement and a strong commitment to religion and culture in the three men. The people of the Northwest might have felt differently. As an editorialist in the *Seattle Morning Times* noted, it was "not a question of men but modes of life; not a matter of nations, but of habits of life. . . . When men who require meat to eat and real beds to sleep in are ousted from their employment to make room for vegetarians who can find the bliss of sleep in some filthy corner, it is rather difficult to say at what limit indignation ceases to be righteous."[13] In many ways, the tension between the white population and the immigrants was not just a matter of race, but of class and culture.

In general, the Bellingham riots and the migration of Indians to the Pacific Northwest produced a complex response from the rest of America.[14] Some who opposed the "Tide of Turbans" (a term coined by San Francisco–based writer Herman Scheffauer) were concerned that money flowing out of the Pacific Northwest and into South Asia would hurt the economy of the region, while others argued that South Asian laborers were physically feeble aliens who, despite their claims to being Aryan,[15] were inassimilable. Still, others were sympathetic to the difficult conditions in South Asia that led to emigration and saw the new arrivals as vital sources of labor. While the *Bellingham Herald* tacitly condoned the riots,[16] journalists such as Will Irwin harshly criticized the violence. In a 1907 article in *Collier's Weekly*, Irwin tells a different story of the events leading to the Bellingham riots. Declaring the tussle over wages a "screaming farce," Irwin argued that the South Asian men were attacked by mill workers who were looking for any excuse to drive them out of town. Recounting an incident that took place

FIG. 1.5 Studio portrait of three unknown Sikh men, date unknown. Photo courtesy of the Henry Brown Collection, Whatcom Museum, 1995.108.117.

a few days before the riots, Irwin notes that there had been a "small disturbance" when two white women were pushing babies in strollers down a street where some Indian immigrants were resting on the sidewalk. When the women asked the men to move, they apparently simply smiled in "their childish way," according to Irwin, and remained by the roadside. Some mill workers who saw this interaction claimed that the men were acting disrespectfully toward the women. The mob attacked the tenements of the South Asian workers that evening, Irwin noted, because the workers were enraged by the idea that these men were not appropriately obsequious to the white townsfolk. Irwin argued that the chief of the Bellingham police, Chief Thomas, housed the victims of the attacks at the police station not to protect them, but to imprison them in order to prevent a Sikh uprising and to ease the collective ousting of all South Asians from town the next morning. After locking away the men who survived the mob's attacks, Chief Thomas had deputized two thousand men to hunt down and find the one hundred South Asians still at large. Irwin wrote:

> Three cheers rent the Bellingham fog, the mob scattered to hunt
> Hindus. The victims lay down like rabbits. Not one fought back.
> Two were running away. The first tried to scurry like a cat up a
> twenty-foot wall. Near the top he lost his hold and fell. The other
> running along a wharf in the dark tripped on his fallen turban and
> fell into the water. The rest were led like lambs to the police station.
> At eleven o'clock a boy in knee breeches brought in two six-footers,
> one in each hand. At midnight an interpreter called the roll. Every
> Hindu in Bellingham was safe at the station. Next morning the
> chief swore in deputies and sent them to accompany the Hindus
> back to their mills, from which they decamped and vanished over
> the border.[17]

Irwin was clearly opposed to the violence directed at the Indians and also critical of how the city authorities reacted. He did not hesitate to note the racial prejudices motivating the riots. However, his language also reveals that even the most liberal and pro-immigrant intellectuals of the time thought of the Indian workers as "childlike" and not able to withstand the strength of a "boy in breeches." Irwin's comparison of the Indians to small animals— cats, rabbits, or lambs—reveals his own racial biases that would read the dark-skinned immigrants as closer to animals and in need of protection. Irwin's coverage exemplifies the undercurrents of racism that affected even the more liberal supporters of immigrant rights.

Following the riot in Bellingham, a similar uprising against South Asian workers took place on November 2, 1907, in Everett, Washington, then another lumber town a few miles south of Bellingham. Newspaper accounts show that while Everett residents condemned violence, they still were grateful that the South Asians were gone from the city. An article in the *Everett Daily Herald* expressed relief that Everett was able to avert the violence that had so tarnished Bellingham. The article goes on to argue that Indians did not belong in Everett because they were still outsiders who could never really become part of the majority population. However, the report did not blame the immigrants, but instead underscored class conflict as it condemned the mill workers and merchants who sought cheap labor.[18] The debate in the newspapers in the Pacific Northwest and across the nation recognized that the central issue between the white population and the Sikh workers was the willingness of the latter to work for lower wages, thus leading to unemployment or depressed wages for white workers. While some writers like Irwin were troubled by the violence and the inhumane treatment of the foreign workers, all of the newspaper reports characterize the immigrants as occupying an ambiguous, but ultimately inassimilable, racial space: they were identified racially as Aryans and therefore akin to the whites through a common claim to Caucasian heritage, and yet their darker skin, their clothing, their food habits, and their religious beliefs marked them as an exotic and threatening alien group.

On the hundredth anniversary of the Bellingham riots, the *Bellingham Herald* published an editorial on September 2, 2007, recognizing the gross injustice done to the region's early South Asian laborers and making an apology:

> It's time to apologize for the venomous racism, for the demeaning talk, for the refusal to defend human beings against a mob because of their skin tone and ethnicity. We apologize to the East Indian people in our community today and to any right-thinking person who is disgusted by the actions this newspaper took in one of the darkest times in our community's history. We are disgusted too.[19]

Some ninety miles south, in the greater Seattle area, where the largest South Asian community in Washington State resides, this anniversary and the newspaper's apology remained largely unnoticed. These incidents—the anniversary and apology and the overall lack of knowledge about the event—indicate a fundamental paradox in the history of South Asians in the Pacific Northwest. Even though South Asian immigrants have some of the longest and most complex early histories in the United States, neither the contemporary South Asian communities nor the few scholars studying them make connections between the experiences of the early South Asian immigrants and those of latter-day migrants. A film made in 2007 by the University of Washington on the Bellingham riots, *Present in All That We Do*, interviews several contemporary Bellingham residents and queries them about the riots. No one had heard of the 1907 riots, but they all claimed that the one event they knew from that time period was a mine disaster involving Chinese laborers in which many Chinese died due to the negligence of the mine owners. The film's narrator notes that there is no historical record of such a disaster and yet it circulated as fact amongst contemporary citizens of Bellingham while a documented event like the riots of 1907 is absent from the historical understanding of the region.

The Bellingham riots exemplify the many hardships faced by the working-class Indian immigrants living on the Pacific coast in the first decade of the twentieth century. But these immigrants were resolute in their desire to continue to explore the West Coast in search of work. They were not passive victims of racism; they organized politically to fight for immigrant rights and for independence from the British in India. These two political agendas came together in 1913 when Indian laborers in Astoria, Oregon, formed the Gadar party.[20] The Gadar party was the culmination of a growing network of transnational activists seeking the end of British colonial rule in South Asia. The Gadar party was also significant because it cut across not only national lines, but also class divisions, as it brought together working-class laborers and middle-class students under a common banner. Although the Indians who came to the Pacific Northwest were mostly laborers and farmers, middle-class migrants were also drawn to the area and came to take advantage of local educational institutions, including the University of Washington, as students.[21] The first student from India to arrive on the West Coast came circa 1901–1902, at the behest of a mathematics professor who came from Lahore. The professor secured scholarships for three Indian students to study at an agricultural college in Oregon. By October 1906, the American consul in Calcutta had written twenty-five letters of introduction on behalf of Indian students seeking admission to schools in the area.[22]

Although separated by class, and often caste or religion, students and laborers found themselves part of a new brotherhood inspired by a sense of displacement from their home countries and the discrimination they faced in the new land. They also created camaraderie as many students joined the full-time workers in the lumber mills and agricultural laborers in the summer months. These students left behind more documents about their lives than did the full-time workers,[23] and through their writings it is clear that both workers and the students played important roles in the development of the Gadar party. In her study of the Gadar party,[24] Maia Ramnath argues that this political organizing arose from a combination of two elements: a smaller number of mostly middle-class intellectuals who came primarily from the Bengal region in India, and a more substantial population of peasants originating in the Punjab region. Among the latter group, over half were Sikhs who had served in the British Army. Ramnath notes that "the first group staffed the printing press, propagandized, theorized, and lectured. The second group, which comprised about 95 percent of the active membership, provided the mass of fighters and funded the operation through donations and subscriptions."[25] The collusion of working-class communities and the student radicals created a vibrant movement that supported the anti-British nationalist spirit gaining momentum across the subcontinent and also sought to challenge anti-immigrant prejudice in the United States.[26] While much has been written about the specific aspects of the Gadar movement during this period, an examination of the documents and narratives left by these activists and visionaries, alongside the works of other students and travelers, nevertheless provides an intimate look into the experiences and lives of some of the first South Asian settlers in the Pacific Northwest.

PERSONAL NARRATIVES AND STORIES OF RESISTANCE

The stories and writings produced by Shree Swami Satyadeva Parivrajaka (1879–1961), a sojourner who traveled the United States, Taraknath Das (1884–1958)[27] and Jogesh C. Misrow (1886?–1915), two student activists who studied at the University of Washington, and Kartar Dhillon (1915–2008), the daughter of a working-class immigrant family in Oregon which was among the founders of the Gadar party, explore the multifaceted nature of budding South Asian nationalism and transnational activism as it thrived in the Pacific Northwest. We turn now to their narratives, which include a travelogue, *A Glimpse of America* by Satyadeva Parivrajaka, political writings by Jogesh Misrow, newspaper articles from *Free Hindusthan*, the newspaper created by Taraknath Das, and the personal memoirs of Kartar Dhillon.[28] Aside from Dhillon, who was born in the United States, the other three came from South Asia to study at American universities. While all three of the students began as visitors in the United States who were not intending to settle permanently, only Satyadeva eventually returned to India and became a well-known political and spiritual thinker, whereas Das and Misrow settled in the United States.[29]

Satyadeva Parivrajak, born Sukh Dayal, arrived in Seattle in 1905 and stayed in America until 1911.[30] He had left India in part because he was considered to be a seditious radical by the British government for his involvement in the nationalist movement in India. After arriving in the United States, Satyadeva wandered through the heart of the country, purportedly walking nearly 2,300 miles during his visit. Dabbling in studies along the way, he attended the University of Washington between 1908 and 1909 after spending time in Chicago and Oregon. He was a prolific writer and published thirty-two works of philosophy, religion, travel, and autobiography in his lifetime. Written originally in Hindi and privately translated by Raj Joshi,[31] *A Glimpse of America* is one text written by Satyadeva that examines the early-twentieth-century United States and offers a unique view of Seattle. In this piece, Satyadeva explores the many cultural differences that face the Indian traveling abroad. For example, he documents the cultural challenges of being a strict vegetarian Hindu and finding enough to eat without meat. Adding insult to injury, he took a job at a farm at one point during his travels and was deeply discomfited by working at a facility that raised animals for slaughter. His story unfolds over five and a half years,[32] however, one of the two most significant sections in his narrative concerns his time in Seattle during the 1909 Alaska Yukon Pacific Exposition (AYPE).[33]

The AYPE was a very important event not only for the growing city of Seattle, but also in the history of the United States. With the success of large exhibitions such as the French Industrial Exposition of 1844 and the Great Exhibition of the Works of Industry of All Nations, also known as the Crystal Palace Exhibition in 1851, world fairs became popular in the industrialized world as a way to showcase a nation's technological progress and modern advancements. The United States held several world fairs prior to the AYPE that emphasized America's industrial and agricultural innovations. In *Fair America,* Rydell and colleagues[34] note that the world fairs that took place between 1895 and 1916 in the United States had two major purposes: the first was to convince Americans that the United States' future progress was possible only through the expansion of international trade and military presence. The second involved "winning the support of white Americans, regardless of social class, for a view of the world that held progress toward civilization could be understood in terms of allegedly innate characteristics."[35] That is to say, the world fairs promoted the idea that all cultures could achieve the status and privilege of western cultures, if they

too moved through the same stages of economic, political, and social development as western nations. The AYPE fulfilled both missions as it celebrated
overseas trade, emphasized the importance of the Pacific Northwest as a
military and economic center, and showcased exhibits comparing the varying levels of development of the cultures of the Pacific Rim, with America
as the most modern and nations such as the Philippines occupying a lesser
status.

Although the AYPE was originally intended to celebrate the Klondike
Gold Rush, it evolved into an event that marketed the rapidly expanding
economic opportunities in Alaska and the Yukon. The focus on the Pacific
Rim was intended to showcase the growing role that Asian trade played
on the West Coast, though the only large-scale exhibitions of Pacific trade
were by Canada and Japan.[36] Originally scheduled to take place in 1907, the
fair finally opened in 1909 on the lush and bucolic grounds of the recently
relocated campus of the University of Washington.

At the time of the AYPE, Satyadeva was in Canada and very enthusiastic
about visiting the exposition. He invited his friend Munshiram to travel
with him and the two men set sail from Vancouver to Seattle in search of
adventure. In his narrative, Satyadeva relates a dramatic dialogue, allegedly
overheard by him en route to the AYPE, between a Canadian father and
his young son, who were also visiting the exposition. The Canadian father
tells the boy, "The Exposition has been opened to let the world know about
Alaska."[37] When the young son queries further, the Canadian goes on to
outline the economic advantages of this display: all countries associated
with the Pacific, he notes, will increase trade amongst themselves. Older
states in America will recognize the richness of the new western states,
enticing people to settle there. As a result, interactions between Pacific
nations will increase and prosperity will befall everyone. The father praises
the growth of trade since the opening of the AYPE in June, pointing to
the increase in land values in Vancouver as an example of the exposition's
effects. At this point, Satyadeva and Munshiram move from observers to
participants in the conversation. Munshiram asks the man whether Canada
would welcome immigrants to settle permanently; the Canadian answers in
the affirmative. Comparing the low population of Canada and its vast land
resources to India's large population and relatively smaller land resources,
the father argues that land wealth will translate to enormous industrial and
agricultural growth in Canada with the help of immigrants. Only by devel-

oping natural resources and growing the population through immigration would Canada remain independent enough to stave off encroachment from the United States should the British lose interest in this territory. Although the conversation is related as a first-hand encounter, Satyadeva uses it as a parable for his Indian audiences to relate the importance of economic and industrial development to the sovereignty of a nation. The Canadian man's argument about the importance of immigration to the economic development of the West Coast also allows Satyadeva to indirectly state his disdain of the anti-immigrant policies that affected South Asians both in Canada and the United States in the early twentieth century.

Satyadeva goes on to describe his and Munshiram's arrival in Seattle. Along with their local host Biharilal, they make their way to the University of Washington campus in time for the AYPE's "Seattle Day" on September 6, 1909. Upon seeing the newly unveiled statue of George Washington that welcomes visitors to the AYPE at the entrance to the campus, the travelers extoll the first American president for his role in liberating the United States from the evil clutches of British imperialism—a feat they hope India will soon accomplish. In drawing parallels between India and the United States, Satyadeva expresses his anti-British sentiment and hopes that India will soon become as modern and technologically advanced as the United States. He lauds the American pursuit of scientific agriculture and the education of farmers as a model for India to emulate and is awed by the military advancements on display such as a Civil War exhibit and a presentation by the United States Department of War on weapons from 1785 to the present. He also notes, however, that "All this was presented to open the eyes of the citizens. There were mothers telling their children how proud they should be of America and its war powers. All I was thinking was, when will they stop making these fearsome war machines?"[38] On one hand, Satyadeva is fascinated with the global economic and industrial reach of the United States displayed so prominently in the AYPE. At the same time, he is troubled by the American assumption that such imperial power was inherent and foundation to the strength of a nation.

Satyadeva is also critical of the representations of other cultures at the AYPE. He and his friends visit the Oriental Building, which was constructed specifically for the exposition and modeled after Grecian and Romanesque architecture prevalent in Italy, complete with displays of Greek and Italian statuary. Satyadeva is surprised by the incongruence of the building's name and the exhibit's contents. He writes, "But we thought the Oriental Building would have exhibited some crafts from our old country which would make us thankful. But we left disappointed about this omission."[39] While Satyadeva points to America's limited understanding of the "Orient," he remains curiously silent about exhibits such as the Igorot Village, which depicted the indigenous cultures originating in the Philippines as barbaric and prehistoric. This silence might be reflective of his and other Indians' understanding of their racial identity as Aryan and thus be complicit with American perceptions of indigenous peoples. Latter day historians of the AYPE such as Robert Rydell and Nard Jones have noted the problematic representations of race and culture that permeated the AYPE. Nard Jones writes that although the AYPE did much to promote Seattle as a boom town and a significant player in Pacific trade, this legacy was almost entirely presumed to emerge from the ingenuity and persistence of white European settlers. Jones writes, "Today it seems odd that among these movers and shakers were no blacks, Indians [Native Americans], Eskimos, Japanese or Chinese. These omissions were not calculated; it simply did not occur to the whites that there should be representations of these races."[40] While Jones might see these as errors of omission, the exhibits and the histories recorded about the development of the Pacific Northwest and Alaska-Yukon regions might also illustrate the ways in which white supremacy was foundational to America's narrative of industrial progress and imperial ambition. The Pacific Northwest is hailed as the site of technological innovation and military supremacy through the AYPE; at the same time, this progress was achieved in part through the decimation of the native populations, who were reduced to living at the edges of this modern panacea, and on the backs of Asian immigrants who made up an important proportion of the local labor force.

Shifting from his reflections on the AYPE, Satyadeva continues his narrative by writing about his life as a student at the University of Washington. Though he was a student, he spends considerable time addressing the difficulties faced by immigrant laborers in Seattle. After touring the country and starting his studies, he found his purse lighter than expected and decided to look for a job to support himself. He was optimistic that although the country had been experiencing an economic recession, the success of the AYPE would help him find a job. He partnered with another Indian student, Vishnudas, who was studying electrical engineering at the University of Washington and needed work to help pay for the second year of his education. The third person in this group of job seekers was a Mexican, Cicerino Magella, who had also come to the United States in search of work. Satyadeva recounts a trip to downtown employment agencies in Seattle that advertised a variety of jobs. After inquiring about an advertised government position, the three men were told that they were unqualified because they were "black." Satyadeva writes, "The clerk showed us a write up from a government official. In it was clearly written that the worker must be an American or Irish white. Do not send us black Hindus."[41] Incensed by this deliberate racism, he continues, "After reading this I was upset but the thoughts that crossed my mind would be inappropriate to express here."[42] Satyadeva goes on to describe his experiences with an employment agent who overcharges them for referring them to a job. The motley crew finally found work in construction, which required that they haul large cartloads of concrete up and down hills. Despite committing to this back-breaking work, they still suffered the indignity of dishonest employers who tried to cheat them out of their hard-earned wages. Satyadeva's reflections are a glimpse into the imperial and racial ideologies of the times from the perspective of someone who experienced the exclusions first-hand. If the AYPE exoticized the imperial subject and rendered him savage, then Satyadeva's narrative offers us a colonial subject's complex response to imperialism, which includes both admiration and criticism of western notions of progress.

Like Satyadeva, who left behind reminiscences of his experiences in the Pacific Northwest, other Indian students at the University of Washington also provide insight into how South Asians experienced the region and the United States in the early twentieth century. Taraknath Das and Jogesh C. Misrow were contemporaries of Satyadeva at the University of Washington and provide eyewitness accounts of South Asian student and political life. Taraknath Das was an activist in the anti-colonial resistance to the British during the Swadeshi movement[43] and was involved with the militant Anusilan Samiti movement[44] in Bengal. Das fled India when he learned that he was about to be arrested.[45] He paid for his passage abroad by accepting monetary gifts from some sympathetic supporters and, according to some accounts, money stolen from a fellow revolutionary.[46] Using this money and disguised as a *sadhu* (a religious ascetic), Das departed for Japan on a French ship carrying livestock. Japan held a fascination for Indian revolutionaries at this time because of its victory in the war against Russia in 1904–1905. Indian revolutionaries saw this as a positive indicator that the white nations were not indomitable.[47] However, the reality of life in Japan was a far cry from what Das had imagined. Although he had learned some Japanese, he found the people to be unenthusiastic about Indian aspirations and he was unable to gain admission to a Japanese university or penetrate the society socially. With the help of an Indian merchant company in Yokohama, he raised money to pay for his fare on a ship traveling to the United States. Das and his friend Pabitra Kummar Roy set sail on the *Tango Maru* on June 20, 1906.

Das arrived in Seattle on July 12, 1906, but ran into immigration problems once on shore. Das had given his name on the passenger manifest as Jogendranath Das. It is not clear whether this was an act of subterfuge or a desire to start life anew under a new name. Whatever his intentions, this lie would later haunt his citizenship applications in the United States and become a stumbling block in his ability to provide documentation about his arrival to the country. A few days after arriving in Seattle, he left for San Francisco, where he made connections with members of the local Vedanta Society[48] and continued his revolutionary work. He remained in contact with activists in India and became part of a growing community of Indians seeking protection against the racism of the United States. Das quickly recognized that in order for him to fight for freedom in India and to work for immigrant rights in America, he needed to ensure his right to stay in the country. He began to contest U.S. immigration regulations that precluded Indians from becoming citizens. Like Dr. Bhagat Singh Thind[49] would do later in front of the Supreme Court, Das challenged the Bureau of Immigration and Naturalization by arguing that Indians were Aryans and eligible for citizenship. U.S. Attorney General Charles Bonaparte rejected the claim on the grounds that natives of British India could not be regarded as white persons.[50]

In the meantime, the burden of transnational revolutionary work and his studies at the University of California, Berkeley, left Taraknath Das financially challenged. These pressures led Das to take the Bureau of Immigration and Naturalization Service exam, which he passed with the highest grade. He then found work as an interpreter in Vancouver, B.C., undoubtedly troubled by the irony that though he could not become a citizen himself, he could still work for the Bureau of Immigration and Naturalization processing the applications of others who sought to settle in the United States. While Das's job was to sift out applications from Indians seeking to immigrate and to act as an interpreter when needed, he used his position

FIG. 1.6 The officers of the Cosmopolitan Club at the University of Washington. Jogesh Misrow is pictured in the first row, first on the left, and Taraknath Das is in the second row, second from the left. Seattle, Washington, 1911. Photo from *The Tyee: The Book of the Class of 1912*, vol. 12.

to help new immigrants find legal representation that would enable them to stay in the United States or Canada. While living in Vancouver, B.C., he began publishing his newspaper, *Free Hindusthan*, in 1908.[51] Because the newspaper argued passionately for Indian independence and also for immigrant rights in Canada, he came under the scrutiny of both Canadian and American authorities. *Free Hindusthan* had a circulation of two thousand copies internationally among diasporic Indian communities and its popularity and seditious content also caught the attention of the British authorities in India, who promptly banned it on the subcontinent. The Canadian government also seized copies of the newspaper, and the American government, which presumably believed in upholding the First Amendment guaranteeing freedom of speech and the press, asked Das to either resign his job or cease publishing the paper. Under pressure, Das resigned, but he then moved to Vermont briefly, where he resumed publication of the *Free Hindusthan* with the help of the editor of the *Gaelic American*, which was another anti-British publication aimed at Irish immigrants and activists. In June 1909, Das returned to the Pacific Northwest and enrolled at the University of Washington to study political science and history. *Free Hindusthan* moved along with him and found a new home in Seattle.

The inaugural edition of the newspaper documented the struggles of the Indian immigrants. The paper was a powerful voice that articulated their experiences with racism, colonialism, and prejudice and also detailed how these early settlers mobilized and collaborated with a range of sympathizers to advocate for their rights as equal subjects in a land of immigrants. *Free Hindusthan* emerges in the historical record as a political document and also a commentary on the challenges of immigrant life. Even the masthead of *Free Hindusthan* boldly declared its emancipatory mission: "Resistance to Tyranny Is Obedience to God." In an article entitled "Our National Life Is at Stake," Das argued that if the British could freely migrate to India, then Indians must have the freedom to migrate to other parts of the British Empire without having the doors of other nations shut to them. He commended the United States for not excluding Indians as thoroughly as the Chinese, but was convinced that if Canada shut its doors to them, then the United States surely would as well.[52]

In another essay titled "Famine in Hindusthan and the Only Remedy," Das argued that famine was not a consequence of crop failure but a consequence of colonial policies, including a high irrigation tax that bankrupted the farmer and a dearth of technical education available to the average person. He noted that more than monetary relief, what the Indian people needed was support for self-government and for practical education. He went on to say, "They [the American people] can really help the cause of humanity by maintaining a few energetic and independent-spirited students of Hindusthan in the western countries so that they can get thorough practical and scientific education which they will properly utilize and spread when they return to Hindusthan." At the end of the article, Das praised Professor Edward T. Mathes, principal of the State Normal School at Bellingham, as a "good friend" of India. He wrote:

> His practical sympathy is sufficient proof of it and we are indebted to him for his kind services. He is taking care of one Hindu student in his institution. He expressed his desire and capacity to help a few more Hindu students in different institutions. The students must be of good moral character and bearing recommendations from respectable and reliable parties. Recommendations from nationalist leaders of Hindusthan will be preferred. Students desiring to avail themselves of the opportunity may communicate with him.[53]

According to Das, the real potential for transformation in India came through an alliance between American educators and institutions and future Indian leaders. Undoubtedly, Das himself was an intellectual, but he saw his education and expertise as necessary to help uplift the working classes and poor masses in India. At the same time, he also felt compelled to make a plea for the financial support of Indian students who were at risk of being regarded as "laborers in the guise of students." This plea also shows how the lines between the working-class and the middle-class students were blurred through the immigration and settlement process. While literacy and fluency in English separated these students from their working-class compatriots, they often experienced the same financial hardships and barriers to work, which created a shared sense of injustice. Das eventually went on to receive a Ph.D. from the University of Washington and to fight for many political causes in India and the United States while working as a professor at Columbia University. He established the Taraknath Das Foundation using his personal funds in the 1930s and the foundation continues his legacy by supporting Indian students with scholarships to this day.[54]

Another Indian student who passed through the University of Washington in the same period, Jogesh C. Misrow, took a different approach to the anti-British politics and immigrant rights work in the United States. Like Das, Misrow worked for the Immigration and Naturalization Service as an interpreter after he earned his degree from the University of Washington. He went on to a master's program at Stanford University, where in 1915 he completed a thesis on Indian immigration to the West Coast. Misrow recognized how important a thoughtful and careful study of South Asian immigration would be to promoting rational discussions about what was increasingly a controversial subject in the United States. Misrow drew on sources such as Washington State politicians' statements to the Congressional Committee on Immigration and Naturalization to underscore the overt racism running through public discourses on immigration. He quotes a notable Washington State politician: "In our state we have kept the East Indian on the move, if there had not been local agitation commencing four or five years ago [the Bellingham and Everett riots], the large number that worked their way to California would have remained in our state [Washington]."[55] In addition to drawing attention to this blatant discrimination, Misrow also noted that the American immigration authorities used more subtle means to restrict Indian immigration by arguing that Indian immigrants would be unable to earn a living if allowed into the country, suffered from mental or physical defects as a race, and were likely to become public burdens.[56]

To counter these claims, Misrow provided statistics that showed that the number of denials markedly increased after the riots and had little to do with the reasons cited above. He argued that immigration should be regulated, rather than restricted, and suggested holding United States immigration officials responsible for the efficient and fair enforcement of existing laws, instituting restrictions at the port of embarkation rather than at the port of entry, fostering better understanding between India and the United States about immigration policies, and extending greater rights to immigrants, such as the opportunity for naturalization.[57] Finally, Misrow advocated for legislative action that would create a fair process for immigrants while mitigating the concerns of American and Canadian citizens. He eloquently concluded his thesis by noting:

The racial aspect of the problem of East Indian immigration just
discussed will find its solution in a closer approximation of the
two races by mutual understanding and social assimilation. As to
the Economic aspect, another method is called for, namely that of
limitation or restriction of numbers of those desiring to enter the
country. In order to effect this purpose, no drastic or discrimina-
tory means need to be resorted to, since general public opinion
does not seem to sanction such measures. . . . Unrestricted immigration from India to America is not conducive to the interests of
both parties. While the right of Naturalization has been extended
to the educated or high caste East Indian, it has been denied to the
laborers, and keeps that class as perpetual aliens in the land of their
adopted choice. The privilege of citizenship should be extended
to them on the basis of character and intelligence, rather than by
the accident of race or geographic origin. It will be a forward step
consistent with the American spirit of political growth.[58]

These suggestions reveal Misrow's remarkable foresight: he outlined in 1915
some of the same principles that would eventually shape the Hart-Cellar
Act of 1965 and opened the doors of America to immigrants around the
globe. As an intellectual, Misrow demonstrated his nuanced understanding of the social and economic issues underlying the problem of exclusion
of South Asians. He pleaded the case for immigration reform based on his
careful examination of available immigration data and provided solutions
sensitive to the perceived needs of North American governments and the
plight of the South Asian immigrant. After completing his master's degree
from Stanford, Misrow moved to Chicago to pursue a doctoral degree in
foreign affairs. Today he is known as an early South Asian American literary
figure for his poetry collection *Usha Songit* or "Songs of the Dawn," which
was published in 1919.

As the works of Satyadeva, Taraknath Das, and Jogesh Misrow demonstrate resistance to British imperialism, articulate a political vision for
an independent India, and support equality for Indian immigrants in the
United States, the memoirs of Kartar Dhillon provide insight into the political and social life of early immigrants in the Pacific Northwest.[59] Her reflections offer an intimate look at family life from the perspective of a woman,
which was rare in a community dominated by men. Dhillon was the daugh-

ter of Bakshish Singh Dhillon, who came to the United States in the 1890s, and his wife, Rattan Kaur, who migrated in 1910 and was among the first South Asian women to settle in the United States.[60] Kartar Dhillon, born in 1915 in the United States, lived with her family in Astoria, Oregon, where her father worked for a lumber mill from 1916 to 1922. The Dhillon family eventually moved south to California, following other members of the Sikh community to which they belonged.[61]

The film *Turbans*,[62] written and directed by Kartar Dhillon's granddaughter Erika Surat Andersen, fictionalizes the Dhillon family's experiences in Astoria. Andersen uses her grandmother's voice-over narration to tell the story of Dhillon's young brothers who wore turbans to school. They were the only Sikh children in Astoria because Dhillon's father was the only Sikh immigrant to bring his young wife with him.[63] Dhillon's brothers suffered from bullying and racist taunts because of the family's decision to honor the tenets of their faith that require men to wear turbans and keep their hair long. Documenting the family's agonizing decision to cut their sons' hair so that they might better fit into their new land, the film poignantly unearths the isolation, alienation, and adaptation that the family experiences. The film also depicts the closeness of the few Indian immigrants who lived on the street that the locals called "Hindoo Alley" and shows how community members supported one another through daily hardships. In doing so, *Turbans* paints a touching portrait of how communities survived in the face of tangible and often violent obstacles to their settlement while learning how to deal with the small and large abdications of their culture in light of new customs and expectations.

As Andersen researched her film, she and her grandmother took a trip to Astoria, which Dhillon chronicled in her essay "Astoria Revisited." As Dhillon tries to find the place where she had lived as a young child, she notes that in contemporary Astoria, there is very little evidence of the existence of Sikh immigrants. When she and Andersen searched for information on her parents' old home, the town librarian asks them why they were looking for information on a house that no longer existed. Grandmother and granddaughter respond: "For the record, to find a trace of our existence here."[64] However, when they drove past the site of the Hammond Lumber Company mills, which employed the immigrants, and the plot where her parents' home had once stood, those traces proved ephemeral. She writes, "We talked to a family who were enjoying the summer evening in their backyard, which would have been our backyard. Their house now occupied the meadow of my memories."[65] Not even a museum exhibit about early Asians in Astoria mentioned the existence of any South Asians in the community.

Nonetheless, during the research trip Dhillon began to uncover pieces of her family's history through visits with some older women who were daughters of other immigrants in Astoria. One woman recalls going to school with Dhillon's older brothers and another remembers that the men of "Hindoo Alley" marched together to the Hammond Lumber Mill in groups to avoid harassment from locals. One person recalled that the Indians "didn't bother anyone. . . . They kept to themselves. Went to work in a group and came home from work in a group." Such a reaction would be understandable, as Dhillon notes: "Why wouldn't they? . . . They had no social halls, or church of their own as other immigrant groups had. They had only the security of their numbers together. They were not welcomed into the larger society and were scorned in the press for being men without families." It was in this milieu of a closely knit group of mostly men living and working in hostile conditions that the Gadar party was born in 1913. Although the Gadar party eventually established itself in California, it was in the "Hindoo Alley" of Astoria that the revolutionary seeds were planted. The ghettoization of the Indian workers, the abysmal living conditions, the exclusion of women through immigration policies, and the lack of advocacy from an imperial government at home were all factors that gave rise to the Gadar political movement.

Astoria served as a formative place for another important figure in South Asian American history: Dr. Bhagat Singh Thind of the landmark court case *United States v. Bhagat Singh Thind.* Thind made his way to Astoria, where he was employed by the Hammond Lumber Company and lived in Alderbrook, near the same "Hindoo Alley" referenced by Dhillon. He lived in a bunkhouse with three other workers and was a member of the Gadar party, though he eventually enlisted in the United States Army in 1918 and was stationed in Fort Lewis, Washington.[66] He applied for U.S. citizenship in Oregon, a move that resulted in the landmark case for which he is most famous. There is no evidence that Dhillon met Thind as a child, but given the small number of South Asian immigrants in Astoria, it is likely that he was among the many young men who became part of her extended family.

Although Dhillon was very young when she lived in Astoria, her memories of that experience are significant and they are among the few sources available about early South Asian immigrant life in the Pacific Northwest.

While *Turbans* and her writing about Astoria are efforts to retrieve memories about the South Asian community, Dhillon's well-known essay "Parrot's Beak"[67] documents how marriage and family relationships were affected by the immigration and acculturation process. At the time that the narrative was written, she was living in California, her father was dead, and her mother was ill in the hospital. Although she was part of a larger Sikh community in 1932 in California than she was during her childhood in Oregon, there were constant reminders about her difference from mainstream culture and the burdens borne by the few women that were expected to keep customs alive for the community. Dhillon recalls her mother's life as shrouded by hard work, isolation, and loneliness:

> I marvel at her survival as the family trekked around California and Oregon, living as they could wherever my father found work. He had the company of other men, friends and workers on the job. My mother had no one, no other Indian women to keep her company, no sisters or relatives to give her a hand with the housework. She had to do it all—all, that is, until her daughters grew old enough to help.[68]

This pioneering life without the company of other women left indelible marks on her mother and Dhillon remembers her as harsh and abusive.[69] The absence of Indian women also had an impact on the men who migrated. As Karen Leonard has documented in California's Imperial Valley, many single Punjabi men who worked on farms in the region married Mexican women in part because there were few Indian women to court and antimiscegenation laws in California made it illegal for white Americans and people from different races to marry.[70]

As a second generation Punjabi, Dhillon also experienced her own marital challenges. After her mother died, her oldest brother, Kapur, planned to send her and the four other children in her family to India. His plan was for Dhillon and her sister to marry and settle there. Much to her brother's dismay, Dhillon fell in love with a Gadar activist, Surat Singh Gill, who was then a student at the University of California, Berkeley. She was caught in a dilemma: either move to India to fulfill her family's expectations or stay in the United States, risking her brother's wrath, and marry someone she knew and loved. She worried that she would not be able to use or further

her education if she moved to India, which was a land that she had never experienced in person. She chose to defy convention and marry her America-based suitor, though the marriage did not last. Dhillon's recollections of her early childhood and her adult life as a single mother underscore the double bind that immigrant women faced as they learned how to navigate a new land as well as manage family responsibilities and gender expectations.

CONCLUSIONS

Although the stories of Satyadeva Parivrajaka, Taraknath Das, Jogesh Misrow, and Kartar Dhillon reveal a dark period in the history of American immigration, they are connected to contemporary immigrant communities. Unlike the earlier immigrants, contemporary immigrants are citizens of free nations and have more rights and privileges, such as the ability to attain permanent residency, apply for citizenship, sponsor spouses, children, or other family members, and build a life in the United States. At the same time, the same feelings of isolation and loneliness and the struggles and joys of making one's way through a new environment echo across the centuries that divide early pioneers and contemporary settlers. There is no doubt, however, that these early immigrants' activism and efforts to establish communities paved the way for South Asian communities in the Pacific Northwest today; we now turn to their stories of departure and arriving to the United States.

2

ROUTES AND ROOTS

I was excited . . . in those days people traveled by big boats. Ships rather than plane, because plane was very expensive and we couldn't afford it. So when I got on the ship and was standing [on the deck] and all the rest of my family and friends were on the dock, then I realized I was going far away and I didn't know when I'd see them again.

—Shanta Gangolli

At that time, a lot of people had moved out of the state because Boeing had laid off about 70,000 people. And there weren't many job opportunities in the Seattle area. There was no Microsoft, or Amazon, or Starbucks at that time. It was just Boeing. But it was kind of a pleasant experience also. The weather was good. It would be raining most of the time, but it was a change from weather in India. So for the first couple of years it felt really good, you know, even if it rained, it was okay.

—Alok Mathur

HER sari fluttering in the sea breeze as she waved to friends and family gathered on the shore, Shanta Gangolli felt a wave of excitement wash over her as she prepared to embark on a new life alongside her young husband. Only after the ocean liner pulled away from the dock in Calcutta and the familiar faces faded into the masses did the enormity of her voyage sink in. Although all journeys begin with a departure, many South Asians such as Shanta Gangolli did not realize just how far that journey would take them from the land of their birth and how transformed they would become in the process. The memory of leaving a beloved home and arriving in a new place, no doubt an experience rife with excitement, anticipation, and trepidation, is held close to the heart of nearly every immigrant.

A family member's teary face, a ship or jetliner bound for new lands, or a crowd of loved ones lingering in the distance are seared into the mind's eye. For the South Asian immigrants who came to the United States at the turn of the twentieth century, the journey overseas was long and arduous, and there was no guarantee that they would ever see their homelands again. After World War Two, the world was a changed place and advancements in transportation, technology, and communications during the war meant that travel between far-flung places became much easier and more accessible to a wider variety of people.

Whether by sea, sky, or land, South Asians made their way to the Pacific Northwest and began the task of creating communities and building homes. Their modes of transportation, their motivations for leaving home, and their initial encounters after arriving make up an archive of immigrant experiences that provides detail to larger patterns of international migration and tell a story of global and national transitions. While each story of departure and arrival can be considered exceptional in some way, several common threads run across these narratives: the individual's family or community circumstances that prompted her or him to leave; the desire to pursue educational or work opportunities; and the often frightening, lonely, absurd, and invigorating experience of fitting into a new culture. Just as the students and workers who came from South Asia in the 1890s and early 1900s did, contemporary immigrants learned to navigate their new terrains by supplementing their favorite foods with new cuisines, speaking mostly English rather than a more familiar native language, and replacing favored styles of dress with western fashions.

Over time, these transitions have become easier, as new immigrants often enter into well-established communities that have resources for helping new arrivals adjust. Just as these communities have changed, so too have the experiences of traveling abroad and communicating with those left behind. The Pacific Northwest as a region has also evolved in the latter half of the twentieth century and today is a place where people from all around the world find themselves at home. Before examining how the Pacific Northwest has been shaped by these contemporary settlers and vice versa, we explore the personal stories about departure, arrival, and initial adjustment as immigrants transitioned from South Asia to their adopted land.

THE CREATION OF A DIASPORA:
MIGRATION WITHIN AND OUT OF SOUTH ASIA

While the reasons behind individual migration from South Asia to the United States are complex, key moments in South Asian and American social and political history shaped these flows, such as the Partition of British India and the subsequent independence of India, Pakistan, Sri Lanka, and Bangladesh; the restriction of immigration in Great Britain and the expansion of educational and work opportunities in the United States; and the growth of global and interconnected economies. Within the subcontinent, people have always moved from one region to another for political and economic reasons. Even though communities might live in a region for generations, it is common to trace family lineage back to ancestral locations well after any material connection has ceased to exist. While the SAOHP focuses on narrators' experiences with migration to the Pacific Northwest, many of them had histories of prior migrations within or outside the subcontinent. Raj Joshi, who came to the United States in the late 1940s, is part of the Maratha community, which is predominately concentrated in the central Indian state of Maharasthra. His family moved to Gwalior in the state of Madhya Pradesh in the nineteenth century; as Joshi notes, "My family got stuck up north because maybe my grandfather's grandfather moved there in the 1800s. They kept their language intact, but they put a lot of Hindi words in there too." Although his family was long-established in Gwalior by the time he was born, they still maintained cultural, linguistic, and family ties in other places on the subcontinent.

Intra-country migration became increasingly common in the twentieth century as transportation infrastructure improved and new opportunities opened in urban centers. Najma Rizvi, who came to the United States from Bangladesh to study geography and anthropology in the 1960s, notes that her family became established in Dhaka when her grandfather migrated from his village to the fast-paced capital city to pursue his education. His migration set in motion a series of events that would lead to Rizvi's own journey out of Bangladesh. Even though Rizvi moved from her home in Dhaka to various cosmopolitan cities including Seattle and Los Angeles, today she splits her time between the United States and some of the small Bangladeshi villages where her family still has roots, working as an anthropologist on issues of health and hunger. For others, migration was more of an accident of circumstance than a deliberate decision.

Bharti Kirchner, who traces her family history to Bangladesh, explains that she was actually born in Kalimpong in West Bengal in India, in the cool and lush shadow of the Himalayan Mountains. Her family had been dispersed on both sides of the India-Bangladesh border. She explains: "Actually I was not born exactly there [in Bangladesh] because as you know, in India, women go to visit their mother, wherever their mother is living. I was born in a smaller town. Now it falls in Bangladesh, but at that time it used to be India." Kirchner's family moved from East Bengal (modern-day Bangladesh) to the Indian-held territory of West Bengal during the Partition of British India. After she grew older, she, her siblings, and her parents moved from town to town as her father sought work in a variety of occupations. By the time she was six years old, Kirchner had already lived in three different cities, a portent of her journey from the eastern part of the Indian subcontinent to a variety of locations such as Chicago, San Francisco, Paris, Tehran, and finally Seattle.

In Kirchner's and Rizvi's cases, class, caste, and language shaped how they experienced moving from place to place and their familiarity with the cultures they encountered. The emphasis on education in Rizvi's family meant that she was fluent in English at an early age, which helped her quickly adjust to living in the United States after she came with her husband to study at Cornell University. Kirchner's college-educated mother also encouraged her children to pursue their dreams, no matter how far away they might lead. The experience of multiple migrations in both Rizvi's and Kirchner's families also meant that it was not entirely unexpected (though a bit unconventional considering the conservative environment of mid-century India and Bangladesh) that these young women would pursue life paths that led them away from their towns and familial networks into the wider world.

Some South Asians claim that the desire to travel the world is something that is culturally fostered. For example, South Asians from the northwestern Indian state of Gujarat have a long history of migration dating to the fifteenth century,[1] and today Gujarati shops and businesses are found everywhere from London to Nairobi to Jersey City. Zakir Parpia, a business owner and master builder in Seattle who is part of the Ismaili community that originates in Gujarat, notes, "We hail from Kutch. As a group, [we] are Banias, who have, apparently, a tremendous instinct for business." This

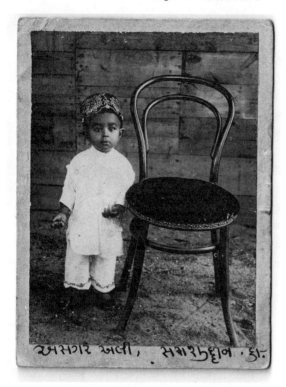

FIG. 2.1 Asgar Ahmedi as a toddler, Madagascar, circa 1930. Photo courtesy of the Ahmedi family.

instinct for business, Parpia implies, has led members of the community to move around the globe to pursue economic opportunities. Although he was born and brought up in Mumbai, Parpia came to the United States in order to further his education and settled, first in Spokane, Washington, and then in Seattle after founding his own business. Of course, the representation of a specific ethnic group in a particular occupation does not mean that some innate cultural proclivity predicts an individual's line of work; however, ethnic, religious, and cultural networks have facilitated the movement and settlement of future generations and have provided vital cultural links across geographically dispersed communities. Such global networks sometimes lead to local concentrations, as in the case of the Punjabi community that has grown in the Pacific Northwest, or the large population of Gujaratis living in East Africa.

Others, such as Asgar Ahmedi, were no strangers to traveling across oceans and continents and came from families that were already in diaspora. He came from a Bohra Muslim family that traces its roots to a town called Kutiyana, which is in the Porbander district in Gujarat and is most famous for being the birthplace of Mahatma Gandhi. In describing his own route to the United States, Ahmedi notes that his family has been long in circulation thanks to his grandfather's desire to explore other parts of the world. He explains:

> My grandfather, in early [19]20s, left India. The story goes that they would supposedly go to East Africa, but the ship they were sailing ended up in Madagascar. [Laughs] I cannot authenticate the story, but that's what I've been told. In this little town—right here on the map—it's a natural port, very small town. My grandfather and my dad were in importing and exporting coffee, vanilla beans, and a product called raffia.

Though he was born in Madagascar, along with his mother and two younger siblings, Ahmedi returned to his town in Gujarat when he was a young boy of four or five. His father requested that Ahmedi be left in the care of an uncle in Mumbai so that he could start his education in India after his mother returned to Madagascar. Recounting his move to India, he remembers:

> Mother and we came to India; my dad stayed in Madagascar, he didn't come with us. But it was also my grandfather—he wanted to come back—and my uncle, we were going to get him married, so that's the reason we came to India. And they left India in 1939, just before the war started. So I was left in India and from 1939 to 1945, I had absolutely no news of my mom and dad and all about five new brothers and sisters that were born while I was in [India]. Right after 1945 and the war ended, we heard from them.

Though the family had gone to India for a joyful occasion—the marriage of an uncle—they found themselves caught up in the political turmoil besieging the world in the late 1930s and 1940s. After Ahmedi's mother returned to Madagascar, he was cut off from all communication with his natal family. Ahmedi's family were subjects of a still-British India living in an island nation off the coast of Africa (which was under the control of Vichy France at the time), and they did not entirely belong in either India or Madagascar. As Indians, they were sympathetic to the mounting move-

FIG. 2.2   Asgar Ahmedi with his parents and brothers, Madagascar, circa 1938-40. Photo courtesy of the Ahmedi family.

ment for Indian independence from Britain; at the same time, they were also residents of a territory controlled by the Axis-allied Vichy French regime and therefore enemies of the occupying regime. This placed the Ahmedis in an uncomfortable position: "So we had two things going on in India in the [19]40s," Ahmedi relates, "India fighting for its independence [and] India also involved in war [supporting the] British, fighting the Germans and Italians and Japanese." The wars also ravaged India's economy and society, curtailing opportunities for education or work for someone like Ahmedi, who had not lived in the country for most of his life. Although his family did not have the means to send him abroad, his father was convinced that Ahmedi would have greater success as a student in relatively neutral America than he would if he stayed in India, moved to England, or even returned to his home in Madagascar.

THE END OF AN EMPIRE:
THE EFFECTS OF PARTITION AND INDEPENDENCE

All across the Indian subcontinent, rumblings of independence in the wake of World War Two forced relocations and prompted voluntary migrations as in Ahmedi's and Kirchner's cases. Sat Kapahi, Kris Gupta, and Padmini Vasishth were all born in what is now Pakistan and migrated to India in the period leading up to the independence of both nations. The Partition Act of 1947, which was the death knell signaling the end of the British Raj,[2] split British India into two nations along religious lines.[3] The division resulted in the displacement of nearly thirteen million people as Hindus fled toward India and Muslims toward Pakistan. This was perhaps the most significant and disruptive event in the lives of many immigrants of this generation. Padmini Vasishth recalls the horror that raged across the newly born countries as entire communities relocated from one place to another in a matter of months:

> You can't imagine it until you have gone through it. It was a very horrible, very sad event. When you see [savagery in] neighbors— you know, we had lived there so long; all my life I was there. The raids were so criminal that it is very difficult to even talk about it, because you well up with the sadness of the story. It was very sad. People were just crazy about religion; it was religion-motivated. And there was a hatred, sort of like something has gone over your brain. Best of friends would start doubting [each] other. And yet the best of friends were the best of friends, even at that time. Many people were moving to India, many people from India who were going to Pakistan, their own friends would defend them, keep them in their places, so that the mob doesn't attack them. It was the mob mentality that was very bad. It was very, very sad. Burning of buildings, killing people, looting their own friends—it was very sad. It was sad. It was, I think, not even under control. The police at that time, they are also human beings. So the mob mentality was too great even for any law and order.

Partition was an experience that changed the lives of Vasishth and her family. Uprooted from a diverse and previously close-knit community, she and her family were forced to leave Pakistan and moved to the Himalayan hill station of Shimla in what is today the Indian state of Himachal Pradesh, and then finally to Delhi. Sat Kapahi's family also left Pakistan for India under similar duress. He explains how his family experienced Partition:

> And then I went to college in Lahore. In 1947, Partition of India took place and then we all had to [migrate to India]. . . . Now Punjab was the state where we lived—like Washington State—and that was further subdivided into two parts. One part went to Pakistan and the other part to India. So there were all kinds of speculation—where will Lahore go? Some people said it'll go to India, others said it'll go to Pakistan. [Because of my father's business], we had all kinds of transportation. Most people do not have any transportation. So my father had moved the family over to Amritsar, which was sure to go to India because of the Golden Temple, which is the most religious, most sacred place for the Sikhs. So my father had moved the family over there [to make sure that the family would be safe in case Lahore went to Pakistan]. The decision was to be announced August 15th, 1947. When the final decision came, we found that Lahore was going to Pakistan, so we could not go back [to Lahore] and get any of our [belongings]. So my father lost all his business, all his property and everything.

The relocation meant that Vasishth's and Kapahi's families had to relinquish their land holdings in their hometown and start anew in unfamiliar cities.

While the division of the subcontinent along communitarian lines led to geographic dislocation for many, others such as Balraj Sokkappa had grown up feeling like outsiders in their own hometowns because they belonged to a religious minority. This feeling was heightened in the wake of religious violence sweeping the new nations. Sokkappa grew up as a Tamil Christian in an American mission compound in the Hindu-majority town of Madurai. The town is famous for the Meenakshi temple, which annually draws thousands of devout Hindus making pilgrimages to the ancient shrine. Though Sokkappa did not necessarily feel excluded from town life because of his religious background as a child, he remembers: "We were a very small minority. The Protestants are one half of one percent of the population and there are one and a half percent Catholics. So it was a total of about two percent Christians." The place of religious and other minorities in postcolonial India has long been a struggle for the nation, which is predominately Hindu. When it came time for Sokkappa to apply for college (he had intended to pursue a medical degree), he was able to qualify for a seat reserved for religious minorities in state-run universities. However, thanks to the mishandling of his application file, Sokkappa wound up on an engineering track where seats were plentiful and less competitive than in the medical field. He remembers: "The guys who organized the files, I guess one of them knew the guy from the state, another Christian, who was the second rank. So he knew that if he bypassed my file, [the second ranked student] would get the seat." Reflecting without regret on the incident, Sokkappa was channeled into his occupation partly as a result of national and cultural politics.

EXPLORING AMERICA:
SOUTH ASIANS ARRIVE (AGAIN) IN THE UNITED STATES

While the end of the British Raj was undoubtedly a significant event for the denizens of India, Pakistan, Bangladesh, and Sri Lanka, immigration policies in the United States and the United Kingdom also had a tremendous impact on where those citizens would eventually travel and settle. Although Taraknath Das, Satyadeva, and the activists of the Gadar movement had idealistically fought for independence from the British and had imagined that once a modern democracy was established, many of South Asia's problems would be resolved, their successors found that there was a large gap between those dreams and the reality of life in a postcolonial nation. As a result, many sought education and work abroad. Some returned to India after their education was complete with the intention of serving the still-developing country. But others stayed overseas because of personal circumstances or because they found that they were no longer suited for the political climate or culture of work in South Asia.

While 1965 is often marked as the turning point in American immigration history because of the passage of the Immigration and Nationality Act, the 1940s and 1950s saw a small but steady number of middle- and upper-middle-class South Asians migrating to study or work. These immigrants often came from families that had the resources to send their children abroad or secure visas through personal or professional connections. Padmini Vasishth, for example, came from a well-connected family that had ties overseas. Her father and grandfather were both lawyers in the British civil service. Her father had been educated at Cambridge University and had practiced law after being admitted to the British and Indian bar. When she and her husband decided to move to the United States to continue their education, her family supported their decision fully, as she was following in her father's footsteps. Likewise, Raj Joshi's father was a professor who specialized in animal husbandry and had an important position in the new Indian government's Department of Agriculture. His father's work brought the family to the United States when Joshi was still a teenager and opened the door for his eventual settlement there. In comparison, though Sat Kapahi's family did not travel outside of the subcontinent, his father was in the brick-making business in Pakistan and started a lucrative stone-crushing business in India after Partition. Having financial support made Kapahi's move to America possible because his family could afford to send him abroad. For others who were less economically endowed, such as Asgar Ahmedi, the opportunity to come to the United States opened partly because of extended family support and a fortunate encounter with an American Foreign Service official. He recalls:

> In Bombay there was a library—U.S. Information Library. It was one of the few places air-conditioned. So I would go there and pick up a *Look* magazine or *Life* magazine and read it and everything. My dad wrote to me, "If you want to, go ahead and apply for a school in USA and I will take care of it. I'll ask for dollars from government of Madagascar." Reserve Bank of India wouldn't give us any money because my dad didn't have any money. So I stopped into that library and I asked—I still remember his name, Mr. Hartwell. He was a director of the U.S. Information Library. I said, "I want to go to USA, I have admissions here—this Colorado School of Mines or University of Denver. But my dad doesn't have money here; he has some money in New York." When he was exporting vanilla, he had put some money there. I'm talking about 1950s. Not now, now it can't happen. He picked up the phone, called Mrs. Sanderson. She was the U.S. Consul in Bombay. He said, "I've got a young fellow sitting here and he wants to go to USA. How can we help him?" And he explained to her what my situation was. So she told him that if this company in New York—the company's name

was Gillespie & Co.—wrote to them that if I went there they'll take care of me. I said, "All right." I was doing my third year in college, studying chemistry and botany. All of a sudden, one day . . . the phone rang. And [someone from the American consulate in Bombay] said, "All right, you can come and pick up your visa to go to the States." My goodness. All of a sudden—"What do I do now?"

That phone call altered Ahmedi's life course and sparked his journey to the United States. However, he still needed to fund the costly trip. Fortunately, he was able to borrow money from his maternal uncle to travel to New York City and then on to Denver to start his education in 1950. Although the decision to migrate is often narrated as a personal choice, the connections and resources available to these narrators were vital in supporting their migration.

For those immigrants who left South Asia immediately after decolonization, such as Vasishth, Sokkappa, Joshi, Kapahi, Ahmedi, Gangolli, and Gupta, travel abroad was a leap of faith into an unknown land and culture, and one that carried with it a great sense of adventure. Flights were still incredibly expensive in that period, and ocean liners were by far a more common way to travel. Coming to America from South Asia by ship meant the journey was long and often involved several stops in exotic locations along the way. Kris Gupta, who emigrated from the state of Kashmir in North India to Seattle, recalls:

I came by ship from Bombay to England. It was an old troop carrier, so part of the reason was it was cheaper. But one of the engines blew on the way, so instead of two weeks, we spent two and a half weeks getting there. Then I was supposed to fly from England to New York, but I was on a waiting list. So I ended up, somebody cancelled, and I came on *Queen Mary* from Southhampton to New York back in [19]51.

After landing in the United States, Gupta made his way to the Pacific Northwest, where he enrolled in an aeronautical engineering program at the University of Washington. Padmini Vasishth and her husband, who came from Delhi to Seattle in 1954, also traveled by ship: "It was a very nice, fine steamer, an Italian boat [the *Lloyd Trostino*]. From Bombay we came to Colombo, Ceylon, and then we went to Hong Kong." During one of her layovers, Vasishth had the chance to tour the British territory of Hong Kong and meet Indians working there:

> India had just got Independence; there were a lot of Indians there, and they were hovering around us—"How great it is that we're an independent country," and "Did you see Nehru, did you see Gandhi?" Because those were our champions of freedom, and they would want to hear all those stories. They were so proud that we had achieved independence. And a lot of them were doing good business—you know, taxi drivers and hotels, and they were running their own businesses. And because we had come from India, it was like they had to look after us—where we should go, where we should eat, this and that. So we had a good time there.

Young, newly married, and full of the energy generated by being a citizen of an independent and increasingly respected new nation, Vasishth and her husband thoroughly enjoyed the voyage and the encounters they had along the way. Not even the seasickness wrought by a typhoon en route could diminish her excitement. More than fifty years later, the memory of landing in Honolulu and making her way to Seattle lingers in her mind in extraordinary detail:

> We reached Honolulu and there they had these leis and all. It was like touching ground after a long time on the ocean. . . . We took some movies there—first time we saw a drive-in movie. It was a big open-air drive-in movie. We could never have those in India. You can drive your car in; we were sitting in the car and watching the movie. And then you got out and went and bought your little something to eat and brought it back. That was, you know, an experience by itself.

In a similar way, Sat Kapahi's journey in 1952 was an adventure that involved multiple stops, modes of transport, and new experiences. Including air as well as sea travel, Kapahi's journey almost did not commence as planned. After his family had made the decision that he and his cousin would travel to the United States to attend school, their plans were delayed by a rather provincial hitch. He recalls: "There's always a family astrologer who picks the auspicious date for us to leave home. The date he picked and the date we were going to sail from Bombay was about ten days apart, so we had to leave home ten days before. [Laughs] Then we went to Bombay and stayed there." After getting celestial clearance to set sail, Kapahi and his cousin sailed from Bombay to London: "We stayed in London for a few days and then we flew from London to New York by Pan-Am flight. Then we went from New York to Baton Rouge [by bus, and joined Louisiana State University]. It was quite an experience." Kapahi and his cousin had embarked on their transcontinental trip with the bravado of young men, but quickly found that they longed for the comforts and familiarity of their homes. While the physical journey took its toll on them, the emotional pressure of leaving behind their friends, families, and wife (in Kapahi's case) was much greater. He recalls:

> We never had been out of the country before, so we were both really very scared. First night we spent at the YMCA in New York—I remember we paid five dollars for sleeping overnight. In those days, it was about 25 rupees—we are talking about 1952. And we both would cry—sat and cried all night. We didn't sleep at all; we were really very scared. Then in the morning, there was one friend of our uncle who came to our YMCA; he took us to the bus [station] and talked to us. We felt a little relieved that there's somebody who knows us.

Likewise for Ahmedi, cross-continental travel was grueling, but filled with new experiences. Getting from Bombay to New York City was no easy task and required several detours:

> Actually, when we left Bombay, there were just about two or three of us [on the plane]. But when we landed in Dhahran—you know, Dhahran, oil capital, Saudi Arabia—all the Americans, engineers, they filled up the plane. Dhahran to Paris; Paris to, what is that? Ireland's airport—Shannon, is it? I forget the name. I had lunch over there. That was one of my first experiences with a lot of fancy

western food and cocktail drinks and everything. Then came to
Gander, Newfoundland—it was bitter cold. September of 1950. All
I had was twenty-dollar traveler's checks. We would go into the
airport. I wanted a cup of coffee and the fellow said, "I can't cash
your check." There was a Canadian lady; she said, "Give the young
man coffee, I'll pay for it." [Laughs]

After arriving in the United States in major cities such as Washington,
D.C., New York City, or Honolulu for those coming via the Pacific Ocean,
these immigrants still had to make their way to their intended destinations.
Raj Joshi initially lived in Washington, D.C., with his family after his father
took a position in the U.S. capital, but after gaining admission at Washington State University in Pullman, he set off on a cross-country trek that
led him from one Washington to another. On the way, Joshi encountered a
profoundly different "Indian" community than his own during his visit to
the Assiniboine Indian reservation in Fort Peck, Montana:

So I came out by bus—took about seven, eight days, sort of a
wandering trip. Stayed in Montana with Assiniboine Indians. I
was expecting to live in teepees and stuff—Mrs. Powers fixed it up
for me—so this guy comes in a Cadillac. [Laughs] Anyway, I had
three or four great days with the Assiniboine Indian Tribe, Fort
Peck Reservation. They even made a record of Indian music for me.
They asked me to give a speech. I was reading Karl Marx, so I said,
"Indians of the world, arise!" in Hindi. [Laughs] When you're 18,
you're crazy anyway.

These stories of departure, travel, and arrival are foundational to the
experience of living in diaspora, as South Asian immigrants had to bridge
the homes they left behind and the new worlds they were encountering. For
the South Asians who came in the 1940s and 1950s, international travel was
rare and to go so far abroad for work or study was not an option available
to most people. Many of these migrants had witnessed firsthand the end of
an empire, become citizens of new nations, and embarked on journeys that
took them away from a familiar, but quickly changing home. Though small
in number, the South Asians who came in this era opened the doors for later
generations of immigrants to establish themselves in the Pacific Northwest.

MIDNIGHT'S CHILDREN: IMMIGRATION REFORMS
AND PROFESSIONAL MIGRATION AFTER 1965

The next wave of South Asians arrived as American immigration laws shifted in the 1960s and new work and education opportunities sprouted throughout the country. Many of the narrators who came in this period were born just prior to or after India, Pakistan, and Sri Lanka become independent nations. Though most did not experience the atrocities and uncertainty of Partition in India and Pakistan firsthand, they did recall the realities of living in a postcolonial nation that still bore the scars of war and civil unrest. Amy Laly, who migrated first to Oregon and then moved to Washington State in the 1960s, was born in the mid-1940s in Mumbai. Her family is Parsi, which is a small but deep-rooted community in India that traces its roots to ancient Persia and predominantly practices Zoroastrianism. Although Zoroastrians (and therefore Parsis) were considered neutral in the religious politics of Partition that split along Hindu, Muslim, and Sikh lines, they were nevertheless deeply affected by the pain of that era:

> So my father was in the railroads and if you know about what
> happened in Northern India, there were three factions, you know,
> that clashed. And those were the Hindus, Muslims, and the Sikhs.
> And my father, being a practicing Zoroastrian, would take his shirt
> off and then he had the Zoroastrian underwear, which identi-
> fied his religion. So they wouldn't touch him. The carnage was all
> around him. And so, he would tell us stories about taking the train
> from Delhi to Lahore. And he would carry Muslims from Delhi
> to Lahore on their way to a new Pakistan, a new state. And when
> the train would arrive at the station, there would be dead bodies
> in the buildings or even in the [rail] compartments, the passenger
> cars. And when he brought the Hindus from Lahore back to Delhi,
> that happened in the same way. There was no innocence left in the
> sense that all these communities—the Hindu, Muslim, and Sikh
> communities—they were on a killing spree.

Laly's family suffered economically because her father found it difficult to cope with the traumas he had witnessed and, in time, grew distant and was unable to work. The horrors of Partition continued to cast a long shadow on the lives of narrators who grew up after the event. For Zahid Hossain, war was a present reality when he was a young man in Bangladesh during the nation's struggle for independence from Pakistan in the late 1960s and early 1970s. He recalls how his family literally "dodged the bullet" of military escalations:

> Our house was probably a block off the main army camp in Khulna. And close to the beginning part of the Independence War, we came very close to being dead. An army [person] was shoot-ing at our house and a few bullets missed my father by few inches. And . . . so like every family in Bangladesh, everybody was affected. We did not . . . we were fortunate that none of our immediate fami-lies were murdered or killed. So, that was a good thing, but many of our slightly distant relatives, friends, they were killed.

His family quickly vacated their home and moved to a suburb to wait out the bloodshed, which made travel and moving around the city a daily struggle: "Nobody in their right mind would go from one place to another unless they had to. Every day, you know, was viewed as your last day. There was no guarantee that you would make it to the following morning."

Bangladesh eventually won its freedom and became an independent nation in 1971 and Hossain went on to finish his university education. After he received his master's degree, he began teaching in a university. However, he found that the education system in Bangladesh could only get him so far and in order to pursue his dream of a doctoral degree, he would have to move abroad. As young people raised in newly sovereign nations, indi-viduals like Hossain and Laly were tasked with becoming the future work-ers and leaders expected to help promote development and progress. For many, however, this task proved daunting and migration became a means of gaining valuable experience that could be put toward the project of nation-building or, in some cases, an escape to a better life. High rates of unemploy-ment plagued the subcontinent; the escalation of worldwide oil prices in the 1970s and famines across countries such as India created intense pressures for young people who wanted to contribute to their national economies, but were hard-pressed to find work. For this generation, the economic and psychological impact of living in postcolonial nations was great. This experience, coupled with opportunities offered in other parts of the world, laid the foundations for the departure of many young people from South Asia.

While earlier generations had favored migration to Britain because of their status as Commonwealth citizens, Britain began shutting its doors to Asian immigrants in the 1960s and 1970s. Enoch Powell, a prominent member of the British Parliament, created a flashpoint of controversy when he gave a publically broadcast speech decrying the immigration of former colonial subjects to the British Isles on April 20, 1968. His infamous oration, dubbed the "Rivers of Blood" speech, along with growing anti-immigrant sentiment across the United Kingdom, paved the way for reactionary forces to gain momentum. Using immigration as an election issue, the Conservative Party came into power in 1970. Under the Conservatives, new legislation was introduced that made migration extremely difficult for foreign-born nationals. For instance, until 1970, most people holding a British passport could immigrate to the Commonwealth. In 1972, new laws mandated that former British colonial subjects could only settle in the United Kingdom if they obtained work permits and could prove that they had a parent or grandparent who had been born on British soil. This policy change had the intended effect of severely curtailing the immigration of subjects from the Indian subcontinent and other parts of the former empire.

At the same time, in the post–World War Two boom years, the American economy was expanding at an unprecedented pace. The United States had claimed its place as a world "superpower" and was hungry for new labor to help build up its burgeoning scientific, medical, educational, and military industries. A self-professed land of immigrants, the United States began to draw increasing numbers of Britain's former colonial residents. With the passage of the 1965 Immigration and Nationality Act, more people could acquire student, worker, and family reunification visas as country of origin quotas were eliminated and new preference categories were instituted. The Pacific Northwest was a particularly attractive destination for South Asian immigrants because it was home to key institutions such as the Boeing Company. Rajinder Manhas was drawn to this sense of greater opportunity in the region and notes that his familiarity with the aerospace industry in the Pacific Northwest contributed to his decision to move there: "Some of the people who had been here before from my college kind of knew a little about Seattle. But also Boeing was here and my bachelor's degree was aeronautics. So that connection had something to do with coming to Seattle."

South Asian immigration after 1965 differed from that of the previous generation partly because of the changes in immigration laws and demand for technically skilled labor in the United States, but also because the kinds of people who were able to immigrate changed as well. The expansion of educational institutions throughout South Asia created opportunities for people born in smaller towns and rural areas, as well as urban centers. Women began to immigrate in greater numbers, not only as spouses or dependents, but also as students and professionals. This had a significant impact on the class and gender profile of the South Asian community: while the majority of pre–World War Two immigrants were mostly single men who came as workers and students, many of the narrators profiled in this book came from middle-class and elite families that were able to provide their children with access to higher education or as part of family units.

Another significant shift was the relative ease in communications and travel. By the time immigrants started coming to the United States in the 1960s and 1970s, air travel had become more commonplace, though the journey from South Asia to Seattle was still long and occasionally hazardous. Dev Manhas recalls his trip from Delhi to the United States in 1967 when he came as a medical resident:

> I came by Pan-Am over the Pacific. The West Coast is sort of dia-
> metrically opposite from India and you can come either east or
> west when you come to the West Coast. So I came via the Pacific.
> So it was a long flight, of course. It was sort of an eventful flight in
> the sense that when we landed—the jets used to be 707 and they
> were not very long-distance, not what we have now. So we flew
> from New Delhi to Bangkok. And then we got down to Bangkok for
> a short period of time, and then we flew from there to Hong Kong.
> And in Hong Kong, we landed and we were supposed to take off
> in an hour. An hour went by and then nothing happened. Almost
> five-six hours went by and still they were not clearing our plane for
> taking off. To make a long story short, we learned later on that the
> plane that came after us, when it landed, half of the plane landed in
> the water. So apparently there were some casualties and the airport
> was closed for that reason, which nobody told us. [Not] until late
> in the evening, [did] they finally say that some accident happened.
> And they said that our flight was going to be leaving the next

morning. So they put us in a nice hotel overnight and then bussed us back to the airport the next morning. And then we flew from there to Tokyo . . . and we stopped in Honolulu . . . the flight then brought me from Honolulu to Portland . . . and then to Seattle.

Arriving with less than fifteen dollars in his pocket, Manhas entered the country in a way remarkably similar to the immigrants who came nearly twenty years earlier; however, his journey was significantly shorter and was a matter of a few days rather than weeks. Manhas, like so many immigrants before him, was sure that he would return to his family and friends in India. In the end, his medical career, family in the United States, and life constraints quickly steered him toward a different path. In contrast, Zahid Hossain was more frank with himself as he boarded the flight that took him from Dhaka to Honolulu for his studies:

Well, I mean I knew the pain of leaving the family before when I came to Dhaka. So that part was, you know, I was used to that part. But when I was coming to the U.S. I was leaving my country. I was leaving my parents and that . . . that was painful. Especially when the plane took off, when I saw the country disappear before my eyes. And I felt that . . . that maybe one day the universities in Bangladesh would be of good quality, so that people like me don't have to go abroad for the degree. It would be right there. So that was primarily the reason. I was not coming to the U.S. for "good life" or to have fun. I was coming because I wanted that education.

The departure of qualified individuals like Hossain and Manhas, however, was not without its problems for those left behind. As the rate of out-migration spiraled upward, many of these emigrants were criticized for being disloyal to the nation. In India, the term NRI—non-resident Indian—came into popular use to describe residents living outside of the national borders, but it also took on a mean-spirited quality as it came to refer to "not really useful Indians" or "not relevant Indians" who were abandoning the nations in search of greener pastures.[4] Some of these concerns over what became known as "brain drain," however, were complicated by the large amounts of money remitted back home from immigrants around the world.[5] Immigrants found themselves in a difficult position: either they could stay in the United States, develop their own careers, and help family members back home financially, or they could return to their home countries and contribute to the growth of industries there. Prem Kumar notes that when he, his wife, and daughter made their first trip back to India in 1984, they had intended to settle there after living and working in Idaho and Washington State for over a decade. Both he and his wife had doctorates and tried to find teaching jobs in India. He recalls, "We traveled mostly in the north. There were fewer universities at that time than there are now. So, our choices were pretty much limited. There is a university in Amritsar, but bigger universities were in Chandigarh, Patiala, and Delhi. So we tried at various universities without much success."

Discouraged by the lack of opportunities for two highly trained researchers and educators, Kumar and his wife decided to return to the United States and pursue their careers there. Ultimately, his move to the United States as a student resulted in a permanent break with his homeland. Thus, the immigrants who came after 1965 experienced what immigration studies identify as classic push-pull factors: the education of a middle class in South Asia coupled with high rates of unemployment pushed people out of their nations, while the increasing demand for trained professionals pulled them toward the West.[6]

NEW MIGRATIONS AFTER 1980:
DISPLACEMENT, REUNIFICATION, AND GLOBALIZATION

While the immigrants after 1965 were affected by deliberate changes in U.S. policy intended to attract technically skilled immigrants, the generations coming after 1980 were more heterogeneous largely due to expanded family reunification policies which allowed people to enter on various types of visas. Others came through new provisions that opened American borders to refugees fleeing from nations such as Sri Lanka, where a vicious and bloody civil war raged through the 1980s and 1990s. Finally, changes in the global economy and the rapid growth of technology industries in the Pacific Northwest brought South Asians to the region for work. Like their predecessors, many South Asians who came in this period were predominantly urban. Many of them had already been exposed to different parts of the world because of advancements in travel, mass media, and telecommunications. Even if they had spent most of their formative years in one region, they were aware of worlds and cultures beyond their nations, and many already had family members long settled around the globe.

While some of these narrators grew up in experiencing cultural and political stability and relative middle-class ease, political turmoil shaped the lives of others. Nirmala Gnanapragasam, a Sri Lankan Tamil, recalls the horrors of the civil war in Sri Lanka that forced her to leave the country. She was a university student when the civil war severely disrupted her home life and education. A middling student before, she was transformed by a series of bloody riots in 1983 that devastated the Tamil community around the country: "After the [19]83 riots, it clearly gave me the motivation. So if you look at my transcript, my grades were so much better after the [19]83 riots than before, because I knew that I had to make something out of my life and I had to get out of the country." During the riots, she and her family were forced out of their house in the capital city: "We basically left the house with just the clothes that we were wearing and took a few things from the house. And everything we owned was burnt." Heartbreakingly, she recalls what life was like as a refugee driven from her cherished home:

> We were in the refugee camp for about five days, which was at the airport in Ratmalane. . . . So we were in the camp for about five days and then we went to the north, North Jaffna, in Sri Lanka, which is a predominantly Tamil area. And we went and lived with our relatives for about two months possibly and then I came back to the university to finish my junior and my senior year.

The pain of multiple migrations within the country also made the idea of leaving Sri Lanka more tolerable. Gnanapragasam married her college sweetheart in 1984 and decided to leave permanently. She had the opportunity to come to the United States with her husband, who was coming to Chicago for graduate school. Recalling her departure, she notes, "So if you asked me when I was growing up as a child, I would never have thought I would settle down in another country. But I think we were forced in a way." Prasanna Samarawickrama had a completely different experience of departing Sri Lanka in the 1980s. Born into a Sinhalese family also living in the capital city, Samarawickrama and his family were affected differently by the wreckage of the civil war. After attending a school in Colombo run by Americans, he was eager to experience life halfway around the world and embarked on a high school exchange program in 1982 at the age of seven-teen. He first came to a tiny town in Oregon, where he completed a year of high school. After he finished his program he returned to Sri Lanka and joined a national airline as a flight attendant. He recalls,

> That was a very high-paying job, in Sri Lanka, because, you know, you travel overseas and you get a stipend. And I saved, you know. pretty much every penny of it. And I didn't even, you know, bring it back to Sri Lanka. I sent it directly to the United States and banked it here. So my commitment to myself was [that] I will do that for two years. In the summer . . . for the fall semester in [19]85, I was going to come back to the United States.

Samarawickrama kept his promise and came back to Oregon to start his degree in engineering. As a flight attendant, he spent two years beginning the day in Colombo and ending it in Paris; as a result, Samarawickrama was well-acquainted with different cultures and lifestyles before he settled in the Pacific Northwest. Similarly, Akhtar Badshah's travels with his fam-ily in South Asia helped cultivate his curiosity about the world: "We went to South India, went to North India. We also went up to Nepal. Of course, Gujarat, lots of trips into Rajasthan, to Madhya Pradesh." He studied abroad in Switzerland as part of his undergraduate education in architecture and afterward, he spent several months backpacking through Italy, Austria, Ger-many, and other European countries. By the time he came to the United States in 1981, travel was not an unusual or dislocating experience for him, so much so that he could not even recall in which city he first arrived, unlike earlier immigrants who could retrace their routes hour-by-hour.

Rizwan Nasar developed a similar cosmopolitan sensibility from his childhood spent in the Pakistani port city of Karachi. He was the second-youngest of seven children and had siblings and other close relatives settled in the United States. He remembers, "My siblings used to travel quite a bit and come here and go back. So it was not as if [it were a very strange thing]. The clothes that I would wear would mostly come from the U.S. most of the time." His family and urban upbringing instilled a sense of worldliness in Nasar and he also credits his exposure to multicultural communities to his education at a Catholic high school in Karachi: "You know, growing up in Karachi, I grew up with Catholics and Protestants. . . . I had friends who were Christians, who were you know, of different religious background, like Afghanis or Parsis or Boris and I have all sorts of friends." His social circles and family abroad piqued Nasar's interest in traveling outside of Pakistan for his education. At the same time, changes in family reunification policies in the United States meant that his sister was able to sponsor him to come to the country on a green card, rather than a student visa. A far cry from the early sojourners who were unable to become citizens when they arrived in the Pacific Northwest in the 1890s, Nasar was able to immigrate to the United States as a permanent resident when he came in the 1980s and apply for citizenship soon afterward.

These stories of departure reveal how the revolution in air transportation not only gave South Asians access to faster and more comfortable travel, but also facilitated greater, more frequent contact between immigrants and their homelands. As regular routes to South Asia were established by international airlines and jet travel became more affordable, South Asian immigrants returned home for family vacations and maintained connections to their regional cultures. Some found that as the global economy expanded and new forms of work brought people from all ends of the globe together, not only their lives, but their jobs also became transnational. Whereas Shanta Gangolli bade farewell to her friends and family not knowing when she would see them next, contemporary immigrants who came after the 1980s traveled the globe with relative ease and found that moving abroad was not as much of a rupture as they had anticipated.

TRANSITIONS AND TRANSFORMATIONS: SETTLING IN THE PACIFIC NORTHWEST

After making the journey to the United States, South Asian immigrants quickly found themselves thrust into new environments and cultures. Though their experiences of departure, travel, and arrival differed depending on the era in which they were migrating, South Asian immigrants across all three generations had to adjust to new climates, develop strategies for keeping in touch with loved ones left behind, and adapt their cooking and eating habits to the ingredients and cuisines available in the United States. Over time, these adjustments became easier as South Asians established cultural centers, restaurants, groceries, and other amenities; however, the initial experiences of arrival were still complicated and unnerving for most of these migrants.

One major aspect of this adjustment was the physical environment itself: though not all narrators migrated initially to the Pacific Northwest, the green and gloomy natural beauty of the region made an impact on many South Asian immigrants no matter when they came. Jeff Siddiqui, who arrived in the 1970s, had been studying at a university in the arid Northwest Provinces in Pakistan. He had grown weary of the dusty and drab landscape that encompassed his campus. Seattle, in comparison, had been described to him as a verdant paradise, which sealed his decision to come to the University of Washington for his master's degree. He recalls his first impressions after he saw pictures of the city: "Green. Rain. I had just come from a university in the desert. Brown, rock, and no rain. And here it was rain and green everywhere. I couldn't believe it. I said 'That's where I'm going.'" Siddiqui was overjoyed to find a place that lived up to his imaginings and quickly explored the region's many forests and parks through camping trips and hiking expeditions. However, for the many new immigrants coming directly from South Asia, where the scent of bougainvillea and jasmine permeates hot tropical cities, the wet and gray winter was an unwelcome shock. Coming to Pullman from Mumbai after having spent a couple of days in New York with a friend, Zakir Parpia remembers:

> Well, I arrived in Spokane. . . . I was supposed to take a flight to
> Pullman but the airport was closed down because of a blizzard. So
> I had never seen snow before. This was an interesting [introduction
> to snow]. There was a gentleman who had to get to Pullman and
> who rented a car. So we piled up, three of us students, into a car
> and [he] drove [us] from Spokane to Pullman in a driving snow-
> storm. . . . We had just met. He did take us to Pullman because
> there was no [other] way to get to Pullman. The airports had been
> shut down. So we drove down the highway in a complete blind-
> ing [snowstorm] in pitch darkness. And of course, there was thick
> snow coming at you as you drove. It's probably one of the most
> vivid memories I have of arriving here.

Rao Remala, who came to Bellevue, Washington, in 1981, was struck not only by the physical beauty of the Puget Sound landscape, but also by the stark difference between the colorful chaos of his native India and the stringent organization of the United States: "I was really mesmerized. I mean, like how orderly the whole thing was, I mean the roads. And then for example one of the [things] clearly I remember, I went to McDonalds. It really kind of surprised [me] . . . I mean, you stand in the line, you order it, and then they give it [to] you in these little containers. They are so clean and neat."

While enthralled with their new surroundings, South Asian immigrants still faced the loneliness and alienation of being so far from their friends and families. While the use of email, cell phones, and video chat to connect immigrants around the world is commonplace today, these technological changes have occurred fairly recently. Today, immigrants are able to keep up with news from home with the click of a mouse and alleviate some of the cultural isolation that earlier immigrants faced. For those narrators who came in the 1940s and 1950s, the changes in telecommunications over time have been remarkable. Sat Kapahi remembers:

So sometimes I would write home, write a letter. You know, in those days telephone was impossible. As a matter of fact, when I came to Seattle and I moved into the house, if you wanted to call India, we would place the call in the evening about six o'clock. And we'll get the connection about four or five in the morning. You called the operator—"I want to call India, such and such number," and then she called you back. And it would always be that you placed the call [at] six in the evening and [she'd] call you [at] four, five in the morning. So I'd always place the call on Friday night so it would be Saturday morning—if she wakes me up at four o'clock, I can sleep a little late. That was a big deal, getting a call through to India [and you had to shout at the top of your voice to be heard on the other end].

The quality of the connection and process of placing a call were not the only obstacles; for South Asian students on limited budgets, the cost of an international phone call was exorbitant. Amy Laly recalls how expensive it was to call India in the 1960s:

Of course, you know, what you missed was in those days, it was . . . I could be exaggerating, but it was like six dollars for a minute to call India. You know, so that was very prohibitive! So I'd call my mother and say "hi—how are you doing?" And then put the

phone down! And she'd hear my voice and she'd be fine. So that's
how we communicated. There was of course a lot of letter writing.
Now that has changed. You can call. You don't even have to write
an email. You just call. So that's all changed.

The India that Sat Kapahi and Amy Laly left behind had no private telephone companies and phone lines were owned and operated by the government. Many Indians did not have phones in their homes and had to use
operators to reach an international line. Often, several families living on the
same hallway of an apartment building would share a common line, or the
fortunate family that had a line in their flat would allow neighbors to use
the phone when needed. It was not until the 1990s that the Indian government created public-private partnerships in the ownership, service provi-
sion, and infrastructure development of the telecommunications industry.[7]
These changes and the opening of telecommunications markets globally
to international competitors have created a sea change across South Asia;
today, India boasts the second-largest telecommunications network in the
world. When calling India today, Kapahi notes, "now you just pick up the
phone and dial and there it is. And the connection is very, very clear—like
you're talking to anybody here in Redmond or Seattle."

Staying connected to South Asia was a challenge for many immigrants,
not only because of telecommunications, but also because of the vast cultural differences between the two parts of the world. Food and access to
familiar ingredients is one area in which those differences are most acute.
The smell of fresh curry leaves, the sounds of popping mustard seeds in oil,
the stickiness of fresh tamarind, the sear of a red chili at the back of the
tongue, the clatter of a stainless steel platter brimming with fragrant basmati rice passed across the table, the warmth of naan hot from the tandoor
on the fingers—these are just a few of the sensory memories that give South
Asians a sense of culture, place, and history.[8] The South Asian immigrants
to the Pacific Northwest who migrated after World War Two did not find
staple ingredients such as long grain rice, yogurt, or spices easily available.
Immigrants would have to request items from people traveling to and from
South Asia or journey to other cities with large immigrant populations
to acquire goods. In time, they also learned to substitute ingredients and
gathered together with others to pool resources and cook familiar foods.
Enterprising immigrants, Asgar Ahmedi included, resorted to importing

ingredients and selling them to others in the Pacific Northwest. Still, for many of these immigrants, part of their experience of migration involved making do with whatever was available. Initially living in Boston in the 1950s, Shanta Gangolli notes that rice was easily available and the presence of an Armenian community helped her find lentils. She and her husband were also able to order food from an Indian store in New York City whenever friends would travel between the two cities. However, Gangolli had limited experience with cooking and an elderly neighbor began feeding her and teaching her how to make American-style dishes when she learned that Gangolli was pregnant. Gangolli remembers:

> Every day she would take me in her house. And once she knew I was expecting a child, she got to feed me—she said, "You have to eat roasts and you have to eat ham." And I was not used to [that], but because I didn't want to hurt her feelings, I started eating. She was a very good cook. I got used to eating all the non-spiced meats because of her, and learned quite a few things like meatloaves and spaghetti sauces and roasts and steaks. She would cook them and then I would ask her how to make [them].

Even though she missed the rich gravies and spices of Indian food, Gangolli grew accustomed to American food and even began to crave certain dishes. More difficult than developing new tastes, however, was the transition to running a kitchen on her own. For many South Asians who had grown up with some sort of domestic help, cooking and cleaning were not well-developed skills.

Those who arrived after 1965 found many more restaurants and shops that catered to an increasingly diverse immigrant population. Amy Laly recalls going to Chinatown in Portland to find coriander, green chilies, and spices. She figured that certain substitutes would make her version of curry bearable, if not completely authentic. Fed up with having to rely on makeshift recipes, Bharti Kirchner went one step further in order to satisfy her desire for Bengali cuisine while studying in Chicago in the early 1960s. She notes:

> I developed a craving for Indian dishes, like Indian students do, and I learned to cook. And I started improving my cooking and I was taking cooking classes here and there. And the idea of an

Indian cookbook was forming in my head. The Bengal region, where I come from—there were no cookbooks available from that area. Only a few general Indian cookbooks were available in the market. I realized that you can't write about all of India, there was such an extensive cuisine and there were so many regional cuisines in India, which people didn't know about. So I had it in my mind that I'd do the Bengali cuisine and initially that happened. Over a number of years later, I'd write that cookbook, but the idea was in my head for a long time.

For Kirchner, who was a trained computer scientist and worked in the technology industry for several years, her craving for Bengali cuisine and her experiments with cooking jump-started a second career as a writer. She has since written several cookbooks and novels in which food plays a starring role.

As recently as the early 1990s, the cities of the Pacific Northwest have historically had a very small number of Indian restaurants and grocery stores in comparison to metropolitan areas such as Chicago, New York, Los Angeles, and San Francisco. In downtown Seattle, people often shopped in the International District at stores such as Uwajimaya (a supermarket established for East Asian immigrants in 1928) for rice, spices, and fresh vegetables or drove to Vancouver in British Columbia to stock up on supplies from the Punjabi markets. When Microsoft experienced its phenomenal growth in the late 1980s and early 1990s, the South Asian community in the Seattle area grew significantly and also brought new business to the region. Rao Remala, the first Indian to be hired by Microsoft in the early 1980s, recalls the difficulty of finding Indian groceries and restaurants when he first arrived. He notes that the engineers from South Asia coming to work for the software giant have made a visible impact on the region's markets and remarks: "We didn't see a big wave of people until, I think, the late 1980s. Then a few people started coming to Microsoft like [19]82 to [19]83. [19]83 there were a couple of people and slowly 4 or 5 [would come] and by end of the [19]80s, there was quite a few people . . . I mean maybe 100 or something like that." By 2000, the South Asian population had exploded. In response to the growing Asian populations, Uwajimaya opened a second store in Bellevue, Washington, and stocks key items such as okra, dal, and pickles that reflect the tastes of South Asian communities.

The many South Asians living in Washington cities such as Redmond, Bellevue, Kirkland, and Woodinville (which happen to be the major communities around Microsoft's main campus) have prompted new businesses, including South Asian grocery stores, restaurants, and halal meat counters. Today, several non–South Asian businesses also cater to the South Asian customer: video stores and Netflix stock Bollywood movies, while grocery store chains such as Safeway and Trader Joe's offer South Asian packaged meals, spices, and vegetables. The bulk retailer Costco, which was founded in Kirkland, Washington, also stocks large packages of uncooked rotis, paneer (Indian cottage cheese), basmati rice, curry sauces, and South Asian sweets. Clearly, the growing South Asian community has created a market hungry for culturally specific products and made an impact on the non–South Asian palate as well.

CONCLUSIONS

Painful, humorous, entrepreneurial, innovative, enduring, exceptional—these are the ways in which immigrants experienced their arrival to the United States and the Pacific Northwest. While family need, coincidence, trauma, and opportunities abroad prompted their decisions to emigrate, changes in immigration laws worldwide drew them to the United States and the Pacific Northwest. Though couched as individual choices, these stories of departure and arrival show how even something that is considered a personal decision is still shaped by state politics, economic conditions, and global migration patterns. In the next chapters, we explore in greater depth how these migrants made the transition from travelers to immigrants, first as students, then as workers who established themselves in the Pacific Northwest.

3

CREATING PROFESSIONAL CLASSES

EDUCATION AND TRAINING

> I was at a school called Barnes High School in Devlali. Devlali is about, I would say, 300 miles from Bombay. It was a British-run school. And I consider [those years] as probably the most enjoyable time of my growing up because it was a beautiful boarding school.
>
> —Zakir Parpia

> But for me, the education up to elementary school was in the same village, you know. I remember we used to walk in a lot of this mud and you know . . . forget about the shoes. And then once we finished fifth grade, then we used to walk to a neighboring . . . it was a little more than a village, and they had power, I think, and they had a high school, and we used to walk, you know, walk all the way to high school every day—one way was like five miles.
>
> —Rao Remala

O N a sweltering August day in 1979, Lakshmi Gaur was filled with trepidation and excitement as she stepped into a large meeting room at the Ministry of Education in Delhi. Leaving nothing to chance, she had dressed carefully that morning in a green sari, as that was her lucky color. Gaur had been studying at Punjab University in Chandigarh when she was called to Delhi to interview for a fellowship through the Fulbright Foreign Student Program. She wanted to pursue her doctoral degree and a Fulbright fellowship was her ticket to the research universities she dreamed of in the United States. But first she had to get through the interview. She took her seat in front of an imposing committee made up of vice chancellors, Indian government officials, and American Foreign Service officers. Though she had hastily put together an application proposal to study transferases, a subfield in human genetics, just days after seeing an advertisement about the fellowship program in a locally circulated newspaper, she confidently answered the questions fired at her by the committee. Finally, the members of the panel asked her one final question: "So, will you come back?" Without skipping a beat, Gaur replied: "Of course! I have to come back and serve my country." With this declaration, Gaur won a sought-after fellowship to leave India and travel to Charleston, South Carolina, and start her Ph.D. Although she ultimately settled permanently in the United States instead of returning to India, Gaur, like generations of South Asians before her, changed the course of her life and that of her family's by deciding to pursue her education abroad.

In Gaur's case, her migration was possible because of the Fulbright program's commitment to promoting international educational exchange and bringing scholars from across the globe to study in the United States; for others, leaving the country for higher education only became possible through a unique set of circumstances. Regardless of how they came, the journey was preceded by countless hours preparing for exams such as the GRE (Graduate Record Exam) and the TOEFL (Test of English as a Foreign Language), meeting with advisors and mentors to learn about foreign educational systems, and applying to various universities. This effort was not the burden of the student alone; parents scrimped and saved to ensure that their son or daughter could continue his or her education abroad. Considering the amount of labor required to move abroad, what brought these students to the United States, and, in particular, to the Pacific Northwest?

On one hand, the answer to that question is simple: South Asians sought a better life and saw education in the United States as one avenue to that end. At the same time, a complex array of forces, such as colonial and postcolonial investments in education,[1] periods of national economic decline in South Asian countries after decolonization, the shortage of labor in the United States during the Cold War, new opportunities through exchange programs such as the Fulbright, and openings in universities across the country after the Immigration and Nationality Act of 1965, all prompted the migration of many South Asians. While each individual might see her or his story as the result of her or his hard work, family support, intelligence, and initiative, this class of immigrants was produced by the confluence of specific socioeconomic events and policies related to education in South

Asia and the United States. Behind the immigrants' personal recollections about their "school days" lies a complex story of how South Asian nations have produced a contemporary educated labor force shaped first by educational policies initiated by the British in the mid-nineteenth century, and then through the rapid expansion of institutions of basic and higher education in the postcolonial period. Education also became the primary catalyst for South Asian immigration to the Pacific Northwest after World War Two, as regional universities began recruiting foreign students in order to supplement the small pool of technically proficient workers in the United States. The legacy of colonial and postcolonial education in South Asia and changes in American immigration laws created a unique moment that resulted in the transplantation of South Asians who were already well-educated, fluent in English, and eager to take advantage of the opportunities now available to them.

LEGACIES OF EMPIRE: COLONIAL MISSIONS AND ENGLISH LANGUAGE EDUCATION

From mission schools in rural areas to modern universities modeled after western campuses, education in South Asia has evolved as an amalgamation of different traditions and influences. As the British East India Company gained political and economic control on the subcontinent in the early seventeenth century, it not only initiated substantial trade between Europe and South Asia, but also opened pathways for social reformers, missionaries, and other groups to engage in formal development projects in the British-held territories. The Charter Act of 1813 sought to make the company more accountable to the British government and invited new constituents interested in gaining a foothold in the region to migrate to the colony. As a result, missionary groups established hospitals, schools, and churches across South Asia and instilled a distinctly British educational system that continues to shape education in nearly all South Asian nations to this day.

Nearly two hundred years later, mission schools still carry considerable weight as premier educational institutions, partly because these were sites where students could learn English. Zakir Parpia recalls the presence of a mission school close to his home in Mumbai. The school housed an orphanage whose students would play near the Mumbai waterfront where he and his siblings would roam. The students and the nuns made an impression on the young Parpia: "So, when I was three, they offered to take me and admit me to the school, which my mother agreed to because it sort of gave her free time." Although his family was part of the Muslim Ismaili community, his parents decided to send him to the school partly because of its proximity to the family's home, but also because the opportunity to send one's young son to a western-style school was rare. Even though educational institutions in South Asia have proliferated, private schools are still often seen as desirable because the quality of education is perceived to be better than that offered by government-run schools. Since private mission schools generally use English as the primary language of instruction and often teach other languages to promote multilingual fluency, they are also highly regarded and considered vital windows into life in the West. Shanta Gangolli describes how important this exposure to English and other languages was to her own family's decision to sending her and her siblings to a mission school in the 1930s:

> Many private schools then were mission schools, and they were not very expensive. People in India, that time, they didn't worry about whether they were Christian schools or Hindu schools. Because until we were in the fourth grade, we were taught in the vernacular language, and then we were given a choice whether we wanted English as a medium or the vernacular language as a medium. So, it was a pretty free choice of languages to learn. Most children learn at least four, five languages when they are growing up. I was surprised here when people fought about prayers or not prayers. I mean, we sang all kinds of songs—Christian hymns, Indian songs. Didn't matter to us, we loved to sing. And parents didn't worry about as much—as long as we didn't harm people, you know. So it didn't matter; the whole idea was that we had good social and moral standards.

Gangolli elaborates that when she decided to pursue the English-language track, it was because she "had planned to go in for higher studies, and in colleges in the Bombay area it was English, the medium of teaching." In order to continue her education, Gangolli found that her proficiency in English was an indisputable advantage.

This ubiquitous presence of English in the South Asian educational system can be traced to 1835 when Thomas Babington Macaulay, historian and East India Company functionary, delivered his now infamous "Minute on Indian Education" to the British Parliament. In his speech, he sought to make explicit how imperative it was to encourage English language education in India. He went so far as to argue that education in native languages was worthless:

> The dialects commonly spoken among the natives of this part of India contain neither literary nor scientific information, and are, moreover so poor and rude that, until they are enriched from some other quarter, it will not be easy to translate any valuable work into them. It seems to be admitted on all sides that the intellectual improvement of those classes of the people who have the means of pursuing higher studies can at present be effected only by means of some language not vernacular among them.[2]

Macaulay's candidate for this exemplary language of a higher order was English. He proposed that while the British could not educate everybody in India, they needed "to form a class who may be interpreters between us and the millions whom we govern: a class of persons, Indian in blood and colour, but English in taste, in opinions, in morals, and in intellect."[3] It was the task of this class of middlemen then to "refine the vernacular dialects" and to enrich them with "terms of science borrowed from the western nomenclature," rendering these languages "fit vehicles for conveying knowledge to the great mass of the population."[4] Macaulay's arrogant pronouncements on Indian culture and languages reinforced the idea that only English could bring so-called backward South Asians into modernity.

Mission-educated Shanta Gangolli and Zakir Parpia in some ways represent the brown-skinned English elite that Macaulay had hoped to socially engineer. However, they each saw English as the means to a brighter future where they could connect with the wider world. This intention differed significantly from the expectations of colonial-era imperialists who saw education as a tool for improving the management of the colonies for the British. Under that logic, English education should be limited to the study of language, literature, and western culture for Indians, rather than carry a focus in the sciences or mathematics. This was in part because Macaulay and his contemporaries did not see the need for scientific education in India because Indians were perceived as intellectually inferior and thus incapable of learning those subjects. In short, they were unfit to participate in the Victorian ideal of industrial and technological progress, which were assumed to be the prerogative of the British. Not surprisingly, many Indian nationalists rejected this belief and strongly advocated that the future of the Indian subcontinent lay precisely in building national scientific and techno-logical curriculums. Despite the racism at the heart of Macaulay's vision, his desire for a class of English-educated Indians came to fruition and many of those individuals went on to form the powerful Indian National Congress and the Muslim League, which were emblematic organizations that headed systematic anti-colonial resistance and eventually led to the decolonization of the region.

CREATING A NEW CITIZENRY: EDUCATION, LANGUAGE, AND POSTCOLONIAL IDENTITY

Across South Asia, the emphasis on English as the medium of education also generated a new set of struggles over personal and national identities that continued even after independence. In India, Nehru recognized that mandating English-only education would create inequalities in the early postcolonial period, even as he advocated that a wider network of govern-ment-funded schools ought to offer greater access to English as a subject. In a letter he wrote to Ramdhari Sinha Dinkar, a nationalist poet and intel-lectual in India, he noted that Hindi should be the medium of instruction for most subjects in Indian schools, though studying English should be com-pulsory for all students.[5] The paradox for Nehru was the practical need to create comprehensive educational policies that recognized the utilitarian value of English for promoting global commerce and international connec-tions, while at the same time attempting to mitigate its hegemonic impact on native cultures and language. The supplanting of regional languages with Hindi or English was primarily an attempt to create a more unified citizenry who would identify themselves as Indians, rather than by their state or com-munity affiliations. However, this perspective was extremely contentious, and local language advocates decried the homogenization that would result if regional languages gave way to Hindi or English. Nehru was sympathetic to this point and did not want people to feel alienated by the new attempts at nation-building. More worrisome was the possibility that English-medium education would create new stratifications in society or what Nehru termed "a new caste system . . . an English knowing caste separated from our people."[6] At the same time, he did not want the newly independent country to be insular or to fall behind other nations in terms of technical advancements; thus, he argued that learning English and other non–South Asian languages was ultimately necessary for communicating with scientists and other thinkers around the world.[7]

The result of this tension between curricula in English and those in indigenous languages was the promotion of bilingual education. Although Nehru supported bilingual education (and particularly that children learn regional languages in elementary school and then English in the higher grades), English-language education has continued to develop rapidly in India partly because of the presumed link between fluency in English and success in a global economy and partly because it is now an integrated vernacular in the South Asian landscape.[8] One legacy of this emphasis on English education is that today, many middle-class, urban South Asians claim English as a language native to India. Zakir Parpia remarks that though he and his siblings were familiar with regional languages such as Marathi, Hindi, and Gujarati, his and his parents' education in mission schools made English the lingua franca of his childhood home.

In contrast, Dinesh Keskar learned English as a third language. Keskar was born in the state of Gujarat and spoke Gujarati almost exclusively until the age of five. When his father, a professor of chemistry, found a job in a small town in the neighboring state of Maharashtra, Keskar quickly had to learn Marathi to adapt to his new environs and later began to study English seriously in school. Similarly, Rao Remala recollects that much of his primary education was in Telugu government schools, which is the language that predominates in his home state of Andhra Pradesh. In high school, he entered into an English-medium school, which proved to be a difficult experience initially. Switching between English in the classroom and Telugu among friends, Remala was challenged to find his footing in a linguistically complicated university world. As a result both Remala and Keskar found that they had to actively negotiate their cultural and linguistic identity on a daily basis.

In other cases, having a deep understanding of various languages was not simply a tool for upward mobility, but a tool for survival. Jafar Siddiqui's family had roots in modern-day India and was uprooted during Partition.

Siddiqui spent his youth moving around different provinces of Pakistan, from Peshawar to Karachi. In the process, he learned Pashto, Urdu, Sindhi, and Punjabi, as well as the requisite English. Although Siddiqui developed a love for languages, his fluency in languages indigenous to Pakistan was tied to his ability to "pass" as a true Pakistani.

Najma Rizvi and Zahid Hossain, who grew up in modern-day Bangladesh, found that issues of language and identity were deeply intermeshed into their educational and personal experiences, as well as the larger political landscape in which they lived. Both were born in East Pakistan and spoke Bengali at home. Rizvi's father had been working on a degree in English literature and was a vocal proponent of learning English. However, his untimely death precluded Rizvi from going to elite schools because her mother was left to manage a large family. Instead, Rizvi and her siblings attended less expensive government schools where the primary medium of instruction was Bengali, though they learned English later in high school. Bangladesh, which was considered part of Pakistan until 1971, was a hotbed of language politics through her adolescence and young adulthood. The official state-determined language was Urdu (to keep in line with the language of then West Pakistan), but the majority of the people in the east were Bengali speakers. By adopting Urdu as a national language, Bengali speakers felt forced to relinquish their rich linguistic and literary traditions.

Language, then, became one of the most potent aspects of Bangladesh's independence struggle. The clash over language and culture came to a crescendo in the late 1960s when the Bengali-speaking portion of the population, aided in large part by the Indian government, launched a full-blown offensive against the Pakistani government. These politics did not impinge on the personal realm for Rizvi: she married an Urdu speaker who had family roots in India, though her marriage to a non-Bengali man was a source of consternation in her family.

Following a bloody war and massive political turmoil, Bangladesh was born in 1971. Bengali became the lingua franca for state-supported schools, while elite education in Bangladesh continued to be in English and modeled on a British curriculum.[9] Still, nationalistic ideals and economic imperatives were at war with one another in the new nation: the country needed to build its indigenous socioeconomic infrastructure and create strong local political leadership in order to deal with the challenges of building a new nation-state.[10] At the same time, the historic class divisions wrought by access to schooling had material effects. Today, a wide gulf persists between the English-speaking middle classes and less well-educated working and lower classes. Although there have been concerted efforts on the part of national and transnational development institutions, such as the World Bank and Asian Development Bank, to invest in education, access is limited to a small number of people and the literacy rate, which is defined as the ability of an individual to read a newspaper and to write a simple letter in any language, hovers just above 55 percent. Bangladesh faces challenges at both the primary and secondary levels of education; when Zahid Hossain was growing up in Bangladesh, there were few avenues available in the country for pursuing education beyond the college level.[11] Hossain found that after he finished his undergraduate and master's degrees in biochemistry, he was unable to move further ahead because his options were limited. He recalls, "In Bangladesh, you study where you get admission into. Getting into university, any kind of university, and it is [that way] still now, is highly competitive. So you just take admissions tests from different institutes and then [in] whichever one you succeed, you study there." Hossain wanted to take up a Ph.D., which was difficult to find in his field. As a result, he applied to international programs and fellowships, which eventually brought him to the United States. In Hossain's case, the lack of graduate opportunities in Bangladesh led him to seek his degree elsewhere.

Linguistic, religious, and ethnic identity also shaped the educational experiences of Nirmala Gnanapragasam and Prasanna Samarawickrama as citizens of postcolonial Sri Lanka. Like other South Asian nations, Sri Lanka established its current educational system while it was still under British rule. After gaining independence in 1948, Sri Lanka undertook substantial educational reforms and began offering free education to the majority of the population. As a result, the country has the highest literacy rate in South Asia, at nearly 92 percent. However, education in Sri Lanka is split along linguistic lines: Sinhala and Tamil are the two major languages, though English is widely spoken and taught in schools. Growing up in a Tamil family in Colombo, Gnanapragasam studied at a government school, which had begun as a mission school. Her education through second grade was in Tamil; after that, she studied English as a second language and was encouraged by her parents to practice speaking and writing English at home. Her family hoped that she would use her English-language skills to go into a scientific field. Though Gnanapragasam played the *veenai* (a string instrument) from a young age and enjoyed performing in her school's theater productions, her educational trajectory was determined by government selection policies. She recalls,

> The government actually picks who goes to the university there [Sri Lanka]. They have a standardized exam there by twelfth grade and the government actually selects who will be going into the different programs like medicine or engineering. And just like most of the Asian communities, medicine and engineering are supposed to be the two top professions. So I think only 7 percent of the Sri Lankan population is selected to go into university. So, yes, after my twelfth grade I got into university there.

National quotas and family pressures together played an important role in shaping Gnanapragasam's professional career as a civil engineer. In contrast to Gnanapragasam's government education, Prasanna Samarawickrama, who also grew up in Colombo, studied at Ananda College. The college was founded by the American missionary Colonel Henry Steel Olcott in conjunction with the Buddhist Theosophical Society in 1886. While Anglicans and Catholics had established mission schools in Sri Lanka, Olcott established schools that incorporated Buddhism, while maintaining an American-style curriculum. Samarawickrama's exposure to American education shaped his desire to study eventually in the United States. He recalls,

> I did high school in Colombo and I always, you know, wanted to come to the United States, but that was kind of a very distant goal for me. I couldn't really figure out how to make that happen, but I did, you know, apply for a scholarship. There was an AFS [American Field Service] scholarship for high school exchange.

Samarawickrama's application to the American Field Service program led him to live with a host family in Oregon for his high school years. He later returned to the Pacific Northwest to finish his post-baccalaureate degrees in engineering. For these narrators and many other South Asians, their educational trajectories and opportunities were shaped by state-engineered policies that attempted to navigate a complicated linguistic and cultural terrain, personal and family circumstances, and the perceived labor needs of their postcolonial nations.

LAYING THE FOUNDATIONS: TECHNOLOGY, DEVELOPMENT, AND THE POSTCOLONIAL NATION

As South Asian nations began to seriously consider what kind of education would best meet their needs, the nascent governments of India, Pakistan, Bangladesh, and Sri Lanka overwhelmingly embraced the development of science- and technology-related curriculums. Among the foremost of these technocratic visionaries was India's first prime minister, Jawaharlal Nehru. Nehru, who had studied at Harrow School and the University of Cambridge in the United Kingdom, was deeply influenced by a vision of a socialist economy driven by Western-style scientific and technical progress. In the inaugural address of the 36th session of the Indian Science Congress in Allahabad in January 1949, Nehru plainly argued that the nation had to take on the mantle of technical education if it was to survive:

> We have to concentrate on the advancement of scientific research and the application of science. The Government is building up laboratories, institutes and the like to give opportunities to youth to further the cause of science, because we realize that a country must be good in regard to scientific research and application of science if it is to play its proper part in the world and because we also realized that we cannot solve our problems economic or otherwise without the help of science.[12]

In the decades following independence, India established a network of higher education institutions that included the Indian Institutes of Technology (IIT),[13] the Indian Institutes of Management (IIM), several regional engineering colleges, and the Indian Institutes of Science. Several private institutions, such as the premier Birla Institute of Technology (which was founded in 1964 through a collaboration between the Ford Foundation and the wealthy Indian Birla family), were also created in this period.

The western influence on education in India persisted well into the post-colonial period and also created new inequalities as technical education developed into a multi-tiered system that privileged the upper castes. The

All India Institute of Medical Sciences (AIIMS) and Armed Forces Medical College (AFMC) led the way for state-sponsored medical programs that borrowed from the British system, while the IITs were high-level schools funded by the central government in collaboration with Germany, the former Soviet Union, the United Kingdom, and the United States. Five IITs were initially established starting in 1950 and located in major cities or small towns: Kharagpur, Mumbai, Chennai, Kanpur, and Delhi. The IITs were followed by the RECs (regional engineering colleges), funded at the state level to mimic the education of the IITs and also to create more opportunities for students all around the country. The Indian Technical Institutes (ITIs) catered to working-class professionals and provided training for plumbers, technicians, machinists, and electricians.[14]

Despite the proliferation, gaining admission into these institutions was difficult for the average student. Rao Remala recalls that when he graduated high school in the early 1970s, there was only one regional engineering college per state and admission was quite competitive. In order to foster national integration and encourage students to move to other parts of the country, the national government had decreed that 50 percent of the seats in each regional engineering college should be reserved for students from other states. Remala did get into a regional engineering college in the district of Warangal in his home state of Andhra Pradesh, but found that many of his classmates did not share his cultural or linguistic background. While the educational policies in the postcolonial period were aimed at developing a much-needed workforce, they also had the effect of promoting a vision of an Indian-trained and -identified civic population. At the same time these scientific and technical education programs continued colonial policies that privileged upper-class and caste elites and worked to establish a national bourgeoisie, even while trying to create a broad, nationally-based workforce.

While postcolonial India heavily invested in technological and scientific education, Pakistan, Sri Lanka, and Bangladesh also turned to education as a major tool for national economic and social development. Rizwan Nasar, who was born in Karachi, Pakistan, came from a family of *muhajirs*, the individuals that moved from India and settled in Pakistan after the Partition of 1947. His parents were Muslims who had lived in East Pakistan (now Bangladesh). After the independence of Bangladesh, they moved permanently to Karachi, where Nasar studied at elite American and British schools through his Cambridge "O"-level exams. Though he was receiving a strong English-language education, when he was in fifth grade his parents moved him to a different school so he could study Urdu. He recalls:

> I started my schooling with the American school. In around fifth–sixth grade, my parents realized that I cannot read and write Urdu, which is the official language of Pakistan and which is my mother tongue as well. I was kind of interested too—one of the things that I said was "Hey, I can't do that!" So what they did was—they put me in a Catholic private school.

Ironically, the best place for Nasar to get a proper Urdu education turned out to be a private mission school. Nonetheless, literacy in Urdu was necessary for the son of a *muhajir* to help solidify his Pakistani identity, particularly because his family traced their roots to mainland India and Bangladesh, rather than Pakistan proper. Even though Nasar was born in modern-day Pakistan, tensions remain over who is considered a "son of the soil" and who is a transplant.

Nasar's vignette is embedded in a complicated story about the national politics of Pakistan. The country was formed in 1947 when British India was partitioned into two nations along religious lines. Like India, the new nation was concerned with what direction education policy would take. Much of the debate in postcolonial Pakistan focused on the role of Islam as the ideological foundation for educational institutions and practices.[15] While the nation went through many political upheavals (such as repeated military coups, a civil war that led to the formation of Bangladesh in 1971, recurrent border skirmishes with India, and the assassinations of political leaders), several five-year plans and national initiatives were launched to promote and develop the national educational infrastructure. However, education in Pakistan remains divided along class lines today: the upper- and middle-class urban elite education continues in the colonial English tradition, whereas Islamic schools seek to provide a religiously grounded education to lower-class populations whose needs are not met by underfunded government schools. Despite the many attempts of the government since 1947 to provide free and universal education to all its citizens, the results are poor: Pakistan has one of the lowest literacy rates in South Asia. Literacy in Pakistan remains at 49.9 percent. Of this, too, male literacy outstrips female literacy—61.7 percent of men are literate while female literacy hovers around 35 percent.[16]

Despite these uneven outcomes, the emphasis on technical and widely accessible education has been a major hallmark of the transition from the colonial to the postcolonial period across the South Asian subcontinent. As citizens of newly formed states came of age in an era rife with political and social struggles, they found that while access to different forms of education expanded, new inequalities and questions over the quality of training available in their home countries lingered. As a result, the emphasis on English as the language of modernity and economic and technical progress, the availability of western-style schools for the middle classes, and the limited employment opportunities for the educated urban elite created a population ready to pursue new opportunities around the globe.

EDUCATION ABROAD:
CHALLENGES, SURPRISES, AND TRANSFORMATIONS

South Asians' experiences with education in the colonial and postcolonial periods of their home nations, as well as the opportunities presented in the United States, paved the way for their migration abroad. South Asian immigrants often present the decision to migrate as one motivated by their personal achievements and aspirations, and the role of U.S. educational policies in actively courting international students is relatively minor in their narratives. And yet, American universities have been admitting foreign students since the late nineteenth century.[17] After World War One, American universities began recruiting international students as new programs facilitating foreign study exchanges were created. As a result, a small number of South Asian students began arriving in the United States.[18] In the early twentieth century, there were approximately one hundred students from India enrolled in American colleges and universities, including Rathindranath Tagore, the son of Nobel laureate and Bengali poet Rabindranath Tagore.[19] In 1942–1943, a census of foreign students enrolled in American universities and colleges recorded fifty-four students from India (only nine of whom were women).[20] As World War Two reached its climax, U.S. Senator J. William Fulbright established the Fulbright Fellowship Program as a way to facilitate greater cultural knowledge between various countries and the United States. The program initially sent six American students to Burma and invited several Burmese students to enroll in U.S. universities.[21] After World War Two, the need to internationalize curriculums in order to

secure American foreign policy interests became an even stronger imperative for many major universities to admit foreign students.[22] As a result, by
1949, only a few years after the earlier census, the number of students from
India had grown to 1,493.[23] The number of international students, particularly from South Asia, in the United States has continued to increase steadily
since the 1960s.[24]

The University of Washington, Washington State University, Oregon
State University, and the University of Oregon have all played a significant
role in recruiting and retaining these international students. The University
of Washington was one of the earliest educational institutions to open its
doors to students from South Asia. Between 1908 and 1915, the University
of Washington admitted twenty-five Indian men to its programs, including Taraknath Das and Jogesh Misrow.[25] In 1969–1970, shortly after the
passage of the Immigration and Nationality Act of 1965, the University of
Washington was among the top ten institutions in the country enrolling
international students, who made up 5.1 percent of its student body at the
time.[26] These numbers have grown steadily since the mid-century: according to the "Open Doors" report of the Institute for International Education
(IIE), India was the number one nation in 2007–2008 to send students to
American universities.[27]

Lakshmi Gaur, whose story opens this chapter, and Owais Jafrey were
direct beneficiaries of these new programs facilitating foreign exchange and
study abroad. Gaur came to South Carolina as part of the Fulbright Foreign
Student Program, which helped her eventually apply for and receive permanent residency. Jafrey had been working as an educational counselor at
the United States Information Services (USIS) in Rawalpindi, Pakistan, and
completed his master's degree in English in the early 1970s. As a result of his
hard work and distinguished service with the USIS, he received an award
from the U.S. government that came with a coveted immigrant visa to the
United States. Though he had not intended to travel abroad, the opportunity presented itself. With the advice of some of his American colleagues in
Rawalpindi, he decided to come to the University of Washington to further
his education and to bring his family with him.

While statistics on visas and foreign student enrollment clearly demonstrate the role of American universities in fostering student immigration,
they do not give insight into the funny, intimidating, confusing, and enrich-
ing aspects of South Asian student life on American university campuses.

Getting admission to a university was only half the battle; once here, South Asian students had to prove that they were every bit as worthy as local students. Rizwan Nasar was in an English class at Michigan State University when he encountered some of the more challenging aspects of being a foreign student. Nasar recalls an incident early in his student career, when he turned in his first essay in a literature course. The instructor told him: "Oh, I have graded your paper and I will give it to you, but I am not going to discuss the paper in class. You have to come to my office hours after class to discuss the paper. I am going to put the paper on your desk and we will continue with class." Understandably shaken after having worked hard on the paper, Nasar felt confused about how to proceed. He recalls:

> I turn [it] over. He gives me a zero and says, "This paper is not written by you." So, I see this and I say, "Wait a minute. What do you mean this paper is not written by me? Have you ever seen a paper from me?" He says, "No. But didn't I tell you that we will not discuss this in class? You come to my office hours." I said, "You will damn well discuss this in class because you gave it to me in class. So you will discuss." This is the first time I spoke in the class. And everybody kind of stopped and looked at me. I said "Yes, you gave me the paper in class. We are going to talk about this in class. I am not going to come to your office to talk to you." And probably he heard me speak in English for the first time—a long sentence. . . . He said, "You are from Pakistan and this is the best-written English paper." I said, "If you have your history correct, Pakistan was a British colony for 200 years and I guess the British know a little bit of English." He went red.

Nasar's experience not only underscores his teacher's ignorance but also highlights the discrimination that South Asian students faced on American campuses. On a more humorous, but equally frustrating note, Pramila Jayapal remembers arriving at Georgetown University as a freshman and trying to sort out her first-year dorm assignment:

> So I went to the Foreign Students Office and I said, you know, "I am a foreign student and I never got my room assignment and can you tell me where I am going to live?" And I think all the guy

heard was "foreign student," because he looks at me and he goes, "Do . . . you . . . speak . . . English?" [Laughs]. And I thought, I can't believe he is asking this. I was like, "No, that was just a rehearsed speech. If you ask me anything else I won't be able to answer." Then he turns bright red, you know, he realized what he had said and he turned bright red. But I did think "Oh my god! I picked Washington, D.C." It's supposed to be the center, you know, for foreign policy, and here is this guy asking me if I speak English.

Once Jayapal settled into the campus, she continued to find that her peers were not nearly as educated about the world as she would have hoped. Feeling homesick one day, she bought a poster of the Taj Mahal to hang on her dorm room wall. She recalls her roommate's reaction to the poster: "She came in and she said, 'Wow! Is that your house?!' And I said 'Yeah!' I said, 'Actually that's the servants' quarters to the house.' I couldn't believe she was serious! And she said, 'Really?! You must be really rich!' I said, 'I am. I'm a princess.'" Nicknamed "Princess Pramila" from that moment, Jayapal reflects that her adjustment to the United States was a mixed bag: "I had instances like that that were so funny in retrospect and I think at that time they were funny, but also incredibly alienating because you realize, oh my gosh, these people don't even know where India is. They have no idea what the Taj Mahal is."

While Nasar and Jayapal highlight the struggles of being foreign students, Bharti Kirchner, who came to the United States in 1962, had to navigate life on the other side of the desk, as a graduate assistant who was responsible for teaching undergraduate mathematics. She was accustomed to a vigorous regime of math classes in high school and college in India and found the students in the United States to be less adept in the subject than she had expected. It was not just dealing with ill-prepared students that challenged her; she felt like a fish out of water when navigating classroom culture in the United States. She recalls:

I found [teaching] a little difficult also because I came from a very strict background where you have to be in class, you have to take the exams and you have to pass them, whereas it was much more lenient here and actually I don't think the students—I don't think I was very popular with the students in the beginning because I didn't understand all that. I kind of gathered that as I went on and so I was a little bit strict with them. I didn't give them all A's

FIG. 3.1 Rizwan Nasar settles down with a cup of tea to read a newspaper at his student apartment, East Lansing, Michigan, 1987. Photo courtesy of Rizwan Nasar.

like they wanted. I didn't give them B's even when they wanted it [laughing] and then I found that things are a lot different here.

Not only was the American classroom a site of estranging encounters for many South Asian students at first, but they also had to struggle with the expectations of their families back home. Often, families had made substantial financial and emotional investments in their children's educations abroad. Pramila Jayapal, whose parents are from the state of Tamil Nadu in India, grew up in Indonesia and moved across Southeast Asia because of her father's work. Her father was determined to send his daughter to the best school that he could afford and felt strongly that education in America was her best option. Her older sister had already come to the United States for college, but when it came time for Jayapal to make the journey in 1982, her family had fallen on hard times. She recalls,

And actually in that period my father went through some very, very tough times with his job. And we struggled financially like the last three-four years. So my sister went to college in the United States in [19]79, and by [19]80 my father was going through all of his job problems. I mean it was really, really tough . . . there was a time when he didn't think I would be going to the [United] States. So we had investigated going back to India, going to the Philippines. We were looking at, you know, potentially doing education and college in the Philippines. And so I really didn't know . . . it was very . . . it was tough. I didn't know where I was going to be going. When he did finally send me to the [United] States, it was kind of amazing. He had, my mother only told me this recently, but he had about $5,000 dollars in a bank at that time. And he was committing to an education that was, at that time, like $12,000–$15,000 a year. Of course now it would be $60,000–$80,000. But at that time that's what it was and he was committing to that because he was so, you know, and I got scholarship and things, but he . . . he was so determined that I should get the best education I could, but in his mind that was in the United States.

Jayapal arrived in Washington, D.C., aware of the efforts it had taken for her to enroll in an elite American university and quickly committed to an early career in business, hoping to become financially independent and economically successful, though she later changed course.

Similarly, Jeff Siddiqui felt the weight of family pressures as a young student at the University of Washington in 1974. Upon arriving at the University of Washington, he signed up for several graduate classes in aeronautical engineering. After a term of balancing an enormous workload and various odd jobs to stay afloat financially, Siddiqui finally reached a breaking point. Facing failure in several of his classes and afraid of disappointing his parents, who had hoped their son would pursue an engineering track, he was feeling hopeless: "I could see it and I knew there was no way that I could pass. It was just impossible. And I just freaked out. I had my bags packed. I said, 'I'm going home, I can't do this. This is ridiculous.'" Eventually, the kind intervention of an International Students Services counselor helped Siddiqui decide to come clean with his parents about his academic and financial troubles:

I was as close to a breakdown as you can get. They had the International Student Services at Schmitz Hall at that time and there was a wonderful fellow called Ted Carpenter. He was the head of the

International Services Office, or something like that. And some-body told me I should go talk to him. So I went and I sat down and he talked to me. And he could see that I was just wrecked. It was unfathomable how bad off I was. Just freaking out. So he calmed [me] down a little. He got me appointments with the counseling office, which was across the hall. I didn't know what the counsel-ing office was. And he did something for me that I remain grateful [for] to this day. I told him that I could not talk to my parents and tell them I'm leaving engineering. Because that's what I'm going to do—I am not going to be an aeronautical engineer. I was done with aeronautical engineering. [Laughs]. And he said, "Well." And I said, "I don't know how I can tell this to my parents, they would be incredibly disappointed." He said, "Well, maybe you should try it." I said, "I can't. And plus, I'm broke!" I mean, I used to work on campus with these twenty-one credits. I was also working at that time, up to thirty hours on campus, to make my living. And he picked up the phone and he dialed my parents' phone number, from the university. And he gave me the phone and he walked out of the office. I don't know how long I spoke, but he let me talk. And I tell you, that saved my life. Because I spoke to my parents and they finally . . . they said, "It's okay. It's okay." And then the counsel-ing office helped me decide that, "Alright, you're not going to be an engineer. Don't worry about it." So they said, "What will you be?" I said, "I have no idea! But I'm not going to be an engineer in aeronautics!"

The counselor helped him to switch majors and to take classes in business administration, which Siddiqui found to be much more manageable and interesting.

As the recipients of their families' gifts, many, like Siddiqui, felt enor-mous pressure to succeed and not disappoint them. Even if he or she had a passion for another field, family expectations compelled the pursuit of a "practical" career. After his family settled in Delhi following Partition, Sat Kapahi recalls his father's insistence that his son leave the country to finish his education: "One day he [my father] was talking to one of my uncles who had been to USA and was educated in USA, and he suggested, 'Why don't you send him to USA for studies?' So one thing led to another. I had no idea that I would really be going." Kapahi's father had it set in his mind that his son would earn a technical degree and use his education to further his work prospects. Though Kapahi played the piano beautifully and loved to study music, he became an engineer. He recalls, "You do what your father wants, not what you want to do. He always wanted one son to be an engineer, so I had to take up engineering." And so in 1952, Kapahi, accompanied by his cousin, left India for America to pursue a life of calculated reasoning rather than the artistic endeavors he so enjoyed.

Likewise, Amy Laly, who was educated in a mission school in Mumbai and came to Portland State University in the mid-1960s, also struggled with her educational choices and familial aspirations:

> I loved history and . . . you know, history, literature, English, stuff like that. I was also very good in math, believe it or not. But all of that fell by the wayside. Even after college, I got a degree in finance and whatnot. It just goes over my head. I mean, I think I made the wrong choices. But for me, at that time, that was the right choice. And I wanted to go into film and my mother said no. She said . . . "Good girls" . . . no . . . "girls from good families don't go into film." Something like that. So I cut a deal with her. I said, "Okay, I won't go into film if you let me go to America." So that's how that happened. That was the compromise we made. But in a sense, I really kind of ran away from home because I couldn't do what I really want to do. And I ended up with a degree that I didn't care for.

Laly, Kapahi, and Siddiqui all felt pressure from their families to pursue certain educational and career paths; at the same time, the realities of their experiences once in the United States and their own desires created conflicts that they had to resolve on their own. Kapahi indeed became an engineer, whereas Siddiqui went on to a career in real estate and Laly spent several years with the Boeing Company, while also nourishing her interest in film by producing two documentaries and participating regularly in the Seattle International Film Festival.

Despite these challenges, South Asian students engaged actively in academic and campus life. The presence of long-standing organizations like the Cosmopolitan Club[28] at the University of Washington helped connect South Asian students with other students on campus. For Jeff Siddiqui, his

FIG 3.2   Jeff Siddiqui at the University of Washington's Foundation for International Understanding through Students (FIUTS) office, Seattle, Washington, 1978. Photo courtesy of Jeff Siddiqui.

time at the University of Washington allowed him to get involved in campus politics. He served as president of the Pakistani Students Association and as vice president of the Foreign Students Association at the University of Washington while doing his master's degree. He also worked with the Commission for Foreign Students and helped facilitate camping trips for incoming international students in the mountains of the Pacific Northwest. He recalls that despite initial pushback for funding such trips, he was able to persuade the committee to pay for them:

> They said, "We're not going to do that." And I said, "Yes, you are." Because these students were coming here and they are going to be the decision-makers of their countries when they go back. They need to learn about the environment and they need to know what the environment is like. So I told them, "These kids need to know what ecology and environment is like. So when they go back to their countries, which are developing countries, they'll have at least some awareness and some sensitivity. And if they get to the

position where they have some influence, it can be very good for
their country and for the world at large." And I managed to sell that
program.

The rich community of South Asian and international students inspired Siddiqui as he negotiated his own academic trials and he went on to work with
the Foundation for International Understanding through Students (FIUTS),
which still exists at the University of Washington.

Prem Kumar, who studied at Washington State University, was part of
the vibrant cultural life sponsored by Indian students on campus. Because
most non-international students on his campus went home for the summer,
the foreign students were often left to their own devices and passed the
hot summers in eastern Washington by camping and traveling together.
Throughout the year, the South Asian students also came together to watch
movies and celebrate festivals. Kumar remembers:

> And movies were not readily available in those days. So I remember
> distinctly that we used to get these Hindi movies from Chicago or
> New York [by Greyhound bus]. I remember as president of Indian
> Students Association, I used to sit at the bus depot for hours
> waiting for the movie parcel to come. And at least once or twice
> a month, we would screen those films on campus. Nobody ever
> missed [coming to watch those movies]. That was pretty much the
> only entertainment. In addition, we did observe Indian festivals.
> We would celebrate Diwali and Holi. And we even did some pro-
> grams at the University, which was greatly appreciated and enjoyed
> by non-Indian students as well.

While Kumar found solace in the South Asian community on campus,
not everyone felt as strongly about wanting to make a culturally specific set
of friends. Zakir Parpia also attended Washington State University in the
1970s around the time when Prem Kumar was working on his Ph.D. there,
but chose not to join the Indian Students Association. He notes, "I thought
in my mind, I didn't leave India to join the Indian club! What I wanted to get
was the feel from students here." Amy Laly, too, found that she was drawn
into broader movements for social change and she befriended a wide spectrum of people as a wide-eyed student at Portland State University in the

FIG 3.3 Rizwan Nasar celebrates Halloween on the campus of Michigan State University, East Lansing, Michigan, 1986. Photo courtesy of Rizwan Nasar.

1960s. Rather than stick with international students, Laly threw herself into various causes and became an activist:

> I came right in the middle of the Civil Rights movement, the women's movement, the anti-war movement. And as for many of my friends who are my age, the coming of age for me was that I saw a lot of my male friends go into the Vietnam War. They were drafted. And that became a sort of huge experience, you know, to see the angst, and the anger. The desolation in families. And also, in those days, there were many movements that you could [be a part of]. Not that you had to join, but that was open for you to broaden your horizons. So I was involved in that. And it was a big, for me at that time, it was a big learning experience.

Whether part of cultural groups or integrated into the wider community, South Asian students on American university campuses facilitated cross-cultural exchange both formally and informally.

CONCLUSIONS

While many of the narrators viewed their early time as foreign students as an opportunity to see the world or to gain valuable life experience, most recognized the importance of education for economic advancement. However, few consciously recognized that they were also laying the foundations for life as an immigrant in the United States by choosing to enroll in a program of study in an American institution. While South Asians often view their experiences with educational institutions in the United States as unique and guided by personal and familial choices, their decisions to move abroad and pursue certain fields were deeply shaped by postcolonial educational policies in South Asia, American higher education and immigration policies, and the shifts in the global labor market. The growth of high-tech and service industries in the Pacific Northwest after World War Two and the world-class universities that fostered education in science, engineering, and medicine also made the region a new homeland for many South Asians as they transitioned from students to workers.

4

ALL IN A DAY'S WORK

EMPLOYMENT, MIGRATION, AND IDENTITY

Later on, I could not become a planning director—that glass ceiling thing hit, pretty much. This is in the [19]60s. Dick Slavin, who was the Director of Planning and Community Affairs in Olympia—we were having lunch. He says, "Raj, you keep complaining about this discrimination, prove it to me!" I said, "Look at it, all the planning directors are WASPs, and all the consultants are either Jewish or foreign-born. What more do you want?" It was very true in those days. But anyway, I became a consultant, made enough money. They had to pay me. But it's true—discrimination played a big part in my life, because I could not get certain jobs which I was quite qualified for later on.

—Raj Joshi

As I said, if I have to sum it up, this country is a great country. I think when you work hard, if you're willing to give a hundred and ten, twenty percent, there's no way anybody can not be a successful man. Or a successful person. . . . I'm talking about the American dream; I didn't have a dream except that I just wanted to become a cardiac surgeon.

—Dev Manhas

WHEN Raj Joshi arrived in Seattle in the 1950s, he found a predominantly white city with a segregated educational system, de facto redlining that marked where people of color could not rent or buy homes, and a working environment that made Indians like him feel like outsiders. Although he was well-credentialed and trained in Washington State universities, when it came time for Joshi to apply for jobs as a municipal urban planner, he fell behind his classmates who were graduating with the same degree. Out of his cohort of eight urban planning master's students, seven were hired immediately in director-level positions; he was the only one who had to go through additional layers of screening before he was considered for a similar job in the city of Renton, Washington. At the time, Joshi had a strong ally in the city's mayor, who considered Joshi his favorite candidate. However, thanks to the machinations of the city council chairman who did not get along with the mayor, Joshi was shut out of the position. As an immigrant, his ability to hold a publicly funded position *at all* was questioned and his case made it all the way to the Washington attorney general's office.

Nearly ten years after that incident, Joshi still found it difficult to move ahead in his profession. After he applied for a position with the Washington State Land Use Commission in 1971, one of his potential employers remarked publicly, "Raj Joshi's pretty good, but how can he talk to Walla Walla commissioners? He is a foreigner." This experience of being a perpetual alien shaped Joshi's working life, even though he eventually found success as a consultant. While in retrospect Raj Joshi is an example of a thriving South Asian professional who established his career in the Pacific Northwest, his experience with working in the United States sums up the contradictions facing many immigrants in the United States: although he was educated and qualified in his field, occupational advancement was not as easy as he had imagined it would be in the land of opportunities.

Like Joshi's, many South Asian immigrants' decisions to come to the United States are grounded in the desire for advancing their educational opportunities or earning more than they would have in their home country. In his examination of South Asian racial politics in the United States, Vijay Prashad argues that the success of people coming from South Asia is often pitted against that of minority American citizens who fare poorly economically and socially compared to immigrants—a phenomenon that leads to South Asians being viewed as "model minorities" and their material advancement attributed to cultural norms instead of historical, economic, or social advantage.[1] Whether the differences are cultural or not, work is arguably one of the most important ways in which immigrants define their relationship to the United States. Being a productive member of American society and its economy is foundational to how many South Asians view themselves. At the same time, work is also a complicated terrain scarred by the lingering effects of discrimination, the uncertainty created by indeterminate immigration status, and other psychological and material barriers. Although immigration policies in the United States and education policies

FIG 4.1   Raj Joshi as a graduate student at the University of Washington campus, Seattle, 1955. Photo courtesy of Raj Joshi.

in South Asia have combined to create workers who are valued in the West, the actual experience of working in America as an immigrant is more complicated than many success stories might make it appear. Thus, we consider the following question: how do the contradictions that accompany working life in the United States shape South Asians' identities and experience as workers?

SCORING A "GREEN CARD":
IMMIGRATION STATUS AND WORK

Before entering the workforce, immigrants who plan on finding jobs in the United States must navigate a complex system of visas and permits establishing the type and duration of work for which they can apply. Many immigrants intending to settle in the United States are eager to apply for and obtain a Permanent Resident Card, which is colloquially referred to as a "green card." The green card establishes an individual's right to work with impunity in most fields and is considered to be the penultimate step before citizenship. Generally, immigrants can apply for permanent residency in the United States after living in the country for five years on a legal visa. However, the path to getting a green card is far from uniform and today, there are backlogs in green card applications that will take several years to clear. As a result, some immigrants are stuck on temporary visas for years before they can establish themselves. Immigrants on temporary visas are often in precarious positions: if their employment is terminated for any reason, they have little recourse but to leave the country unless they can find another employer to sponsor them. Those with permanent residency status have the ability to stay in the United States without fear of deportation if a similar fate were to befall them. The green card has other advantages: it opens up avenues of employment that are restricted for students or other temporary workers. Whether they use permanent or temporary workers, several companies and industries have been transformed by the influx of foreign workers from South Asia. Raj Joshi remembers that the landscape in Seattle changed dramatically after the passage of the Immigration and Nationality Act of 1965, which made new fields of employment available to noncitizens:

> In those days, when there were so few Indians, if you saw an Indian
> across the street, you would walk across the street and introduce
> yourself, which nobody does now. It all changed in the middle
> [19]60s, after the Immigration Act was changed in [19]65. That's
> when all the Indians started coming here. But before that, there
> were very few. Also in the [19]50s, foreigners couldn't work for
> the Boeing Company. So that's one of the reasons there were no
> Indians there. Once that was changed, then Indians started moving
> to Boeing. [But] there were no jobs here, I mean, unless you were
> working for the government, if you were a civil engineer. [B]ut for
> aeronautical engineers or mechanical engineers, there were
> fewer jobs.

By the 1970s, the aerospace industries, led by companies such as Boeing, attracted increasing numbers of South Asians who had trained as engineers. However, immigration restrictions still influenced where they could work.

For Dinesh Keskar, who came to the United States in 1975 to study aerospace engineering, the green card was essential for him to work and advance in his field:

> When I was working at NASA and finished my Ph.D. . . . there were a lot of companies who do subcontract work for NASA . . . one such company, they picked me up and got me a green card at the same time. And so once you have a green card, the sky's the limit, because companies like Boeing, at least in those days, would not hire you unless you had the legal paperwork to stay in the country. . . . Even before I had the green card, I had an offer letter from Boeing saying that subject to confirming that I had the paperwork to work, I had a job offer here to come anytime.

Keskar found that although he was well qualified to work in the aerospace industry, companies were loath to undertake the legwork necessary to hire foreign nationals. Luckily, he was able to find sponsorship from a subcontracting firm and to start working after he finished school.

While the Immigration and Nationality Act of 1965, as noted previously, prioritized the immigration of technically skilled individuals in order to fulfill the needs of particular industries, employment-based immigration programs have proliferated in the years since the passage of the legislation. Today there is a veritable alphabet soup of visas available to foreign nationals; these visas have greatly increased the number of South Asians moving to the United States overall. The H-1 visa program was initiated through the 1952 Immigration and Nationality Act as part of efforts to lift prohibitions on contract labor migration and was primarily used by Latin American workers. It was only after the Immigration and Nationality Act of 1965 repealed geographic quotas that had been in place since the Asian Exclusion Acts of 1917 and 1924 that South Asians were permitted to enter the United States in substantial numbers.[2] The introduction of the J-1 visa (created through the Fulbright-Hays Act in 1961 to promote educational and cultural exchange), the L visa (created in 1970 to facilitate inter-company employee transfer), and an increase in the allocation of employment-based visas to immigrants and their family members in 1976 all created new pathways for so-called "skilled" and "unskilled" migration.[3] The H-1B visa grew out of the early H-1 program in 1990 and in its current form, it is a migration pathway for "workers in a specialty occupation" who meet the following criteria: the applicant holds a bachelor's or higher degree or its equivalent; "the degree requirement for the job is common to the industry or the job is so complex or unique that it can be performed only by an individual with a degree"; and "the nature of the specific duties is so specialized and complex that the knowledge required to perform the duties is usually associated with the attainment of a bachelor's or higher degree."[4] Workers are eligible for visas that expire after three years, but can be renewed for up to six years. Annually, between 65,000 and 195,000 people come to the United States to work in the technology, finance, and educational sectors on the H-1B visa. Since the H-1B visa program was initiated, it has become closely associated with South and East Asian workers in the technology industries—over half of H-1B visas are issued to citizens of India and China.

However, unlike the green card, the H-1B does not guarantee its holder the right to stay in the country permanently, nor does it allow individuals to sponsor extended family members to migrate to the United States.[5] Only citizens can sponsor additional family members, and having a green card is a precondition of citizenship for most immigrants; thus, only permanent residents can truly make the arrangements necessary to reunify their families if they choose to stay on in the United States. Rizwan Nasar, who came to study in the United States from Pakistan, was able to bypass the long process of converting a student visa into a green card because his sister had already initiated his immigration process:

> My sister had already applied for [my green card] . . . when she got married much earlier, when probably I was a baby, she moved to the U.S. and she was a U.S. citizen. So she had applied for all the siblings, sponsored them to come to the U.S. And you know . . . when I completed my bachelor's, that's when I got a call from the consulate as well that, "Hey your visa is here too. So your green card is done and you can go." So it all worked out pretty well. And in 1985 I moved. That's how I moved here. And I came on a green card instead of a student visa to go to school.

Nasar was a beneficiary of the Family Reunification Act of 1980, which created more opportunities for people to emigrate through family sponsorship, rather than as students or workers.[6] When this and other immigration laws prioritized family reunification as a primary factor for immigration to the United States, new streams of migrants began to flow in, diversifying the communities of students and professionals that had been established earlier. Family-based immigration still constitutes a substantial proportion of immigration from South Asia today, and the labor of wives, children, and extended relations have become an integral part of the family-run businesses that make up a large part of South Asian American economies. While there are many elite South Asian professionals coming to America, there are also plenty of individuals who arrive through these familial networks and provide vital paid and unpaid labor to various businesses.

NAVIGATING CLASS IDENTITY:
TRANSITIONING FROM STUDENT TO WORKER

Despite this diversity, public representations of South Asian work life on the whole tend to vacillate between two extremes: the highly educated, white collar professional or the working-class individual laboring in a small business. The reality is more fluid and it is common to learn that South Asian professionals endured financial hardships and worked in much less glamorous occupations early in their careers to support themselves or left behind their training to start small businesses. The success of the highly educated segments of the South Asian population is not a matter of innate cultural ability, nor has every immigrant followed an easy path to professional and economic achievement. Often, the combination of economic advantage in South Asia and their exposure to higher education positioned them to prosper. For instance, Padmini Vasishth's parents were college educated and her father and grandfather were both lawyers. Vasishth, who was among the first to emigrate after World War Two, came from a colonially educated, urban, elite family for whom schooling and work abroad seemed like a natural trajectory of their social position. It was therefore no surprise to her family when she and her husband decided to migrate in the 1950s for higher education and then to remain for work.

As South Asian nations improved their economic development programs through education, the middle classes grew and emigration was not always presumed. Often families in small towns and rural areas aspired to urban middle-class life and saw educating their children as the pathway to socioeconomic advancement. Shaila Kode, who spent her early years in a small town, moved to Mumbai as a child because her father felt that he would find better opportunities there than he could as a government worker living in a small town. He decided to move his family from Belgaum in the state of Karnataka to a suburb of Mumbai so that his children could have access to better schools. Recalling how her father went to great lengths to make sure that she and her siblings were able to study without interruption, Kode notes, "My father always had ambition for his oldest daughter to become a doctor. He always encouraged and motivated me into getting a good education, even as a child. And that was the reason I think that he sent me to a good school, so I could learn English at an early age." However, the family's move to Mumbai proved economically difficult and her father was unable to find work in his previous occupation. Desperate and financially strapped, Kode's father took up a job as a taxi driver:

> So my father took up driving taxi in Mumbai, just to support the family. And his only motivation and his ambition was to make sure that I go to medical school. So, he used to work about twelve hours a day, seven days a week. He used to come home at twelve midnight and then eat his meals. He never spent a penny outside just to make sure that all the money he earned would go towards our education. So that's how I got into medical school.

Her father's sacrifices and Shaila Kode's determination enabled her to become a doctor and achieve the middle-class status to which her father aspired. Though the shift from being the daughter of a taxi driver to being a medical doctor vastly changed Kode's economic and social position, the notion of who is "middle class" is difficult to define.[7] The narrators profiled in this book are by no means homogenous and their definitions of middle class-ness vary widely: thus, the daughter of a judge, the son of a businessman, and the daughter of a cabdriver all embrace a middle-class identity despite the differences in monetary and cultural capital each person might have.

Although many immigrants came from relatively economically privileged backgrounds in their home countries, many experienced downward mobility when they arrived in the United States. Herbert Gans's research shows that while immigration to the United States is usually associated with economic benefits and improvement in social status, for some upper- and middle-class immigrants, moving abroad can actually result in the opposite phenomenon. Gans argues that "the main cause of immigrant downward mobility is occupational; newcomers often cannot resume old occupations or careers, and so are forced to take jobs of lower status than in their country of origin. Former professors become school teachers; doctors work as medical technicians; and managers wind up as sales persons or store owners."[8] Shaila Kode, for example, had been practicing medicine in rural India for several years before she migrated to the United States. She had spent two years working for the Ministry of Health and though she was a young doctor, she was well-seasoned in clinical situations and used to working independently. She recalls, "There were some challenges while I worked there. Some twin deliveries . . . and see they didn't have, the closest hospital was five hours away . . . every day, we traveled to a different village." She worked as a doctor in these difficult conditions until her family arranged her marriage to a man living in the United States.

After her wedding, she moved to Seattle and found that the man she had married was not as financially or emotionally stable as he had alleged. Although he claimed to be an employed architect, he did not have a job when she arrived. In order to support her new family, as well as her parents and siblings still in India, Kode was desperate to start working. However, rather than continuing to practice medicine, she found that she was housebound because her medical credentials were not recognized in the United States until she passed local certification examinations. She recalls, "I had to go through all the ECFMG [Educational Commission for Foreign Medical Graduates] exams, license, before I could start working here. And you know, I never imagined that I would come to U.S. So I didn't know what the procedure was. I didn't have any contacts. I didn't know anything. So I was completely lost."

Kode resorted to studying in her spare time and took on paramedical work to help make ends meet, working at an obesity clinic for a meager $700 a month. Unable to use her years of medical training, she became frustrated: "Because I was a physician, I had a lot of knowledge but I could not use anything. I was not allowed to say anything there because my job was it. And the doctors didn't like us to talk too much—just do your job and get out." Only after taking a leave of absence from her job and completing a course with other foreign students to prepare for the ECFMG was Kode able to concentrate on the exam required for securing her medical license in America. She eventually passed the tests and finished a residency in New York before taking the unusual step of joining the United States Armed Forces and becoming an Army physician. Kode's story demonstrates Gans's assertion that even for highly trained professionals, work in America can be a complicated and difficult endeavor.

The everyday experiences of middle-class life in South Asia are also quite different than those of middle-class life in the United States. In South Asia, middle-class families often employ servants to perform household work such as cooking, cleaning, and childcare. Many South Asians who arrived as students in America experienced culture shock because of their new economic positions. They discovered that the financial aid or stipends offered to them as students, while seemingly extravagant in South Asian currencies, were much less than they expected when faced with the much higher cost of living in the United States. Kris Gupta, who belonged to a wealthy and distinguished family in India, came to Seattle as a graduate student in 1961 and found that life was more expensive than he had anticipated. After becoming friends with a student from eastern Washington in a summer class at the University of Washington, Gupta decided to visit him in Cheney, Washington. In need of work, he met a farmer who was familiar with India. Taking a shine to Gupta, the farmer asked him: "Do you want to work? What are you doing?" Gupta replied, "I'm going back to the university." The farmer intervened and offered Gupta a job repairing tractors in the community for the summer. As he recalls, "I ended up working the six weeks that I had in between. That kind of was an eye opener, coming from a doctor's [family] to the university and going to a farm. And I stayed right on top of the restaurant where we were working. Working for these farmers was something unbelievable."

Gupta's notions of class were dramatically changed by his experience of working in a small rural community where his education and family background were eclipsed by his status as a foreigner and low economic position as a student. Even though Gupta went on to get his master's degree in transportation and traffic engineering from the University of California, Berkeley, and worked as a civil engineer for the rest of his career, his early time working various odd jobs as a student lingered with him.

Asgar Ahmedi, too, came to the United States as a young sojourner and student in 1950 and was transformed by his first jobs in the country. A few years after he arrived, Ahmedi began working in a steel factory near the

Boeing Company in south Seattle after he had enrolled in a master's program at the University of Washington. Though he never finished his thesis, Ahmedi went through his coursework before relinquishing his dream of higher education in order to support his young and quickly growing family. He eventually abandoned his training in chemistry and engineering altogether and started an import-export business. He went on to own retail shops and even ran a booth at the 1962 Seattle World's Fair selling exotic goods from around the world to visitors. For immigrants who came in the 1940s and 1950s, adapting emotionally and socially was only one part of the settlement process; learning how to take on new jobs as they transitioned from being students to workers was another piece.

Jeff Siddiqui was particularly struck by the difference between his cushy life in an elite family in Pakistan and his lean days as a University of Washington graduate student in the 1970s. When he arrived in Seattle, Siddiqui was both financially strapped and woefully unprepared to manage domestic tasks like cooking. He killed two birds with one stone, so to speak, and found a job with a catering company. Siddiqui recalls:

> You know, I would've probably starved to death if I hadn't found some jobs at catering places, like the kitchen. And you know, I'd just quickly look around and eat. One time, I was working as a cook's helper. There was this wonderful woman, big woman. She was Wally. When I first got in there, she said, "Now look, I'm telling you one thing. If I catch you so much as nibbling on one cracker, you will be on your ear, out on the street before you can turn around. I will not have this." And so we had this on-going game. If there was good food there, I'd say "Wally. Do you see that fly on the wall over there?" And she'd turn around very slowly and say, "What fly, Jeff?" I'd say, "Just look, I swear there's a huge fly over there!" And I'd stuff my face. "I'm still looking Jeff, I don't see anything." "Yeah, well, keep looking!" [Laughs]. "I think I've seen it all!" And all I could think of was "mmm-yeah!" Then she'd turn around, look at me and say, "Were you doing something I shouldn't know?" I'd say, "No, Wally." "Okay, well, get moving then!"

Siddiqui cleverly managed to use his part-time job as a way to supplement his own lack of interest in the culinary arts. Though humorous, Siddiqui's story demonstrates his anxieties about living on the edge financially. Few narrators could afford to finance an entire college education, despite the fact that they often came from financially stable families. They relied on a variety of odd jobs, support from friends and family, and their own ingenuity to make it through those early days.

IMMIGRANT DILEMMAS: DECIDING TO STAY OR RETURN

While the transition from student to working professional was challenging in certain ways, deciding whether to stay in the United States permanently was also tricky terrain. Coming to the United States to pursue higher education was one thing, but putting down roots here was another, and few thought they were making a permanent move. As Rao Remala notes, "I never came here thinking that I would stay on. It was like making money, going back. But then like most of the immigrants, I think they say this. Even today, I think a lot of them think like that, but very few go back. You know, I thought okay, maybe four-five years, but then you get used to it."

FIG 4.2 Prem Kumar and his wife Swaran at the Taj Mahal, Agra, India, on his first trip back to India after immigrating to the United States, 1984. Photo courtesy of Prem Kumar.

Just like so many others who came before and after, a few years turned into a life and career spent away from "home." Retrospectively, it would seem like immigrants make decisions that clearly lead toward settlement—moving abroad, establishing communities and networks, getting involved with local organizations, starting families, and so on. However, most individuals rarely saw these actions as part of a deliberate plan or effort to create a life in a new country.

At the same time, many narrators recall the incidents that influenced their decisions to stay. Often they faced the dilemma of having to choose between conflicting and competing needs, including idealistic desires to serve their homeland, family and economic pressures, the realities of unemployment or underemployment, and aspirations for intellectual and emotional fulfillment. For Balraj Sokkappa, the decision to stay in the United States after he finished his Ph.D. was by no means predetermined. Even though he met his American-born and -raised wife at the University of California, Berkeley, while she was a nursing student, Sokkappa still held on to the idea of returning to India. As he settled in Seattle after getting a job and moving his family there (which had grown with the addition of two children), Sokkappa recalls that he had doubts about whether he would remain in the country:

> I was still thinking of going back. I finished my Ph.D. Just before finishing my Ph.D. we all went to India, in 1961. Part of the reason was to [have my wife] meet my family, and look for jobs. So I went around and looked for teaching positions in various places. It was not very easy there. People were still interviewing candidates like they do in the British system. Because jobs are so difficult to find, they almost treat you like they are doing you a favor, interviewing you. I didn't like that at all. Actually, in one of these institutes that was started by British in Delhi, they were very interested in giving me a job, but just the way they conducted the interview, I didn't like that at all. For example, there were three of them, four of them, I can't remember. The principal, or what you call, the president in this country, I guess, of the institute, and a professor from Britain and another local professor. I had to wait for a long time for the interview. The secretary wouldn't even go tell the principal that I was waiting. . . . While I was waiting to go in, another Indian fel-

low came in and sat next to me and he started talking to me. I told him I was here for an interview, that I was from U.S., from Seattle. Turns out that he was there for an interview also, for a junior position. He was an engineer. And one of the things he asked me was, "Why do you want to come back to India?" So I told him this is where my family is and U.S. is a different kind of society and I always thought of coming back. And one of the things he said was, "If you come back, what you are doing is taking opportunities from people like me who have not gone outside." I thought that was very revealing. [Laughs.] He says, "Obviously, you can get a job in the U.S. Why do you want to come back and take away positions from people like me?" So I thought about all that, and then when we came back to the U.S., I decided I will try to get a green card.

In Sokkappa's memory, a chance meeting with a stranger helped solidify what would become a lifetime commitment to the United States: though his heart led him to explore India as a possible place to use the knowledge he had gained while living and working abroad, his encounter with another Indian in a similar position forced Sokkappa to reconsider his return to India. Sokkappa frames his choice to come back to the United States as not only a safer decision, but also a more honorable one. Competing with a foreign-acquired skill set would have certainly set him apart from other job seekers and made him attractive to Indian employers. However, he found that he was also fundamentally changed by his experience of working the United States and even the interview process ran counter to his expectations. Because of his own transformation and after reflecting on what would ultimately be best for his family, Sokkappa came back to Seattle for good.

In a similar way, Dev Manhas was also confronted with the difficult decision of making a break with his homeland on a trip back to Kashmir after having come to Seattle to do a residency at the University of Washington Medical School. For Manhas, returning to India was heart-warming and it was a relief to see his parents and siblings after five long years abroad. Spending time with comrades from college, old professors, childhood friends, and family energized Manhas, who also had the chance to shine in his community's eyes as a recently published young doctor. Recalling the pull he felt to stay on in India, he notes: "My mother and sister wanted me to come back [to India] and I had gone through those phases myself. But, you know, I decided, obviously my job was already here, when I came back as Assistant Professor of Surgery." Instead of remaining in India, he decided to apply for his green card and establish permanent residency after starting a fellowship in cardiac surgery. Knowing how hard it was to choose his career over his family, Manhas remembers, "I was boarding a bus and [my mother and sister] were absolutely teary-eyed, both of them. And I was, of course, I am too emotional, teary-eyed also. And they said, "You know, if you don't like it there, why don't you just stay back?" Brushing aside the notion of remaining in India, Manhas boarded the bus and began his journey back to the life awaiting him in Seattle.

For others, the move abroad was transformative not only on a personal level, but also on a professional level. Sokkappa recounts, "I got my master's degree in Berkeley, and then since I was thinking of teaching, the University of Washington offered me a faculty position after my master's degree. I thought I will go get some experience teaching at Seattle, and then go back to India. So I came to Seattle and started teaching electrical engineering." After learning that he could teach part-time and work on his doctorate simultaneously, he decided to pursue his Ph.D. His desire to deepen his knowledge of electrical engineering was one motivating factor and the better pay as a graduate student instructor was another. In addition to his personal reasons, Sokkappa decided to specialize in "power" within electrical engineering—or the subfield that explores the generation, distribution, and transmission of electricity. He was drawn to this topic because "that was the area where you could get a job in India more easily and that's what was more common." The possibility of return helped move him into electrical engineering; however, exposure to the cutting-edge fields of science and technology developing at Berkeley in the 1960s exploded his notions of what sort of career might await him in the future. Though an academic advisor pushed Sokkappa to consider the burgeoning field of computer technology, he notes, "I didn't want to do that because I wasn't quite sure how it would fit my objective."

Despite the chance to move into the field of computer science, Sokkappa decided to turn down a job offer and continue on with his engineering degree with the hope of returning to India to help the nation develop. He notes, "I guess in retrospect it was probably a mistake, because if I was going to stay in this country, computer science was the field to go into. In those days computers were just coming into play." Another potential career-shifting opportunity came across his desk at Berkeley in the form of work on nuclear accelerators. The chance to work with several famous scientists, including Linus Pauling, who went on to be one of only two people ever to win both the Nobel Peace Prize and the Nobel Prize in Chemistry, and Ernest Lawrence, who was one of the earliest orchestrators of the American nuclear program that led to the Manhattan Project, was persuasive and drew Sokkappa to seriously explore nuclear physics as a field. Sokkappa recalls:

> All these guys, Oppenheimer and the other H-bomb [guy], Edward Teller—they all worked with Lawrence those days because Lawrence was the pioneer. So I could've worked on nuclear accelerators. I took courses in nuclear accelerators but then I was hesitant because I didn't know whether I can go very far with that because of security problems, being a foreigner. You know, you've got to get special security clearance and all that. So I decided to leave Berkeley and come to Seattle. But if I had thought of staying in this country, I think I would have stayed in Berkeley, got my Ph.D. there.

Instead, Sokkappa made the move from California to Washington State and took up work with Seattle City Light and worked on his degree in electrical engineering. The irony of Sokkappa's educational journey is that he chose his profession based on what he saw as most marketable and useful for finding a job in India. Not only that, but his position as an immigrant who might not be able to pass the various levels of security clearance required in the burgeoning U.S. nuclear industries led him away from other possible fields. His status as a foreigner meant that he could not rise in rank unless he obtained a green card, which he was not quite ready to do at that time. Instead, he applied his talents to the Pacific Northwest and began working there.

An opportunity with a major lab in Boston took Sokkappa away for several years and he gradually shifted his focus to systems engineering. He worked for MITRE labs until an exciting possibility opened at a lab run by the Massachusetts Institute of Technology's Aeronautics and Astronautics Department. This move was not a mere stepping stone for Sokkappa: he joined the design team for the Apollo space program, which coordinated the missions that landed the first humans on the Earth's moon. Sokkappa recalls:

I think very few people get an opportunity to work on something like that. And then I got the job designing what they call steering equation for the rockets. On the Apollo there is a big rocket, the Saturn rocket that launches it into orbit. That was done by von Braun—you know, Wernher von Braun who came from Germany. He was the guy who was in charge of that rocket in Alabama. We didn't have anything to do with it, but once the Apollo vehicle was launched, it had its own rockets. And depending on what orbit you want to get to and when you want to go to the moon, you had to fire this rocket and point it in the right direction so it gets the right velocity to get on the correct orbit. So that's what I worked on, writing the equations. Again, MIT being a laboratory, it couldn't build anything. So we write all the design and the equations and then put it in a document that NASA hands to Raytheon at that time. Raytheon had just built a computer that was called a hard-wired computer. You couldn't put much weight in the vehicle, so it has to be very small. If it was very small, you couldn't write the software, the software has to be wired into it. So we gave the design to Raytheon and they built the computer. And of course—I want to say Northrop—Rockwell Industries at that time in Los Angeles built the vehicle and they assembled everything in there. But we did the guidance and navigation. I did the Apollo vehicle and my officemate did the lunar vehicle—you know, the guidance for the lunar vehicle.

The chance to work on a project of such national significance pushed Sokkappa even further toward considering the possibility of staying in the United States for the long haul and led him to finally take steps to make his settlement permanent. Later, Sokkappa went on to work in Sri Lanka as part of a UNESCO program, where he lectured on astronautics. He came back to the United States and joined the Federal Aviation Administration, which took him on assignments all over the world. Only after retiring did Sokkappa return to the Pacific Northwest. Ironically, though he started in the region as a student and his career path led him around the globe, he ultimately found that it was the place he could most fully call home. His transition from student to worker to retiree began and ended in Seattle. Sokappa's story demonstrates how his internal struggle to reconcile competing desires, and global and national circumstances all played important roles in his decision-making process.

Even though immigrants like Sokkappa may well have decided to stay in the United States as a practical matter, his story also points to the unpredictability of the immigrant experience. Raj Joshi, who came to the Pacific Northwest as a graduate student of geography and settled in the area after marrying his wife Irene, found that he was ready for a new challenge in his life after spending several years working for various city and state planning agencies. Joshi was an associate planner for the King County Planning Department in Seattle, where he helped to write the comprehensive master plan for the entire county. He was then hired by the Puget Sound Regional Transportation Authority as a senior regional planner and shortly after that, he became director of regional planning. After leaving the public sector, he became an urban planning consultant. Having worked in the urban planning field for so many years, he decided at the age of forty-nine to take an unusual step: he joined the Peace Corps. Telling his wife that he was itching to try something new, Joshi made his move:

> I applied for Peace Corps and they took me. I went to the Philippines for two years, and after that, it seems like I was more with Americans than with Indians. . . . [I] loved it. I became less competitive and I said, live and let live. Yeah, that duty changed my attitude towards a lot of things. Two years away. And Irene came and visited me there. I got a nice little bamboo hut built in the mountains, and we stayed there. It was fun. Fun two years. I made a lot of good friends in the Peace Corps. They're still friends. And they were all young kids—I was the oldest guy, but they thought I acted the youngest. [Laughs.] No, that was a good experience; very good. So I did that too. And also I was a reservist with FEMA—Federal Emergency Management Agency. I did that for fifteen years . . . that involved going on the disasters. You know, to Hurricane Hugo in the Virgin Islands, earthquake in California, Mississippi floods, Guam, typhoons, Samoa.

Even though he continued to do work related to urban planning, Joshi used his experience to explore various parts of the world and to try out adventures on his own terms.

Similarly, Bharti Kirchner's career underwent several transformations from her early days as a graduate student in mathematics. She first landed in the Chicago metro area as a student in 1961 and began her career working for the Rock Island Railroad. As she recalls, "The railroad industry was still on and people that worked for it [seemed to love the business]. . . . I was working in the computer department. I was sort of digitizing . . . computerizing their railroad system." She went on to develop expertise in the nascent field of software development and made her way westward. She moved to San Francisco and took a job with Levi Strauss in its software division. She met her future husband while working there. Together they decided to travel the world, taking jobs in areas that were in need of experienced computer programmers. Their desire for a new experience drew them to Iran; she notes, "Those were interesting days. Those were the days of Shah, the last days of Shah. He had a big computer department and hired us with lots of money and gave us the leeway to train. Our job was mainly to train Iranian programmers." However, the political instability following the overthrow of the Iranian government in 1979 led the Kirchners to leave the country and find jobs in Holland.

Eventually winding their way through Europe, they spent time in France. It was in France that Kirchner's second love (aside from software development) began to blossom and she honed her skills as a cook. Kirchner left her career in computer programming behind and recreated herself as a cookbook author and novelist. Food features prominently in her novels, as do the cities that were formative in her own life. She notes, "Interestingly enough, these travels really helped me later on when I wrote my cookbook. I got to bring these influences from different parts of the world to my cooking and also be able to write about them." Not only was her nonfiction influenced by her experiences, but her fiction, too, drew upon her global experiences and multiple passions. For example, in her novel *Shiva Dancing*, the protagonist is a San Francisco-based software engineer who travels to India to explore a traumatic episode from her past.[9] The shift between the cosmopolitan cities of northern California and the poetically arid and almost anachronistic landscapes of north India echoes Kirchner's own movement between India and the United States. Turning her literary gaze to her adopted hometown

for her novel *Pastries: A Novel of Desserts and Discoveries*, Kirchner notes that the book is "my ode to Seattle."[10] After traveling in Japan, Kirchner was struck by the idea that turned into the central plot of the novel: "Actually the story starts in Seattle with a young Indian-American baker, a young woman who is not an engineer or a doctor or . . . but who has gone into the bakery business. It's a new profession for an Indian-American, but she loses her baking skills." The protagonist finds herself in need of a salve for her recently broken heart; she ultimately finds her way back to the kitchen after a transformative trip to Japan. Kirchner notes, "So it's not about baking as much as really finding your place in life and getting your faith back to yourself. Baking is only a metaphor for many things." Kirchner's career transformation and settlement into the city of Seattle as her home clearly inspire this novel.

Like Kirchner, who discovered her literary voice later in life, Pramila Jayapal has also reinvented herself many times over and found passion in travel and writing. After moving to Washington, D.C., to attend Georgetown University, Jayapal worked for the American stock brokerage and asset management firm Paine Webber, focusing on leveraged buyouts in the mid-1980s. She recalls, "It was crazy! I was twenty years old and I was, you know, going and representing bankruptcy clients in bankruptcy courts and firing people. And I mean, I had no idea what I was doing. It was very exciting, great training. [But] doing that, I saw very little value for me." She went back to school and got her master's degree in business administration from Northwestern University. After taking a job with a medical device company, Jayapal recalls that she was "the first woman, much less brown person, to be in that sales district." The job took her to Seattle, but proved unfulfilling after a few years despite the generous paycheck it provided. She left the company and took a job with PATH, a public health nonprofit, in 1991 and never looked back at the corporate world. Jayapal's career shift took her all over the globe, including Thailand, Cambodia, Ghana, Senegal, Kenya, and India. Though she was born in Chennai, India, Jayapal had lived most of her life in Singapore, Indonesia, and then the United States. Having the chance to work in India gave her an opportunity to connect with a piece of her own history that was always slightly out of reach, since she had grown up in the Indian diaspora in Southeast Asia. She wrote a book about her experiences and went on tours around the country, where she met other diasporic South Asians who connected to her journey of self-discovery.[11] After years of working on development projects around the world, Jayapal finally settled in Seattle and began consulting for various local nonprofit organizations. However, on September 11, 2001, Jayapal, like so many other Americans, was personally moved and traumatized by the events that transpired first in New York City and then around the world. She remembers in aching detail:

I just thought, "Everything is going to change!" And I had been doing work in the DV [domestic violence], South Asian DV community and in other immigrant refugee communities from my consulting projects and I started getting a lot of calls from people— you know these people are being harassed physically, the guy was shot in Mesa, Arizona, the Sikh gentleman. And Sikh cab drivers were physically harassed and attacked and it was awful. I just remembered not wanting Janak, my son, to go out and not wanting to wear my own, you know, *salwar kameez* or anything.

Inspired by actions taking place across the country to stand up against the violence occurring in the wake of September 11, Jayapal urged Washington State Congressman Jim McDermott to adopt a resolution that declared the state a "hate-free zone." A week after September 11, Jayapal found herself on a stage at the Seattle Center with several Washington State officials at a press conference where, as she recalls, "They all denounced the hate and said this state stands for, you know, it's a hate free zone and that was the start of Hate Free Zone!" Even though she had not intended to launch an organization, Jayapal then began working on behalf of immigrant communities who were being targeted and named the collaborative group "Hate Free Zone" after a resolution bearing the same message passed in the Washington State legislature. Today, the organization is known as One America, has grown to employ more than fifteen people, and has a national presence advocating for marginalized and immigrant communities.

Jamal Rahman's career trajectory was likewise transformed as he went from being a businessman to becoming a spiritual leader. Born in Bangladesh but raised around the world because his father was a diplomat, Rahman first came to the Pacific Northwest as a student at the University of Oregon in 1970. After first moving to the United States, Rahman began working on campus. Echoing Kris Gupta and Asgar Ahmedi's experiences twenty years before his own arrival, he recalls:

> We couldn't work outside of campus. So inside of campus, all kinds
> of work. I remember cleaning the dorms, working in the offices,
> doing what is called graveyard shifts—midnight to early morning
> and those. Then, on campus all kinds of little jobs in the cafeteria.
> I didn't so much do cafeteria but security jobs and events, helped
> with that. Anything which paid money, where it was legally pos-
> sible to do so, and we managed for ourselves and other friends.

He began studying economics while in Oregon and even started a Ph.D. program in political science at the University of California, Berkeley. Although he never finished the program, Rahman found that he was drawn increasingly to the politics of the day through movements against the Vietnam War and for civil rights. At the same time, an internal calling emerged and he decided to pursue the deeper study of Sufism, which was the religious tradition of his family. Eventually he moved around the world to study with various theological masters. After spending several years studying in France, Egypt, and Canada, Rahman decided to take up more earthly pursuits: "I was thinking, what sort of future I will have? What will I do, with this information and knowledge, and picking up individual experiences?

Let me also understand something about marketing, setting up something, maybe consultancy, like a business. So I took up some business courses." He went on to start a brass company with his brother in the United States and was in business until 1990.

After a series of personal losses, Rahman re-evaluated his career choice again; at the same time, his interest in spiritual life was renewed and he started meeting with a group of like-minded friends. He recalls that the community used to come together every Sunday, but they did not have a regular meeting space: "We were very creative. People said 'we have homes and large homes,' so they volunteered their homes." Calling themselves the "Circle of Love," the community began to expand and eventually found a permanent home in an old church in the Ballard neighborhood of Seattle that had an existing, but shrinking, congregation. The two communities merged in 1999 and created the Seattle Interfaith Community Church. Rahman notes:

And so this place is ours now and we have a particular philosophy where in this place we foster a living, breathing interfaith community. We ask ourselves, "What does it mean to live an interfaith life?" And there are two kinds of people we have. One is a person like me, a Muslim, always a Muslim, who is watering those roots and becoming aware of the beauty and wisdom of other traditions. The other type of congregant is a person who says, "You know, I am a recovering Catholic, recovering Muslim, recovering Hindu. I don't want to be attached to any institution. I am a spiritual person. I want to borrow from here and here and create my own hybrid spirituality." That's another, a growing type of congregant, all over America. So we cater to them also because they need for their sustenance and nourishment, they need a community more than anybody else to support them. That's what we foster in this place. So that . . . it has grown into other ministries and we work with . . . I work with a particular rabbi, and a particular Christian pastor. We have become very good friends, especially after 9/11. And that has grown.

This interfaith community has grown to include over 700 members. Rahman has found no shortage of work; together with Jewish and Christian colleagues, he has written several books, teaches seminars at Seattle

University and the University of Washington, and is actively engaged with his congregation. In a most appropriate expression of how affirming and unpredictable his experience with work has been, Rahman notes, "I decided, as Joseph Campbell would say: 'Follow your bliss. What is it?' I had no conventional parameters or categories to fall into. So I said I must look within myself and create my own and that's when I, with the help of friends in collaboration, I created my own. My own job description, I'd say."

MAKING AN IMPACT: SOUTH ASIANS
AND INDUSTRY TRANSFORMATION

While certainly personally inspiring, stories like Bharti Kirchner's transition from computer scientist to writer or Jayapal's from businesswoman to social advocate also show how work has come to be defining for South Asians. In turn, South Asians have redefined entire fields and industries through their work. One of those industry transformations came out of the recruitment of one South Asian immigrant in particular. Rao Remala came to the United States not as a student, like so many others in the Pacific Northwest, but after working for what would become one of the largest computer companies in India in the 1970s. Born in a tiny village in the Southern Indian state of Andhra Pradesh, Remala describes his hometown as "a village where there was no power, no roads, and no running water, hardly any, of course, obviously there is no drinking water at that place." Remala walked five miles each way to attend his high school—and that was not just a story that he told his daughters to make them appreciate the comforts of their lives in the suburbs of Seattle. It was a remote existence and Remala's parents had minimal access to education. When Remala was getting ready to move on to higher education, his family fell onto hard times: "I would say, we were a lower-middle class . . . by the time I started going to college, I mean, you know, we had become pretty . . . um, those days were pretty difficult." With the support of his older brothers, Remala was accepted into college in a town called Warangal, where he studied electrical engineering. Against all odds, he applied for and won one of six open seats at the prestigious Indian Institute of Technology (IIT) in Kanpur for a graduate program focusing on computer science, which was a new field in India and around the world at the time. Explaining his pull toward computers, Remala recalls,

I remember hearing about all these computers and IBM. Actually there were some computers in India, like the IBM computers. They are like very, very old IBM computers. And then what happened was that when I was in engineering, we had an industrial tour to North India, and then we went to IIT Kanpur. IIT Kanpur actually was the very first institute to have any kind of computers. So they had a computer and then we had a visit to the computer center. And then somebody, you know, showed us a bunch of programs and then they explained to us, this is what it does, and this what you can do. So I thought, I mean, this might be the area I want to be interested in, you know. Also there were not tons of jobs those days in India, but it was an area where it had just started coming up.

After gaining admission into IIT Kanpur, Remala borrowed some money from a friend to pay the tuition deposit and entered into the halls of one of India's most prestigious technology institutes. After graduating, he moved to Delhi and joined DCM Data Products in its efforts to create "mini-computers" and develop other technologies not yet available in India. Along with a few colleagues from DCM, Remala left the company and began a start-up in 1976 known as Hindustan Computers Limited. "HCL, they call it. It's actually one of the biggest companies now in India and I was part of it. I was the first one to set up the software group," says Remala. Today, HCL is one of India's largest producers of electronics, computing, and information technology. Though still headquartered in the outskirts of Delhi, it has a national and worldwide presence with 170 branches and 300 service centers throughout India.

While working for HCL, Remala had the chance to visit a small software company based in Bellevue, Washington, in 1979. That company was Microsoft, which, Remala notes, "was a very, very small company in those days, like 35 people or something. They were selling some software for the microcomputers. Actually, if you remember, Microsoft had [BASIC]. And we wanted to move their [BASIC] to one of the computers, what HCL was working on. I was here for a few weeks, not even [a] month." He began working closely with some Microsoft employees who were impressed by his technical skills. In one casual conversation, the question of Remala joining Microsoft came up, although there was some concern about how to actually hire him as a foreign national. Remala notes, "I mean, for people those days, the way to come here was mostly higher education, you know. Now you see more of them coming for job sources. In those days, it was only higher education. Nothing else. You come here and you find the job." For him, the process of obtaining a work visa was arduous and lasted more than a year. Even after the paperwork went through and the opportunity was finally in hand, it was not an easy decision to leave India and come to work for what was then basically an unknown entity. Asking himself if emigrating was the right choice for him and his wife and young daughter, he remembers, "I started thinking, I mean the place where I was working was doing very well. The company was doing well and I was in two minds whether to come here or not. But then by the time I decided to come here, it was like 1981, June."

Remala came intending to work for Microsoft for a few years and then move on to a more lucrative position somewhere else, for example, with IBM. He also began his Ph.D. in computer science at the University of Washington at that time, but found that balancing the stresses of school, his family, and the increasing demands of work at Microsoft meant that something had to give. He decided to withdraw from the Ph.D. program and instead threw himself into building the architecture of the early software division at Microsoft. Remala's presence at the company also signaled a sea change, not only because of the talents he personally brought to the company, but also because he was the first South Asian to be hired at Microsoft. At the time, the intimate work culture meant that Remala was reporting directly to Microsoft founder Bill Gates. Today, the notion that South Asians were a novelty at Microsoft might seem almost laughable, considering that the company employs thousands of Indians, Sri Lankans, Bangladeshis, and Pakistanis, many of whom work at the campus in Redmond, Washington.[12] The corporation also has a strong presence in India, with the Microsoft India Development Center in Hyderabad and branches in cities like Bangalore, Mumbai, and Delhi.

However, when Remala started working at Microsoft in 1981, U.S. companies were just beginning to hire South Asians. Remala notes a few companies in the Pacific Northwest were ahead of the curve: "Boeing had quite a few Indians by that time. . . . There were quite a few doctors who came during those days." But the relationship between South Asian engineers and the burgeoning software and information technology industries was still in its infancy at the time. Remala was soon joined by increasing numbers of workers from across the subcontinent and Microsoft began recruiting directly at institutions like the Indian Institutes of Technology (IITs) to attract some of the world's brightest minds to join its teams. With the growth of outsourcing firms in India and the United States like Wipro, Tata Consulting Services, and Bellevue-based Aditi Technology, the pathways for greater migration in the technology industries grew even wider.

Remala's entry into the world of Microsoft also paved the way for others like Vijay Vashee, who joined Microsoft soon after him in 1982. Vashee, also a graduate from one of the IITs, was an early innovator at Microsoft. During his tenure, the company grew to acquire such ubiquitous technologies as PowerPoint and launched into the superpower that it is today. Microsoft has become established not only as a technology powerhouse, but also as an important source of philanthropy both in the Puget Sound region and globally. Akhtar Badshah is another central figure who has worked to further cement Microsoft's relationship with the South Asian community worldwide. Hired as Microsoft's senior director of community development, Badshah brought his experience as the CEO and president of Digital Partners Foundation, a Seattle-area nonprofit aimed at mobilizing digital solutions in development projects in places like South Asia, Africa, and Latin America. Badshah recalls that during his time at Digital Partners, "we were focused on, you know, looking at IT for development. Information technology and development and looking at it from a social entrepreneurship [point of view]. You know, so we had a global program and this was really what I built from scratch here."

Badshah is another example of someone who reinvented his career many times over; he notes, "I have actually never really decided what I want to do. I always go from one thing to the other. Just when the opportunity comes in." Starting as a student and eventually working as a professor of architecture at MIT, Badshah is now a key leader who links Microsoft to issues of community importance that cross industries. In May 2010, Badshah collaborated with the South Asia Center at the University of Washington to organize a symposium about the role the South Asian diaspora has played in development projects in the region and the ways it can take on greater roles in the future. Aimed at mobilizing both local and transnational communities, the event brought together first, second, and third generations of South Asian immigrants with technology and development organizations to think creatively about how the copious amount of work originating from the Pacific Northwest might be used to better serve the subcontinent. These immigrants have together transformed not only Microsoft, but also the way in which the South Asian community itself interacts with the software giant.

But as Remala mentions, South Asians were already an established presence in the Pacific Northwest even before Microsoft emerged, particularly in the field of aeronautics because of Boeing. Alok Mathur, who moved to the United States in the late 1970s with his family, was just one of the many South Asians to work for Boeing. His father was a senior employee for the American embassy in Delhi and was offered immigration to the United States when he reached retirement age. Mathur pushed his father to take the plunge. At the age of twenty-five, Mathur came to America along with his parents and brother. After working in the Virginia area where the family settled initially, Mathur wanted to travel westward. He recalls,

> Well, you may call it a dream, but when I was in Washington, D.C., when I had come to the U.S., somehow I wanted to work for the Boeing Company. And I was looking for some way to get a job over here. When I was working for this company in Vienna, I was reading this magazine, *Machine Design*, and there was an ad for Boeing in that magazine. And they had a phone number, so I called up that number, they sent me the forms. I think I got a job within two weeks. They interviewed me on the telephone and I had the job. They offered me about three times what I was making over in Vienna, so it didn't take me very long to decide. And I didn't have very much, very many belongings at that time, so they just sent me a ticket. I flew over here.

Coming to Seattle in 1978 on his own, Mathur quickly settled into life in the region. He notes, "At that time, a lot of people had moved out of the state because Boeing had laid off about 70,000 people. And there weren't very many job opportunities in Seattle area. There was no Microsoft, or Amazon or Starbucks at that time. It was just Boeing." Even though there were other engineers from India, Mathur found that his education was not fully recognized by Boeing and there was only so far he could go with his credentials from an Indian college:

> I was working in, like, a wing skin job . . . the aluminum panels to make the wings. So I was a tool and production planner in the

fabrication division at Auburn. And I worked there until 198[3]. So at that time, I had to go to this, another college because Boeing did not recognize the degree from India, at that time. So, at that time there was a college called Cogswell College, which was based in San Francisco area. They had opened a branch in Seattle and, kind of, Boeing had collaborated with them because at that time there were very few other colleges. University of Washington was there. But there was no engineering college here, so they kind of sponsored Cogswell College [in] Seattle. So they were looking for people to go to that college. So I was encouraged to go there, you know, get a degree. And I had already done all my engineering courses, so I had to kind of go for one year and take about forty-eight credits to get a degree because that was the minimum requirement to obtain a degree. So I said okay. So I went to Cogswell College in night time and I took forty-eight credits . . . U.S. history and business ethics and society and English literature and those things. I took forty-eight credits and then Boeing recognized me as an engineer. . . . And so, after that, in 1987, I did my MBA from City University in Seattle. Yeah, so once I obtained my master's degree, then I took up this job in Customer Engineering.

After spending years as a hands-on engineer, Mathur made the switch to a more customer- oriented job. He rose to become a lead account manager and today works with clients all over the globe, including in his home city of Delhi. Mathur notes that while the United States' economy has been experiencing a serious recession since 2007, sales in places like India have helped keep the company steady: "To Air India alone we sold like sixty-eight airplanes, to the tune of about seventeen billion dollars. And then we have sold, we have already sold and delivered, almost fifty airplanes to Jet Airways." Like Mathur, Dinesh Keskar made the transition from engineering to the business side of work at Boeing. Keskar came to the United States as a graduate student and initially came to Cincinnati, Ohio. He finished his Ph.D. in aerospace engineering in 1978. Not only was Keskar only twenty years old when he finished his degree, but he had the distinction of working under legendary American astronaut Neil Armstrong, who was then on the faculty at the University of Cincinnati. From there, Keskar went on to work for NASA in Langley, Virginia, but then took a job with Boeing in 1980 and

moved to Seattle. After completing his master's degree in business administration from the City University in Seattle, Keskar applied for and took a job
in Boeing's sales and marketing division in 1988. He worked his way up to a
position that allows him to travel extensively in Asia. He explains:

> That's the ideal job anybody can have in the world. Actually, that's
> the second-best ideal, because I used to go to India every month.
> From here, you know? And Boeing would obviously foot the bill,
> but I had work to do there and the best thing you can do is what
> I'm doing right now, is go as an ex-pat[riate] and live in India as a
> senior executive of your company, you know, like the CEO of Boe-
> ing India, and you're running the whole operation for that com-
> pany. And you are Indian but you're actually getting all the benefits
> an ex-pat would get, you know?

Today, Keskar is president of Boeing India and vice president of Boeing
International Trading and splits his time between Delhi and Renton, Washington, where he and his wife still keep a house. In many ways, Keskar lives
the "dream" of being able to move between India and the United States with
speed, ease, and comfort, all the while building his career.

PERPETUAL FOREIGNERS:
BREAKING BARRIERS AND OVERCOMING PREJUDICE

While there is no doubt that South Asians have progressed in extraordinary
ways in the industries in the Pacific Northwest and that some have achieved
phenomenal levels of success, many faced serious barriers and discrimination in the United States as well. Because of their immigration status,
the color of their skin, their religious background, and in some cases, their
gender, immigrant workers in the United States have sometimes suffered.
As in Shaila Kode's case, mentioned earlier, and in the case of other doctors trained abroad, the experience of coming to the United States and not
having their training recognized was a frustration that took an emotional
toll. Dev Manhas came to Seattle after having worked as a house surgeon
in India. He recalls,

> I continued as assistant registrar and during that period of time, I
> did my master's degree in surgery. That I did in 1963. So I became

a specialist in surgery after three years of doing the, you know, the clinical work. So then after that, I became a registrar because that was a qualification that you have to have; a post-graduate qualification. So I became a registrar, I think, in 1964. And then, after that, I became a senior lecturer, which is a faculty position, but the senior lecturer is equivalent of probably assistant professor. So I continued that until 1967, when I left India and came to Seattle.

With such credentials under his belt and having had the experience of not only performing surgeries on his own, but also tweaking and teaching new techniques and methods, Manhas was rudely awakened to the realities of life as a medical resident in the United States. He found himself pitted against the chief resident, who did not have as much experience as he had even though the chief resident was technically in a higher position than Manhas. He recalls,

> My chief resident, who I worked with when I came from India, was
> a very [slow surgeon]. But he was a chief resident. You're already
> in surgery for five years, when you [can] become chief resident.
> Fifth year or fourth year. And they have done the same amount of
> surgery [as I had]. But unfortunately, this particular gentleman was
> not, I don't know why his rotation was such, but he had not done
> much surgery. I could see that when I came. I was a teacher. I was
> teaching, training people over there [in India]. So I had to be hold-
> ing retractors for him. I was a second-third year resident, he was a
> fifth year resident.

For Manhas, the indignation of being considered a second-class doctor in comparison to a lesser-skilled surgeon led him to make a few inappropriate comments about the chief resident's skills. At the end of his first three months, he was called into the residency program director's office and told "my performance was not up to the standard and I'm on probation and I may not have a position at the end of the year." Realizing that word of his frustrations must have gotten back to the chief resident, Manhas vowed never to speak ill publicly about a colleague again and redoubled his efforts to prove that he was an excellent surgeon.

Other narrators who had American credentials still encountered racial and ethnic prejudice in various fields. As Raj Joshi's story at the beginning of this chapter demonstrates, jobs that were related to certain government contracts were out of reach of most immigrants. This glass ceiling meant that immigrants were often clustered in less prestigious work or that it took them much longer to break into their professions. Balraj Sokkappa also experienced the sting of being overlooked for a job because of his nationality. After being encouraged to apply for a job with General Electric (GE) by a professor in his department, he and another student from India met with a representative of the company. He recalls, "We talked with him, but then nothing came out of it. And several months later, the professor told us that he didn't think that GE would hire [us] because [we were] both from India. But we weren't too interested in the industrial job anyhow, so you know, we didn't bother about it. But he did tell us that he probably would have given us a job if we were Caucasian." For both Joshi and Sokkappa, the issues of citizenship and ethnicity played a role in what sorts of opportunities were open to them.

For women, there is the burden of gender discrimination to overcome in addition to race and nationality. Bharti Kirchner worked for IBM for several years and despite having many different types of work experiences that qualified her for her position, she notes, "I always had to prove to them that I could do the work and I could do it not only as good as them but maybe better than them. And they would expect me at their own level only if I was as good or better." Kirchner saw this as an issue of ethnic devaluation: Indians are not accepted or recognized as creative workers or management material. Even when her managers recognized that she was chronically under-employed, she still had a difficult time breaking out of the system to be promoted. Kirchner reflects,

At some point of time I got very frustrated. Especially at IBM, I got frustrated and I saw that I probably wouldn't move up, despite the fact that I was working very hard and I was doing everything I could think of, I would not go very far after that. There were only a couple of more steps for me. And at some point, it was interesting for me, that the writing bug hit me. And it came at the right time because I was getting frustrated with IBM and I was looking for something else to do except I didn't know what. I saw writing being an opportunity for me.

She was able to channel her frustration with an industry that had difficulty recognizing her talent toward more fulfilling and creative pursuits. In a way, feeling like there was only so far she could advance at IBM spurred her into finding a new path and new career. Similarly, Amy Laly, who worked for the Boeing Company for over two decades, notes that her experience there was fraught with tension and victories over gender and racial discrimination.

> At work, I have taken on the battle a couple of times, each time from a position of strength. I won't say I fought it, but I did deal with it in a constructive manner. When I joined Boeing, the culture there was very hierarchical and authoritarian. But over the years, Boeing underwent a huge culture change. Management and non-management employees had to take mandatory training for zero tolerance on sexual harassment in the workplace, gender and race discrimination. Qualified women and minorities are now promoted regularly, although I think that Boeing still has a long way to go. But I have seen a sea change at Boeing and that is good.

Still, Laly notes that even though women continue to get paid less than men and that she herself always had to work twice as hard to prove herself as capable as the men on her teams, she found her work at Boeing to be engaging and rewarding. She notes, "There are so many Americas in this country, and one has to learn to navigate between disparate realities. That's what makes living here so vibrant. But understanding the roots of bigotry helps to challenge the myths that people hold."

Thinking of America in multiplicity can help immigrants reconcile their own sometimes fragmented and contradictory experiences. Sokkappa notes, too, that while he managed to work his way around constraints placed on him, he still sees himself as occupying a position of relative privilege. Speaking of the civil rights movement that he witnessed early in his time in the United States, he notes, "I identified with the civil rights effort as something that [was fixing] wrongs to the blacks. Because I felt that actually the foreigners who were immigrating to this country, Asians, I think they had a better deal than the blacks in this country, and I thought that was wrong." While Vijay Prashad has argued that South Asians in particular hold on to their model minority status by denigrating or discriminating against African Americans or other American minorities, Sokkappa reveals a sensitivity to the disparate ways in which race operates as a dividing force—one that needs to be addressed head on: "See, I could get a job more easily, a technical job, than a black student who got a technical degree. If a black guy graduated with a graduate degree and I graduated with a graduate degree, I probably would have had an easier time than him." Rather than simply deny the effects of race, gender, ethnic, and national discrimination, these stories remind us that the path to South Asian success is riddled with potholes and complicated by factors both within and outside of any single immigrant's control.

CONCLUSIONS

Despite the challenges that South Asian immigrants to the Pacific Northwest have faced in their professional lives, their legacy in the region cannot be ignored. Regardless of whether they came through a work visa or family reunification, today South Asians permeate every field and have had an impact on shaping key industries in the Pacific Northwest. It is no coincidence that huge multinational corporations like Boeing or Microsoft have been strong advocates for increasing immigration opportunities between South Asia and the United States; the value of these workers is stamped on nearly every aspect of their business products and services. However, South Asians have made a living in all sorts of ways and walks of life for over a hundred years in the Pacific Northwest.

In addition to the numerous South Asians working in educational, technological, and engineering industries, there are many others such as the small agriculturists, restaurateurs, and grocery shop owners that also make up an important part of the regional economy. Whether working on cutting-edge technology as Rao Remala did at Microsoft in the 1980s, or participating in business chambers of commerce, as Zakir Parpia did during his term with the Master Builders Association for King and Snohomish Counties, or working as public officials as Raj Manhas did as the Seattle School District superintendent, South Asians have changed the landscape of the region through their hard work and ambition. At the same time, they too have been transformed by the experience of moving in professional worlds as immigrants facing various obstacles ranging from legal to interpersonal. Across the spectrum, however, South Asians have made an impact on the ways in which business is conducted and are vital components of the

American economy. As Vijay Prashad suggests, the status of South Asians as "model minorities" is problematic and predicated on competition among different ethnic groups, but behind that label are many complex stories of distinguished achievement, varied career trajectories, and shifting class identities that also need to be told.

5

FALLING FROM THE TREE

FAMILY, GENDER, AND GENERATIONAL DIFFERENCES

> And so after we came, we were in Boston and I was very homesick
> the first few months because my husband got involved with study-
> ing at the university. And I was not sure what I wanted to do. Then I
> started babysitting. . . . I met a few Indian people, got to know them.
> And within a few months, I realized I was expecting a baby. That was
> a shock because we couldn't have afforded a child then. But luckily
> everything went smoothly and so he was born a year after we
> arrived here.
>
> —Shanta Gangolli

> My family—my mother was very concerned that she wasn't a daughter
> of one of her friends. She wasn't one that she chose. My mother had a
> string of girls ready. She'd write me a letter saying, "Here's a girl. Her
> parents are great friends of mine. You should marry her." Or "Here's
> a girl . . . they are pretty wealthy and she's their only daughter. You
> should marry her. And here I was marrying a girl who came from a
> middle-class family. You know, not a Muslim. Not South Asian. But
> she didn't object much. She said, "Well, at least he's getting married."
>
> —Jeff Siddiqui

WHEN the snow began to fall during her first winter in the United
States in 1958, Shanta Gangolli began to have serious doubts about
her decision to accompany her husband to chilly Cambridge, Massachusetts, as he began his studies at the Massachusetts Institute of Technology.
After the initial excitement of her overseas voyage had worn off, the reality
of having to set up a home in a strange new country began to seep into her
heart. She had married her husband, Ramesh, shortly before they set off to
America, and she was still trying to find herself in her new role as wife. Her

move abroad was also accompanied by a shift in her professional identity: although she had finished her college degree in Bombay and had worked as a stenographer before moving to the United States, Gangolli soon found herself in a cold, lonely apartment in the middle of a Northeastern winter with little to do. Her struggles with settling into a new country, becoming a mother in a land far away from her kin, and learning how to balance her own desires and expectations with the realities of family life in America echo across many immigrants' experiences. Gangolli's stories also raise the question: how do ideas about the family and gender relationships change through the immigration process?

Families can be the source of great joy and consternation for immigrants who must negotiate changing social positions, shifting expectations, and newfound desires. Although family networks often provide immigrants with emotional and material support, the home can also be a site of struggle as immigrants adapt to their new situations.[1] These challenges manifest through marriage choices, the process of family formation, intergenerational conflicts, and changes in gender roles. There is a particular burden placed on women who are expected to maintain customs and traditions of their home countries while also preparing children to fit into mainstream host societies.[2] Many of the stories told by South Asians in the Pacific Northwest show how gender roles in the immigrant family tend to follow recognizable conventions whereby women are expected to take care of the home and children, while men are more likely to move through the public sphere of work and society.

However, the experience of immigration also reorients men's roles as they learn to do more of the "caring work"[3] in their households than their own fathers or contemporaries living in South Asia would do. In a few cases, women took on the role of breadwinner after migration, whereas men faced greater obstacles to finding work—a situation that also created tension within the family as men struggled with their declining social and economic positions. Not all of the stories told by narrators reinforce the idea that families are a place of sanctuary; for some, they became a source of pain as narrators negotiated domestic violence or divorce. At the same time, some immigrants who came to the United States relied gratefully on siblings or extended family members to help pave the way, while others found that they were far from familial networks and had to start anew. The stories of narrators who negotiate this intimate and complicated ground

FIG 5.1 Prem and Swaran Kumar's wedding, North India, July 6, 1970. Photo courtesy of Prem Kumar.

shed light on how central the family, households, and friendships are to the immigrant experience, and how these institutions are transformed through the settlement process.

AFTER THE HONEYMOON: MARRIAGE AND MIGRATION

All over South Asia, the heterosexual family is a significant organizer of society; it is also one of the primary mechanisms through which immigrants enter the United States. In South Asia multiple generations often live in the same household and the definition of the family extends well beyond the nuclear household of a husband, wife, and children. Instead, grandparents, aunts, uncles, and other kin may all live together under the same roof. Endogamous marriage within a specific caste, linguistic group, or religious community is a widespread social practice; as a result, many immigrants who come to the United States are embedded in intricate regional networks and can trace their roots to specific locations and communities in South Asia for generations. Weddings are often an occasion of great celebration, and across communities, marriage is often seen as a melding of two families in addition to the union of two individuals.

As South Asians move to the United States, family reunification has been a vital instrument in helping others cross borders. Approximately two-thirds of immigrants who come to the United States legally as permanent residents arrive under family preference categories,[4] and many of these family "reunifications" actually occur through new marriages. Partly because of the large numbers of immigrants coming as a result of marriage and partly because of the popular representations of "exotic" and colorful South Asian marriage traditions, there is fascination with the institution (particularly arranged marriages), within and outside of the South Asian diasporic community.[5] Despite the allusions to tradition, the institution of marriage has shifted in many ways through the migration process, though there are patterns that persist. In many cases, men came to the United States first and then traveled back to South Asia to get married before bringing their brides over to live with them. In other cases, immigrants ventured abroad together after getting married at home, while others met their spouses after coming to the United States. Still others, such as Sat Kapahi, married in their home country and then came abroad on his or her own. Kapahi's marriage, which took place in Lahore, was arranged by his family in the year just prior to the partition of India and Pakistan. He had not met his wife before the wedding. He recalls:

> And then another very [difficult] thing for people over here [to understand] is that I was married with a pre-arranged marriage by my family. That was a big affair in Lahore, because [my wife's] family was very, very well-known there and they were extremely wealthy. So when I got engaged, there was a teacher who was— there always has to be a man who's a go-between—who knows both families. This [teacher] knew the family of my wife and my family, so he arranged all this. And when all this is arranged, my family went to visit the girl's family and then the girl's family—the girl doesn't come, but the mother [and some close] relative, they come and visit my family. So that was arranged and it was a big, big wedding. It was the talk of the town at that time.

After the wedding festivities were complete, Kapahi came to the United

States in 1952 to complete his mechanical engineering degree at Louisiana State University, leaving his wife behind. It was only after he received a job offer from the Boeing Company and moved to Seattle that his wife joined him two years later. Likewise, Kris Gupta, who came to Seattle to attend the University of Washington to study engineering after leaving his home in Kashmir, met his wife in India. Gupta had come to the United States in 1950, but moved back to India for a period from 1956 to 1961 before deciding to permanently settle in the United States. Soon after making the move back to America, Gupta went to visit Kashmir for his younger brother's wedding. After the wedding, he was introduced to his future wife in what Gupta describes as a "somewhat" arranged marriage: he notes that it was a "'you guys can meet and decide' type of thing. We got married in [19]62." After some struggles with getting a visa for the new Mrs. Gupta, the couple came initially to Canada and made their way back to Seattle.

Dev Manhas and Rao Remala were also young professionals when their families decided it was time for them to settle down, even though they were planning on migrating abroad. Dev Manhas's family arranged his marriage just before he left for the United States for his medical residency in 1967. He arrived in Seattle first and his wife followed six months later. Rao Remala was working in Delhi when his family arranged his marriage with a young woman from a town in his home state of Andhra Pradesh. He married his wife in 1976 and she moved to Delhi with him, where their first daughter was born. They moved to Seattle a few years later when Remala was recruited to work for Microsoft. While Manhas and Remala talk about marriage as almost a natural phase of life that they did not question, making the decision to get married was not so easy for others. Shaila Kode, for instance, was working as a doctor in a government program that required newly graduated medical students to provide service in underserved parts of the country when her family began to pressure her to marry. Kode recalls her father's anxiety about her living on her own, which heightened his desire to find a partner for her: "I had told him, too, 'I don't really need to get married now.' But, you know, parents at that time were different. Their outlook was different. They thought that if I reach 25-26, the girl has to be married. That's how the parents looked at it." Kode was matched after a relative answered an advertisement put out by her future husband. She notes, "He [her future husband] had advertised in the newspaper for a doctor wife. And one of my relatives happened to see [it] and [he] was a friend of one of my relatives'

FIG 5.2 Kris Gupta and his wife, Suman, with Senator Warren Magnusson, date unknown. Magnusson helped Mrs. Gupta secure a visa to immigrate to the United States. Photo courtesy of Kris Gupta and the Wing Luke Museum of the Asian Pacific American Experience, 2003.200.016.

son-in-laws. So that's how my father came to know him. But he only wanted a doctor wife."

Kode's point about her husband's desire to marry a "doctor wife" shows the contradictory importance of women's education to their own marriageability in the diaspora. Even today, a quick scan of the matrimonial advertisements placed in *India Abroad*, the most widely read newspaper of the Indian American community, reveals how many families put out notices about women that emphasize their more fetching attributes, and also their education, their employment, and their desire to move abroad. In the several pages of newsprint (and online forums) dedicated to matrimonial advertisements, it is common to come across notices that emphasize a marriage candidate's profession, family background, height, weight, religious and linguistic group, and other traits.[6] At the same time that families of brides-to-be showcase the women's education and employment, they are also careful to signal the women's domestic skills by emphasizing their "homely" (meaning domestic) qualities and strong cultural values. A man's matrimonial advertisements, on the other hand, are almost entirely devoted to his education, employment prospects, and accomplishments.[7] In these ads, a good education, high salary, and desirable visa status are as important as religious, linguistic, and caste markers. They also point to the strong correlation between marriage, education, and class status, as they highlight qualities that families deem most important when finding suitable spouses for their children.

Not all immigrants followed their parents' marital expectations, however, and after individuals move away from their home communities and enter into western societies, marriage can be the subject of great discord. The act of choosing love over family expectations and obligations is not without consequence. Zakir Parpia, who grew up in an Ismaili Muslim community in Bombay, met his future bride, Chitra, after getting to know her father through a business associate. Chitra's father and family were Brahmin Hindus who took their religious and caste affiliations very seriously. Even though Zakir and Chitra's father enjoyed a warm friendship over an extended period of time, when Chitra revealed her relationship with Zakir to her family, they effectively disowned her. After initially pushing back, Zakir and Chitra decided to marry even though the family pressures against their union increased. Zakir recalls:

> I should say that we actually got married three times. One was when she was having trouble [with the family] in [19]76, when I was here in Spokane. Her father found out [about us] and he was pressuring her to see eligible bachelors. And he took them in there [to see her]. And she was frantic and frightened. So we had a proxy marriage; so we signed some papers. In that sense, it was a legal marriage, which she kept under wraps until. . . . She said if she ever needed to, she would sort of trot it out as a safety route. And when we got back, on the fourth of July, we had a small Muslim ceremony [in my home with a reception]. The other one was more or less a court situation. The second one was a Muslim ceremony. And the third time, what you call it? A reception and stuff like that. After we came back from our honeymoon, it was sometime in late July, we had all of our friends over.

Chitra's father's disapproval meant that the family was unable to recognize Zakir and Chitra's commitment, but there were moments of resistance from sympathetic family members: while Chitra's father had forbidden any family members to attend their Muslim wedding, her mother found the courage to disobey him and came to the ceremony. Over thirty years later, Zakir is deeply touched by her strength and notes, "Like most women in India who don't talk back or fight back with their husbands, this was probably the only instance where she rebelled [and I am eternally grateful to her for that gesture of defiance and support for us]." In Zakir's touching story is a reminder of the deep repercussions for defying family expectations. Even though Zakir and Chitra had been married for over thirty years, her father refused to speak to her or acknowledge their marriage. Likewise, Akhtar Badshah experienced a similar chill from his in-laws after meeting his wife, Alka, in Delhi. Badshah and his future wife were both architects and met at a conference in India. They quickly fell in love and decided to get married. But, like Zakir and Chitra, Akhtar came from a Muslim family and Alka from a Hindu family. Even though his family came to accept the marriage, hers did not, and they cut off communication with the couple for five years. However, hard feelings eventually softened and Alka's family came around to accepting the marriage. Now, they have a warm relationship with both sides of the family.

Of course, there was not always outright family resistance to cross-cultural marriage. Narrators like Raj Joshi, Jafar Siddiqui, and Bharti Kirchner met their non–South Asian spouses in the United States and had to gently convince their families that they were making the right choice, whereas others like Asgar Ahmedi went ahead with marriage without waiting for family approval. Ahmedi recalls his early relationship with his first wife:

What happened was that in 1955, I met this young nurse—Norma Morgan from Bozeman, Montana, working at Providence Hospital. We got to know each other and got married. And then I had finished all my coursework but I didn't do my thesis. She was pregnant with my first daughter, so I got a job in a steel factory. I started working there as a chemist. Our daughter was born, and [my wife was expecting] again!

Even though that relationship eventually ended, Ahmedi's marriage was remarkable for the time considering that interracial marriage was still technically illegal in certain parts of the United States. In fact, it was not until the monumental court case of *Loving v. Virginia* in 1967 that the Supreme Court officially struck down anti-miscegenation laws that would have prohibited marriages like that between Asgar Ahmedi and Norma Morgan, or Raj and Irene Joshi. Joshi came to America in 1946 as a teenager when his father was offered the opportunity to work for the United Nations Food and Agriculture Organization, which was then based in Washington, D.C. When his family left for their next posting in Rome in 1951, Joshi stayed behind and moved across the country to attend Washington State University. He eventually came to Seattle to earn his master's degree at the University of Washington, where he met his future wife, Irene, who was a white, American-born woman. Joshi recounts his first meeting with Irene:

> I was a graduate student and she was a sophomore in political science. She was interested in international [issues]—in fact, that's what she was studying, international politics. There was a place called People's Center on the corner of Campus Parkway and University Ave. It was a left-wing group, and in fact was investigated during the McCarthy hearings and stuff. They had rooms—about ten rooms, I think—and there were a lot of graduate students, mostly foreigners, Indians, staying there. Irene used to come down there. People would meet, and that's how I met her first.

After dating for almost two years, Raj and Irene married even though he had not fully committed to staying in the United States. In fact, he seriously considered returning to India because of the hardships he faced as a foreign worker. Even though Joshi's parents had reservations about the marriage, they were mostly concerned that it would mean he would never return to India, and, as future grandparents, that they would not have much contact with their grandchildren. Luckily, they were assuaged by regular visits to India by the newly married couple and, eventually, by the much-anticipated grandchildren.

Likewise, Bharti Kirchner came to the United States as a young student in 1962 and was taken aback by the American culture of dating. She recalls: "I found the dating system a bit complicated. And I dated a little bit. I dated both Americans and Indians, but I found that people's dating habits were, you know, something difficult for me to get used to." Even though she was initially tentative about exploring romantic relationships, she met her American-born spouse in San Francisco, where they were

FIG 5.3   A party celebrating the engagement of Asgar and Norma Ahmedi, including Raj and Irene Joshi, Seattle, Washington, circa 1955. Photo courtesy of Raj Joshi.

FIG 5.4   Raj and Irene Joshi on their wedding day, circa 1955. Photo courtesy of Raj Joshi.

both working for a technology firm. Unfortunately, they got off to a rocky start: "Interestingly enough my husband was on a leave of absence when I joined there. So he was gone and they gave me his job. He came back and, needless to say, we didn't get along because I had his job and they gave him another job, which maybe he didn't like as much. We argued a lot." They were able to put aside their differences quickly and married after six months of dating in 1976.

While most of the narrators were partnered, marriage was not an end goal for others. Amy Laly, who came to Portland to study in the late 1960s, had married her college sweetheart, but then decided to end the relationship. Proudly single today, Laly does not regret her decision and expressed relief at being able to explore her own passions and interests. Jamal Rahman also found himself in a marriage that was not right for him. He explains, "After my parents died, I thought I should get married. It was sort of a headstrong decision, a rushed decision. So I got married 1997–1998 and it did not work out. It was a good marriage, but it was not fulfilling and we divorced just recently, a year and half ago." While there is a lower rate of divorce among South Asians than in the larger American population, some marriages were simply not meant to last. Living in the United States, where divorce is less of a social stigma, allowed South Asian immigrants in unhappy marriages an opportunity to leave those relationships and to seek fulfillment elsewhere. Asgar Ahmedi, who married an American-born white woman in the 1950s and had children with her, found that the differences between them were too great. He ended up remarrying later in life and had another daughter with his second wife, who was South Asian. Likewise, Prasanna Samaramawickrama married his young sweetheart after traveling the world as an airline host. While that marriage lasted for several years, it ended before they started a family. Today he is married to a woman who shares his Sri Lankan roots. Though they have different religious backgrounds—he is Sinhalese and comes from a Buddhist family and she is a Christian—they are happily married with two sons.

GENDER TRANSFORMATIONS: NEW ROLES AND NEGOTIATIONS

After the initial blush of new love fades, couples are faced with the work of settling into new responsibilities and relationships. When their move abroad coincided with marriage, women who came to the United States found that they had to seriously reconsider their identities as they learned how to be a South Asian living abroad *and* a new wife. When Shanta Gangolli moved to Boston as a young bride, she found the adjustment to life in the United States to be complicated: "It was a little different than what [I expected]—I had pictures of countryside-like things. But Boston was very different. Old and, you know, certain parts were pretty grim." Facing the dark and frigid winter without many friends or acquaintances, Gangolli found it very difficult to maintain even small semblances of the life to which she was accustomed. Finding Indian groceries proved to be a Herculean task and cooking therefore called for creative maneuverings, like using different ingredients to make familiar dishes. Gangolli recalls the lengths she would go to in search of spices and foods: "There was a store in New York that we would write to and ask them to send us [things]. They would give you a list of things they had, and you could ask them to mail you. That's how we started getting some Indian groceries." Of course, it was not just the groceries, but learning how to cook, manage the household, and eventually deal with raising children that placed stress on women. At the same time, Gangolli adapted and sought out support in unexpected places:

> When we first came to Boston, I was so lonesome in the apartment building. My next-door neighbor, I went and knocked on her door. She was an elderly woman. She was also very lonesome because they had no children, and she never went out of her apartment. So when I knocked on her door, she came and opened, and when I told her I was staying in the next apartment, she got very friendly.

This neighbor was instrumental in helping Gangolli learn how to prepare dishes, now that she was responsible for such tasks, and gave her advice on what to eat, especially after she found out that Gangolli was pregnant. Like Gangolli, Padmini Vasishth also had to learn the basics of cooking and cleaning as part of her transition from student to married woman. When living in her mother's household, where there were domestic workers who helped with cooking, she only had to say what she wanted to eat and it would be ready for her after a long day of studying. However, after coming to the United States, she became the cook in charge of making sure the day's meals were planned and prepared. Funny in retrospect, but feeling like a disaster at the time, Vasishth recalls her first attempt at cooking a meal for some American friends:

> So here it was, so I said, "All right, we will make this mincemeat [curry]." You know, this ground meat? "I'll make it, and you boil the rice." And an Indian friend who [lived] close by, he said, "I'll make you some Indian bread—puris and potatoes." That would be perfect—he'll make the potato curry with puris and [I'll make] this ground beef. So here I am gone to the store, I bring the beef, the meat, all ground up and everything. Put it in the skillet. Of course the damn thing has to change color—from pink it is becoming brown. And I didn't know it was going to turn brown. I'm shouting to my husband, "This damn fellow, he has given us bad meat!" I dumped it in the garbage. Went [to try for a] second time. And of course the time was getting on too, and of course, potatoes were put on boil because our friend was going to come and make the curry and do his job. Anyway, second time, again it happened, the same thing!

After asking a friend to step in, Vasishth belatedly learned that meat, in fact, *does* change color when cooked, and the browning was a good thing. Ruefully, Vasishth recalls: "So you can understand how much [I had to learn]—although I was a chemistry student, I never learned this chemistry on meat!"

Though eventually both Gangolli and Vasishth mastered the art of cooking, they each faced readjustments in their own career paths after moving abroad and getting married. As noted in the epigraph of this chapter, Gangolli found that she was pregnant very soon after moving to the United States. Having a child far away from her family posed a new set of challenges as she bore the burden of maintaining family life. She notes, "I think it's more . . . adjustment for a woman [than] when the men come . . . see, when we came, even though we had education, we did not think our career came ahead of [our] husbands' career. We went where he had his job, and then we tried to adjust." When reflecting on the difficulty of raising children who grow up between two cultures, she asks:

> Have you thought of the women who came from India, like me and your mothers, who had to adjust to the life here? Become an American mom, drive kids around to all the activities, participate in

PTAs, do the housework, which she was not used to. Have no help
from the husbands because the husbands were not used to helping.
Learn driving, which they never did [before]; if they could afford a
car in India, they would have a driver. They had to adjust more to
the lives here, having been brought up in India and then adjusting
to their children's needs. And then the children, the question of
dating, drugs. The mothers have gone through more problems than
these children who constantly used to have these panel discussions
about being brought up in two cultures. It was hard for them, true,
but I think it was hard for the mothers also—more than the father,
because father was busy with his work and was still not used to
being an American father. Whereas mothers had to take the role
of an American mother, learn driving, do all the chores that an
American woman does, which she never did before. In the house,
outside, do lawn, get the gardening if they had a house. Entertain.
And then attend to the children's activities, you know. But I doubt
if anybody has given a thought to the woman's part.

Gangolli describes the strain caused by trying to be an "American" mom
while still being an "Indian" housewife: "We were in that middle, sand-
wiched between. We were not in India—we were in this country wanting to
be American, but not quite ready." For her, being a wife and mother meant
preparing three fresh hot meals every day, washing diapers by hand, keeping
up with school activities, and making sure that the home was in order and
her husband's comforts maintained. However, Gangolli notes, while these
competing expectations reigned supreme for women, the reverse was not
always true for men: "They were not used to [doing these things in India], so
it didn't occur to them. Men were not expected to help out in the household
things. Men were expected to go to their work, come home, and all their
needs were attended to. And so when they came here, they did the same
thing." While women were required to adjust in order to meet both American and South Asian demands, men were able to enjoy the sense of male
privilege they had had before.

Dev Manhas echoes Gangolli's assertion that maintaining the home and
children is a task more often delegated to women than men. Manhas, a high-
ranking cardiologist who had his own practice for several years, grounds
the distinct division of labor in his family in cultural terms: "I think that we
all knew our roles. As being from Indian background, I knew what my role

was, more as a provider, and whatever I could do at home, I would. Asha, on the other hand, has just been a model mother and as a wife [and home-maker]." Praising his wife for her work to care for the family, Manhas reiter-ates that his job as a heart surgeon kept him away from home and being on call meant that he was often unable to participate actively in his children's lives. Manhas notes with regret that the stresses of his job created distance between himself and his children, though the demands of his career over-shadowed his ability to make different choices.

Rao Remala, too, mentions that during his time as an early employee at Microsoft, his job often kept him away from his family. He notes,

> It was hard for us initially. First of all, for my wife, it was hard initially because being a housewife and being in the house is very, very hard. And with me dedicating lot of time at Microsoft, spend-ing tons of hours [was hard]. Then also, when my first daughter was born, then she was with her family in Andhra and there was a lot of help and all that. But here all of a sudden, there is no help, nothing. And you know, here my second daughter was born, in Microsoft, remember in those days, it was a very small company. There was no structured maternity leave and things like that. All they did was gave me half a day!

Remala became very successful while at Microsoft; however, despite his personal and financial achievements, he says: "My regret is basically dur-ing those days when I was working at Microsoft, there was nothing but my work and you know . . . honestly I couldn't spend a lot of time with them [his family]. That was actually, I think, the biggest regret I have now." For men like Manhas and Remala, professional success came at personal cost. Prem Kumar found himself in the opposite position in his family when his wife was hired to work for Boeing in the mid-1980s and they moved to the Seattle area. She specialized in supercomputers and developed a high-pow-ered career. After the move, Kumar became a part-time worker and full-time caregiver for his young daughter. He recalls:

> For a two-career family, there are some additional challenges, and both of us had sort of demanding jobs at that time. Bulk of raising our daughter fell upon me because my job was slightly less chal-

lenging than my wife's. . . . I thoroughly enjoyed raising our daughter. It gave me the opportunity of spending time with her, taking her to different types of activities. Taking her to school, back and forth, since there was no transportation to the school that she went to. So, it was a wonderful experience.

Kumar's story is unusual in comparison to those of other South Asian men who stick to the traditionally defined "male" roles of providing materially for their families without too much day-to-day involvement. His experience of raising his daughter was truly transformative and he notes that he most likely would not have taken up the same responsibilities had he and his wife decided to settle in India. Similarly, Raj Manhas points out that being a father in the United States opened up different ways of interacting with his children than what he would have experienced if he had never migrated abroad. He remembers being in the birthing room during his wife's labor and delivery of their first child, which was a fairly uncommon experience for men in his family:

> Because in our culture, in India, you know, [the father] is not there generally. I don't know now, but in old India, you know the way I grew up, and they didn't know when the baby's born. And for me to watch this miracle happen . . . and being with my wife. Being there . . . are those moments that I will never forget because they were so beautiful. As I said, with all the anxiety and the issues, you know, associated with it: "Is the kid going to be okay? And is Inderjit, my wife, is [she] going to be fine?" And it's all of that. But then there's a sheer happiness seeing this little baby who is [an] extension of you.

For Manhas and Kumar, being a parent proved to be a challenging but infinitely rewarding experience that pushed them to reconsider their own gender roles. Though Kumar relished his time with his daughter, he had to compromise aspects of his career to sustain his family. Kumar has a Ph.D. in English from Washington State University and once had ambitions to pursue a career as a tenure-track professor, but found his life moving along a different course:

Well, about six months or so after we moved to Seattle, I found out
that Boeing had a position for a technical editor. And since I had
experience in that area, I applied and got the job. I took that job,
somewhat reluctantly, because I still wanted to go back to teaching
or doing research, those types of things. But I took the job since
teaching jobs in my area of specialty were not easily available at
that time, to me. Eventually, I found the work interesting enough
because it gave me an opportunity to learn in an area which was
not my specialty. And, as time went by, it simply became more
convenient for the two of us to work for the same company, so we
could adjust our timing and our holidays and other things. And so
it was a kind of compromise, more for convenience than my desire
to do the things that I really wanted to do in terms of my career.

Kumar celebrated over twenty years of working with Boeing at the time of
his oral history interview and also had founded and worked closely with
several South Asian community groups in that time; still, he wistfully
remembered his desire to teach and be involved in his first passion, English
literature, throughout his career. Though unusual for a man, Kumar's decision to put his own career on hold for the sake of his family was a familiar
one for many South Asian women.

Nearly thirty years before, Padmini Vasishth had been dedicated to pursuing a scientific career. She was slated to go to Newnham College in Cambridge, but World War Two made travel to England impossible. She decided
to complete her studies in India and her mother pushed her to consider
becoming a doctor. She began her training in chemistry, but that, too, was
interrupted—this time by the partition of India and Pakistan. After her family moved from Lahore to Delhi, she completed her courses, but she never
had the opportunity to fulfill her dream of becoming a doctor:

Of course then the Partition occurred and we moved to Delhi,
and things were different. I took my master's exam in Delhi only.
Did all my work in Delhi for my master's thesis; Dr. Agarwal was
my [advisor]. Punjab University was housed in a portion of Delhi
University before they had their own [building]. So the question of
going to the medical school drifted. I never did go back and I see
I should have gone back. I really feel because there was so much [I

FIG 5.5 Prem Kumar receives the American Literature Award from Vice Principal McCullough at Daring Union Christian College, Batala, India, 1969. Photo courtesy of Prem Kumar.

could do], and I was very good in zoology and botany. But because I had come for master's. . . . But from there I never went back to medicine. I would've been a good surgeon. Another friend of mine, Mira Menon, was also at the University of Washington. She was not married at that time. Menon was also going there. He was in electrical engineering; they got married here. And now she's still doing so well. She got her Ph.D. They moved on to Chicago or someplace on the east side, I don't know exactly where. She continued until she got her degree, got her Ph.D. in microbiology. She was a full [medical] doctor before she came here, Indian doctor, and she took to microbiology. But anyway, I did want to go into medicine, but I didn't. Anyway, I have no regrets. I have no regrets but that was a fond hope.

Even though she was unable to continue her studies, Vasishth continued her interest in chemistry and worked with her husband after he set up a consulting business to develop techniques to stabilize wood used as building material. Eventually, her husband took a job as a visiting scientist at Mississippi State University. Finding herself in a small southern town with little to do, Vasishth finally had the chance to complete her Ph.D. in wood science and technology in an uplifting and inspiring turn of events in 1993.

THE DARKER SIDE OF HOME:
FAMILY CONFLICTS AND VIOLENCE

While Kumar and Vasishth each made professional sacrifices for their personal lives, others found such choices came at a higher cost. Shaila Kode, a young doctor who immigrated to the United States in the 1970s, found that her responsibility doubled when she became a young mother—she was not only responsible for her immediate family and extended family, but she was also the stable breadwinner in her marriage because her husband was out of work for an extended period of time. After having her first child while completing her medical residency in New York, she worked to help support her brother in his education to become a dentist and her sister as she finished her university studies in India. On top of these financial pressures, she had to balance the demand of her medical training and motherhood. Her story twists some of the gendered expectations that require women to put aside their careers for the good of the family; instead, Kode was compelled to ensure that she always had a job in order to provide economically for her family. A quick eighteen months after her first child was born, Kode found that she was pregnant again, but her husband was still only working intermittently. This time she took charge of the situation:

> I became pregnant; I was finishing my residency. This was in 1980.
> I said, "Oh my god. I'm going to go to Seattle and I don't have a job
> and this man doesn't have a job. What should I do?" I joined the
> Army. I recruited myself. I went through recruitment and joined
> the Army. You wouldn't believe it, all I did for this family! I actually
> got recruited on active duty while I was doing my final year of resi-
> dency, while I was pregnant. So as soon as I finished, on the 30th
> of June, we left New York. This was again because I got recruited,
> all of our moving expenses were taken care of. I had a job as soon
> as I'd come [back] to Seattle . . . I'd have a job in hand with officer's

pay. . . . I had to go to San Antonio for six weeks [for basic training]. And I was pregnant! [Laughs.]

Kode still works at the Madigan Army Medical Center at Fort Lewis, Washington, and is a U.S. Army doctor. Her decision to sign up for military service was unusual for a young immigrant mother from India and, among her Army comrades, she was very much in the minority. She not only reversed traditional roles by taking on the responsibility of the primary breadwinner, but she also entered a highly masculinized profession by choosing to become a military doctor.

Kode's bravery and persistence, sadly, were also needed for an increasingly difficult situation at home as her relationship with her (now ex-) husband deteriorated. Kode was fully contributing to her family's livelihood, and yet her husband restricted her ability to spend money as she saw fit and forbade her to help her extended family financially. While she was empowered through her own career, she was disempowered at home because of the skewed dynamics of power and control that she experienced with her husband: "I was working so hard, but I didn't have the authority to send money. It was very controlling behavior. I did my best to save some money and send it [to my family] without letting him know. Things like that." Kode's story is one of perseverance in the face of a bad marriage. The social taboos against divorce in South Asian cultures add a layer of complexity for immigrants living away from their communities. Margaret Abraham's work on domestic violence in the United States' South Asian communities points to the challenges facing immigrant women in escaping difficult situations at home.[8] She argues that "in the immigrant context, although South Asian women were to be economic contributors, they were increasingly constructed in cultural terms with the immigrant home as the site for defining gender relations and ensuring traditional patriarchy."[9]

The cultural barriers faced by South Asian women, including the desire to maintain a seamless façade of a perfect family life and preserve South Asian "family values," make speaking out against violence and abusive situations incredibly difficult. After facing similar difficulties in her own marriage, Lakshmi Gaur relates that because she chose to marry someone who was from a different part of India than her, she felt trapped and unable to tell her family about the challenges she faced in her marriage: "It was tough for some time and . . . remember I chose to marry, [so] I cannot share any of the unpleasant stuff with anybody. Because my mom died so young, my family raised me with so much care and attention. Very tender loving care for me. So they cannot ever imagine my getting hurt." Gaur's desire to protect her family from the unpleasantness she faced at home led her to hide her problems. After several years of struggle, Gaur finally ended the relationship. With the help of close friends and her sons, she moved on to a successful career and today acts as an informal mentor to other young women in her community:

> It's tough for me, probably it was very difficult for the kids. But we did not fall off the wagon. I did not fall off the wagon. I did not ever give up. I had a fantastic [19]97–98, research-wise, career-wise. So we moved on and then I kept my head up, you know, in Indian community. After my divorce, not many people would want to talk to me. None of the North Indian friends want to talk to me. And then I don't have many South Indian friends because my ex [husband] could not speak the language and then he did not like to visit with them. So we had a tough time. I didn't have any friends by then. At the time of divorce, it's only me and my two children. It was tough for them too. But the truth is, we all have inherent energy and then we—I believe that we have to pull ourselves. Nobody is going to pull us. You know we have to help ourselves. And then we did. We came out and then I started getting involved in community after that. And then that's a lot of solace because I did not want any other woman to go through what I went through. I went through several forms of abuse that I don't want anybody to go through. So, anybody that needs help, any young lady that needs help, I wanted to lend a hand.

Kode and Gaur's stories are remarkable because of their courage; however, they are by no means unique. While both Kode and Gaur took the brave step of sharing their stories, there are other members of the South Asian community who are silent about their struggles with family or partner violence because the price of revealing the trauma that they have survived might be too high.

It is important to keep in mind that while many, many stories of joy and love come from marriage and family life, there are also challenges that should not be silenced. In nearly every region of the United States where there are substantial populations of South Asians, there are also culturally-specific organizations aimed at ending domestic violence and supporting survivors.[10] One such organization, Chaya, was formed in 1996 in Seattle to help other South Asian survivors and families who are in crisis.[11] Chaya has merged with the Asian and Pacific Islander Women and Family Safety Center in order to meet the needs of a wider constituency and help survivors connect with social and legal services. The organization not only provides information and services to survivors, but it also has an important presence in South Asian and wider Asian American communities because of its efforts to raise awareness about domestic violence and work to change societal conditions that enable oppression. In her family memoir *Motiba's Tattoos*, Mira Kamdar describes her experience of growing up in an ethnically mixed family: her father was an Indian engineer who came to study and eventually work for Boeing in Seattle and her mother was of Danish-American origin. Kamdar describes her father's tumultuous relationship with his family and the often violent home life she experienced as a child in the 1960s:

> If Dad had to suffer a thousand insults to his authority at home, at work he got even less respect. Changing his name from Prabhakar to "Pete" wasn't enough to turn him into a "good ol' American" white boy who could bond with his peers and superiors in an industry dominated by swaggering ex–Air Force types. Years later, he told me about his disappointment when it had finally become clear to him that no matter how well he did or how many years he put in, he'd never be promoted into management. Money was also tight in those days . . . my mother wasn't working and my father's income had to support both us and the family in India. Between the commute, the money worries, and the constant if most often subtle racism my father had to deal with at work, it's no wonder Dad felt stressed. He had to take his frustrations out on someone. We were the only available candidates. When I think back to the text of my confrontations with my father, they were always about power and authority: his power over us; his right to exercise absolute authority; his rage that even we, his own family, would not grant him that.[12]

Kamdar acknowledges the various social and economic pressures weighing on her father as he learned to play his role in a society where he was continuously marked as an outsider, no matter how hard he tried to be seen otherwise. At the same time, Kamdar tries to reconcile her own anger and pain at bearing the brunt of her father's abuse with the structural and emotional factors that made her father feel trapped by a sense of powerlessness and despair. Kamdar plainly names the twin pillars of power and authority as the principal forces that led her father to berate her and her siblings. Kamdar writes,

> During my entire childhood, I was convinced that my father behaved the way he did because he was Indian, that the yelling and screaming and crying that took place in our house never occurred in any other house in America. It took me years to figure out that not all Indian fathers were like Dad and that "real" American families were perfectly capable of experiencing the same, or worse.[13]

Without absolving him of his responsibility, Kamdar situates his actions in a story of historical and contemporary marginalization faced by immigrants, rather than viewing them as simply a reflection of the patriarchal culture of South Asia or an individual psychosis. Likewise, the stories of survivors of intimate violence reveal the ways in which immigration can trouble personal relationships and create tensions within the home.

CHOSEN FAMILIES:
FINDING FRIENDS AND MAINTAINING NETWORKS

While marriage is a significant path to migration for many South Asians, family-sponsored immigration allows other relatives to come to the United States. For instance, Rizwan Nasar came to the United States as a college student after his sister sponsored him. He arrived in Michigan with a green card in hand, which was a rarity; many immigrants come on short-term student or work visas and then go through the lengthy green card and permanent residency process. Having an uncle and aunt living near his university also meant that he always had a place to go during breaks and holidays from school. Because his sister was able to sponsor him, Nasar was able to establish a permanent base in the United States relatively easily. Likewise,

Jamal Rahman was able to help his sister and her family migrate to Seattle from Bangladesh. Even though he has been settled in the United States for several decades, his sister, who was a doctor in Bangladesh, only made the move in 2005. Ironically, even though Rahman had been on his own for many years, he now lives with his sister, her husband, and their children in a single-family house. Laughingly, he remarks, "So I am enjoying very much that family situation and that is different because I was married for some time. Before that, I was a bachelor for many years. I have gone through a bachelor life, a married life, and now an extended family system in America. Life is made poetic!"

Shaila Kode, whose brother migrated to the United States after her and lives in the Seattle area, was also able to sponsor her siblings and mother. Her elderly mother now splits her time between her son's home and Kode's home. Families continue to diversify as different generations of immigrants come to live together or near one another, and today senior citizens increasingly make up an important part of South Asian communities living in the Pacific Northwest.

While reunification through immigration was one way to maintain family connections, there were, of course, changes in family structures as people moved abroad permanently. In the early period of South Asian migration, the likelihood of losing touch with one's family and personal networks was very high. Raj Joshi recalls the days before regular telephone calls to India were possible. Letters were the primary mode of communication, and even those were simply snatches of a life happening far away. As the years went on, the burning desire to remain connected to India began to fade; he notes, "You get used to it. You have your own life and you live. And they forget you too, you know. [Laughs.] Parents forget you. My father, when he was living, he would write to me religiously, every week or every other week." Over time, the letters waned and Joshi and his father found new rhythms in their less-frequent communication. Likewise, Shanta Gangolli remarks on how family interactions change as a result of immigration:

> I think in India, there are a lot more cousins and relatives coming and going. There is always something happening in somebody's house and all the relatives are together. Not having close relatives here—now my sister's son and his sister's son have moved to this country, but that was later, when they were already grown

up. . . . My children grew up without that, without the contact of the cousins and relatives, constantly, like we had.

For Gangolli and Joshi, being away from their kin meant a loosening of social ties. Others, like Amy Laly, were able to maintain connections across the years and continents. Laly describes friendships from her high school days: "I still have friends, you know, even though we're miles apart and years have gone by. It's been forty years or forty-five years, something like that, from graduating from high school. They still write to me and I write to them. They come and visit me and I go visit them in India." With a sister in Canada and close relatives in Australia, her family and friend network is vibrant and transnational. Alok Mathur also keeps in regular contact with his family living in Delhi. Describing his childhood home, Mathur notes, "My sister is living there in that house now. And we have rented a portion of the house . . . there is a two-bedroom flat on the first floor—we have kept that to ourselves." Mathur and Laly have been able to maintain close relationships despite the distances that separate them from friends and family.

At the same time, "intentional" families created by immigrants as they learn how to settle into their adopted homes are equally important. For example, even though Gangolli might have left her biologically-related family behind, her communities of friends in America have played a vital role in her children's lives: "But my Indian friends here have now become more like an extended family to them, which is nice. . . . And since we are the oldest of them, they consider us [the elders] . . . they all live around here [laughs], so for everything, they are kind of around us, and we spend a lot of time for any special thing." For immigrants a long way from their homes, intentional communities are central to celebrating and remembering what life is like in South Asia. Rizwan Nasar hosted a neighborhood-wide Eid celebration in Sammamish, Washington, for his American friends and Pakistani family, while Santosh Wahi hosted large annual Diwali parties on Mercer Island, Washington, that were important venues for socializing and celebrating. These intentional community spaces serve an important purpose for immigrants from South Asia who often find themselves disconnected from the family and friends of their previous lives or because of the life choices that they have made through immigration.

LOVE AND LOSS: DEALING WITH DEATH AND DISTANCE

Though South Asians have generated an extended family life across continents through regular trips back and communication, the distance created by migration is not as easy to bridge when immigrants experience the loss of loved ones. Shaila Kode recalls the passing of her father only a few years after she moved to the United States. At the time, she was studying for an exam given by the Educational Commission for Foreign Medical Graduates (ECFMG) to become certified to practice medicine in the United States. She had not returned to India since leaving for Seattle until the tragedy struck. Over thirty years later, Kode recalls with heartfelt detail every aspect of how she found out about her father's poor condition:

> I went to [my friend] Maria's [house] and that afternoon, my brother-in-law, he and his wife called me and said, "Where are you?" I said, "I'm at Maria's." [They said] "Oh, we have to come and pick you up. Your father is very sick." I said, "What happened?" They said, "Your father is very sick and he's in the hospital. And they want you to come home right away." I said, "Oh my god!" I just could not believe it. I flew home from Seattle to New York, New York to Mumbai. Nobody was at the airport to pick me up except my husband's sister and her husband. I thought, "How come nobody from my family is here?" They took me to my home in Goregaon. They're driving and from far [off] you could see the common gallery, like a big [courtyard]. I could see my mama-ji[14] standing. I said, "How come mama-ji's here?" My mama lived in Belgaum. I go home and I learn that my father is dead. He had just sat next to my brother. He had no symptoms. No chest pain, nothing. He just didn't say anything. My brother was going to take his dental exam in two days. He told my mom to cook soon so that he [my brother] could eat and go to study. He sat next to [my brother] and just dropped dead. He was 57 [years old]. So I go home and I see, you know, that my father's not there anymore! They don't keep the body because they didn't keep—at that time, it was different. I was just distraught. My brother was still in school. My sister had a little job. And I was immobile—where do I stand today? Do I quit

everything and just stay here? I don't have a job here and I don't
have a job there, you know what I mean? I didn't know what to do.
It was a big decision time for me. . . . I had never seen him [again]
once I had left the country.

Kode's story illuminates the gut-wrenching emotion of a child who finds
out that her or his parent is now gone. Even though she was not there in
his final moments, Kode felt connected to him in his moment of passing.
Upon returning to India, she faced not only the deep grief of the loss of her
father, but also the incredible weight of responsibility for her family as the
oldest child in her family, now abroad. Torn between her husband and new
life in the United States and her obligations to her family in Mumbai, Kode
confronted one of the worst scenarios that an immigrant must face. Now
that her family home was bereft of its anchor, Kode had to take over the role
of provider that her father had played because, as a doctor residing abroad,
she had the most opportunities. Looming large were the specters of her
young brother struggling to complete his education and an unmarried sister
at home. Tempted as she was to just stay in India and help her family, she
ultimately came back to her life in Seattle and worked diligently to sponsor
her family members over time.

While Kode's story demonstrates the heartbreak that can befall an
immigrant while living far from home, Najma Rizvi's story links family tragedy and immigration in a different vein. Rizvi initially came to the United
States with her husband when she was twenty-one, but they both returned
to Bangladesh after completing higher courses of study. After teaching at
the University of Dhaka for a few years, her husband was caught in the
increasing tensions arising from the movement seeking the recognition of
Bengali as an official language of East Pakistan rather than the primary language of Urdu. Since Rizvi's husband was not originally from the region and
was a native Urdu speaker, he began to feel the weight of anti-Urdu sentiments. The language movement supporters were precursors to the nationalist groups who sparked the Bangladesh Liberation War in 1971, which led to
the separation of East Pakistan and the creation of the independent country of Bangladesh. After receiving a job offer from a university in Denver,
Rizvi and her husband decided to leave Bangladesh and come to the United
States as permanent residents in 1965. A week after they made the decision
to come, in a cruel twist of fate, Rizvi's husband collapsed on his way home

from his office: "He was taken to the hospital, but he had a massive attack. And you know, he even said that there is no point in taking me. And how much he loved me. His brain was working, [but] his body was completely cold. And I went almost crazy I think." Rizvi's own father had died when she was very young and left her mother a widow with eight children to support. At the time of her husband's passing, Rizvi herself was the mother of two young children. Feeling like history was eerily repeating itself, Rizvi fell into a stupor and was only able to pull herself together enough to care for her children. She recalls that soon after the news began to sink in, the visa consular officer who had approved her husband's petition to immigrate to the United States came to visit her:

> The consular officer came to express his condolence and sympathy to me. And he asked me to apply fresh, you know. And he had come within a week after my husband died, within ten days, to my home. That was really, I mean, unheard of, that the consular officer himself came because he was very impressed with my husband. And so I remember when he told me, I didn't say much. And at that time, I didn't know what to [do] . . . which would be the right decision.

With the encouragement of her brother, who was already in the United States working on his Ph.D. in engineering, Rizvi took a leap of faith and moved to Oklahoma on an immigrant visa in 1969. Still troubled by the darkness looming in her heart after her husband's death, it was all that she could do to get out of bed each morning. She went on, however, to earn her Ph.D. in anthropology and eventually moved to the Seattle area to teach at a local college. Rizvi's husband's passing was a heavy blow, but she still had the opportunity to seek out a new life abroad.

While Rizvi lost her husband at a very young age as they were about to embark on their new life as immigrants together, Padmini Vasishth became widowed just as she and her husband were about to enter retirement. Vasishth's husband, Ramesh, had been making arrangements to move to Canada for a period of time on a job assignment when he started to feel unwell. He visited his doctor in Mississippi, where they were living at the time, and was given a clean bill of health. At the same time, Vasishth's son was preparing for his wedding to an American-born woman and her daughter's child was about to celebrate his first birthday; the family was filled with excited anticipation. Just a few days before the birthday and wedding festivities, Ramesh became gravely ill. Quickly and without warning, his condition worsened, and he had a stroke only four days before his son's wedding. Amidst heartbreak, the American portion of the wedding went ahead as planned and in the autumn of that same year, the family made a trip to India to return Ramesh's ashes to his home soil and to complete an Indian wedding ceremony. Vasishth recalls:

> It was painful thing, painful. But anyhow, if it was not for my kids, I wouldn't have known what to do. It was a big diversion with the grandchildren and the kids. And then we went to India to have my son's wedding and [saw] all my relatives there. I escaped what could have been very bad for me. Then I decided, children decided, "Mother, why do you want to live alone?" We had sold our home. We had a house in Danville; we had sold that earlier. And then afterwards my children said, "You don't have to live alone. You live part of the time with me. Why do you want to set up house again?" So I live with my son and my daughter, and then I go to India.

In a heartbeat, Vasishth's life was transformed from that of a working wife, mother, and grandmother to that of a single woman. Supported by her many friends and children, today she spends her time between her children's homes in the United States and takes extended trips back to India.

THE NEXT GENERATION: PARENTING IN AMERICA

Vasishth's story speaks to another major transition faced by many immigrants—that of starting a family and raising children in a new culture. This intergenerational transition often means that immigrants must give up the dream of returning home for fear of becoming disconnected from children who are more at home in the host country. Parenting is rarely an easy task; for immigrants who do not share the same social codes, adolescent experiences, or even values around marriage, dating, and sex, raising children in America creates new challenges. For women like Shanta Gangolli, becoming a new mother was a daunting experience that she faced almost completely alone. She notes that while today it is common to see South Asians invite their parents for extended visits when the couple has a child, when she came in the late 1950s that practice was fairly uncommon: "In those days we couldn't afford anyone, and it was very hard to get a visa or anything. So it was very difficult, when I had the first child. And I had no experience of having a child, a baby in the house." Gangolli relied on the help of her friends who had experience rearing children because her husband was busy with school and building his career. Raj Manhas also notes that the experience of starting a family might be one of the most intimidating aspects of immigrant life:

> [It was] one of the most challenging times as immigrants you face. Not that my wife and I [struggled]; we had this wonderful [experience of], you know, both of us kind of, in some ways, learning and growing together here. . . . And I'm still learning. I was learning and learning obviously never stops, as you know. But she, when we had our son [it was tough], you know not having both sides [of our families or relatives nearby]. Her parents had gone back to India and they didn't come back [to Canada]. And my parents weren't here. So not having any side of your family and trying to deal with, you know, something you don't know enough about, having a child and dealing with the issues with that.

The question of navigating the new terrain of parenthood is common across narrators' stories. Some, like Aktar Badshah and his wife Alka, had to manage their dual careers while raising three sons. Like Manhas and Kumar mention above in regard to their own experiences as fathers, Badshah was expected to do more hands-on childrearing than if he had continued to live in India:

> Everything was a surprise. But you know you had to do everything. From waking up in the middle of the night, to changing diapers, to feed the kids, to taking them out for a walk in the middle of the night because of crying, or putting them in the car and driving in circles. Or driving to the grocery store because they wanted something. Taking them to, you know, to visit another child. Everything was a surprise!

Badshah and his wife ultimately relied on paid childcare to help balance the load between work and family, including hiring nannies from regions as diverse as South Asia, Europe, and the Caribbean.

The burden of learning how to deal with the demands of family life falls heavily on women's shoulders, as they are often responsible for not only helping children navigate American culture (as Shanta Gangolli's earlier stories reveal), but also maintaining traditions from South Asia. Intergenerational conflict is a constant source of worry for immigrants, particularly as they have to learn how to deal with their children's exposure to American ideas and lifestyles. Not wanting to alienate their children, but also wanting to make sure that they have some connection to South Asian cultural traditions, immigrants struggle over how to walk that very fine line. Kris Gupta recalls his struggle to raise his children so that they could move easily through American society. Choosing to primarily speak English at home meant that his children had limited exposure to Hindi. He argues, "My philosophy was if you're going to stay here, you might as well compete with the things here. It's nice to have that dual thing, but that doesn't help that much. If you hear them, you won't see any accent or anything like that. Even after thirty years, I still have [an] accent." Gupta is satisfied at having raised well-adjusted kids:

> We always wanted them to be able to stand on their own feet, make their own decisions. But [my wife] went out of the way to make enough trips to try to keep in touch with the Indian thing too. I'm glad to say that they're very well adjusted to both sides. They both have graduated [from the] University of Washington and they both have taken some Hindi classes. So they can understand some, speak a little. But they're not pushing it on their kids, which we never did. But they made enough trips to India; they're close to the family. They like their cousins and all that other stuff, like to do that. Actually, the two of them, when they were I would say in high school, maybe a little older, went on their own and spent time with their cousins.

Even though Gupta professes to want his children to fit easily into American society, a note of pride creeps in as he talks about how they came to learn about Indian culture on their own terms. That they decided to spend time in

India and learn about Hindi after entering college obviously means a great deal to Gupta. In a similar way, Padmini Vasishth's children did not learn Hindi at home, but picked up the language after going to India. She notes that this was in part because of the social circles that she and her husband moved within:

> Actually, we had more American friends than Indian friends because when Ramesh was working in Reichhold he had a lot of American friends there. But every time I used to go to India, the children learned how to speak and talk. Unfortunately, they gave up the speaking part when they went to college. They were too conscious of themselves. But now when they go [to India], they can understand everything, and they can speak, but with an accent. At that time, they were speaking such good Punjabi and Hindi. When I went to India and took them, they would speak in such perfect language that my friends would say, "How have you brought them up, they are speaking [so well]?" I would say, "They have got it by themselves." But they gave it up, which is unfortunate. And neither of my grandchildren, not one of them has picked up any Indian language. I wish they would learn, because this is the age when children can.

While it was important to Vasishth that her children picked up some language skill, she is wistful when discussing her grandchildren, who are yet another generation removed from her own history and do not have much connection to their Indian heritage. Raj Joshi, on the other hand, took a more proactive approach to instilling Indian culture in his children:

> They know the Indian foods and the Indian culture. That's because I sent them [to India] when they were younger—seven and nine. For almost four, five months they were there. They went to school there, but they went to Italian Catholic school, a mission school. And my brother taught them quite a bit, and his wife. They didn't have any kids at that time. My brother, he had [children] very late. His son is now doing his Ph.D. at University of West Virginia. So [the girls] were like their children, so they really treated them nice and taught them a lot of stuff. When they came back they were

almost speaking English with an Indian accent and singing Indian songs. [Laughs.] But then they forgot.

Even though Joshi's older daughter is married to a non–South Asian (and his wife, Irene, was not Indian), he notes that she still has a deep sense of Indian culture. For others, raising a child in two cultures created additional challenges and adjustments. Prem Kumar notes that for his daughter, her life at home actually meant belonging to a different cultural world altogether:

> In our case, we spoke Indian languages at home, we cooked Indian food, and we dressed up as people in India would do and she felt comfortable with that. But when she went out, the language was different, the food, her interaction with other children was different. So, like any other child who has to deal with two cultures, she went through that experience. She had not been to India until she was six, India was just a word . . . a name for her. She sort of questioned how Indian she was. So there was a sort of, I wouldn't say rejection, but reluctance to absorb Indian culture or Indian customs, traditions, at that young age.

Kumar notes that his daughter's acceptance of Indian customs grew as she got older and that he and his wife tried to encourage her various interests. Once the family settled in Seattle, his daughter got involved with summer camps run through local Indian American organizations: "She got to know other children who shared her background and even languages and customs, things of that type. So she developed her own circle of friends. And she looked forward to those camps. And then she got interested in Indian music and Indian arts, Indian movies, et cetera." Santosh Wahi also found that her expectations of her daughters to maintain Indian identities sometimes created friction between them. On the challenge of growing up between cultures, she remarks:

> I'm sure it was very hard. And I think, you can probably relate that to yourself, it is two cultures that they have to work with. At home and what our expectation was of them, was different. Probably more strict, stringent, versus what their school environment was. And there were a lot of things that the other . . . as they were grow-

ing up, there were certain restrictions put on our children [that were different] than what the child who had been living in this country for generations [would have]. You know, their families were here for generations. Of course everyone's an immigrant here. But it's just the length and degree and numbers of generations. Yeah, I think there was a lot more, or a lot, no—less freedom that I wanted for my children comparatively as they were growing up. And they had to live with two different sets of cultural [expectations] . . . they had to, they had to work with the Indian cultural environment and stay with the culture. Also they wanted them, we didn't want them to lose that also. So they had to do double the work [to] keep up with the Indian festivals, keep up with the Indian celebrations, keep up with Indian language, the religion.

Wahi was instrumental in setting up large annual celebrations for the Indian community, and she also started a language school to teach second-generation children Indian languages. It was important to her in every way to maintain a link to India and her notion of Indian culture through her children. However, one of the biggest areas of strife came as American-born children grew old enough to participate in what seemed like very foreign rituals like dating and "hanging out." Rao Remala remarks on the steep learning curve he experienced as his daughters became old enough to enter high school:

People used to say, "Oh, we have th[ese] high school dances." I mean we have never heard of those things. Those are all the surprising things, you know. But also I think one of the realizations is that the whole society is not like, I mean, there . . . there is the notion that maybe the society itself is, like, low moral values or something. Which is, I mean, that's how I think in a way, we had a, you know, even today, probably a lot of the people in India have that kind of a concept—that U.S.A. is a society with low moral values. But which is totally not true. I mean you see lots of families with, you know, good moral values.

Remala was confronted with his own biases of what life in America was like, particularly life as a teenager. Having to deal with new social expectations can be an uncomfortable experience for parents who grew up in a completely different cultural context. Zahid Hossain, who came to the United States from Bangladesh, also homes in on the challenges for children living with a different set of rules than their counterparts:

> I think [there are] many, many, many things that an "American girl" would be allowed to do, and my daughter was not. So sometimes that was hard for her. For example, you know, if [a] few of her classmates are hanging out in the mall, guys and girls, it was nothing for them. But it was not viewed with support from us. So things like that. Or maybe spending the night at somebody's house.

On the other hand, some parents chose to raise their children with fewer restrictions, which created different dissonances. Shanta Gangolli took a very different parenting strategy with her two sons than did Hossain and Remala, though interestingly, she notes that if she had had daughters, she might have behaved differently:

> I mean, they never felt that they had trouble growing in two cultures, because luckily, we didn't have many restrictions or anything. Many Indian families who were very traditional did have many restrictions on dating and things. First of all, I must thank God, because none of them had any problems in school, with drugs, or anything. My older son was so much into music, right at a very young age, that he would come home and start practicing. And so he did not date until he had gone through his senior year. He did not have any girlfriends in high school. He knew girls, and he played in the school music—band and orchestra and things. He went to Roosevelt High School, they all did. The second one, again, was very much into computers. And so he would come home—we had a computer, and he would sit and do things. He had some friends, but none of them had dates until they went to college. They met girls. So I had no problem about that. And I wouldn't have really restricted them, suppose they had somebody that they were going out with. But I'm not sure if it was a girl whether I would have felt differently. I think as a girl's mother, I would have felt a little more responsible. But you have to have a certain trust and also you have to kind of have the home atmosphere and education to know what is right and what is wrong.

Ultimately, like Gangolli, Hossain agrees that his children's lives were improved by being raised in America and notes that among the advantages they have here, "they are getting continuous exposure to different types of lifestyle, different types of people. They are growing up with a much broader mindset." While second- and third-generation children certainly face a tricky landscape where they must balance competing expectations, their parents, too, had to sift through unfamiliar terrain.

CONCLUSIONS

Undoubtedly, the family is a cornerstone institution for South Asian immigrants. Women, in particular, face a special set of pressures, as they are often expected to balance family and community expectations, learn how to run a household in a country with new systems and customs, and maintain cultural connections to their homelands. Often, the family and the home are considered to be sacred sites, a respite from the difficulties and discomfort of dealing with life in a new country. The home is the place where one can feel free to express a "Pakistani" or "Bangladeshi" identity without worrying about how to fit into wider American culture. At the same time, it is a complicated space where generational differences, changing gender roles, and potential conflicts collide. For South Asians in the Pacific Northwest, the household is but one aspect of immigrant life, though a vital one that has redefined the meaning of family and friendship.

6

SEEDS TAKE ROOT

GROWING SOUTH ASIAN COMMUNITIES IN
THE PACIFIC NORTHWEST

I was and have been fascinated by the American way of life. Very
often, there would be groups of Indians or Pakistanis. And they
would . . . offer to take you under their wings, and make you feel at
home. You know, I felt that I had come to this country and I wanted to
associate with and learn from the Americans. I mean, I thought in my
mind, I didn't leave India to join the Indian club! What I wanted to get
was the feel of life from students here.

—Zakir Parpia

[Now] we have community centers. We have places to go. We have
built a network of Pakistani-Indian like-minded people where the
kids can get together and do things and so on and so forth. But I think
earlier on, like . . . a couple of generations before, I think it was much
tougher for them to raise kids here because then there were no community centers. I mean, we have MAPS, which is Muslim Association
of Puget Sound, in Redmond. It's a mosque plus community center
and we go frequently. So you know, they try to keep the culture.

—Rizwan Nasar

As the last days of summer faded and the gray drizzle marked the onset
of autumn in Seattle, each year the Wahi household would turn from
warm-weather pursuits toward preparations for a Diwali party. Diwali, the
Hindu festival of lights marking the arrival of the new year, was a big event
for many Indians living near their home in Mercer Island, Washington.
Every year, Santosh Wahi and her husband hosted a two day–long celebration for their friends and family. Not only was Diwali a chance to come
together for dinner, drinks, and celebrating, it served to help local Indian

children learn more about the culture and traditions of their parents' homeland. On the first day of the holiday, the Wahis would adorn their house with small clay lamps, garlands of flowers, and other traditional decorations. Over thirty children would come over to play games, eat snacks, and listen to stories related to the holiday. After the fun and games were over, they were treated to a sumptuous Indian dinner. The evening after the kids' party, the Wahis hosted an adult-only fête where women were decked out in their best silk saris and glittering jewels and men donned embroidered kurtas and jackets. The party would last well into the night as people lingered over conversation and card games after dinner. This celebration, like many others, represented an important way in which South Asians established communities in the Pacific Northwest—simultaneously remembering traditions from home and creating new ones locally.

Although the term "community" is notoriously difficult to define, the ability to create spaces for gathering—whether for social, religious, political, or cultural reasons—has been essential for South Asians to feel comfortable in their adopted home.[1] Zakir Parpia's and Rizwan Nasar's reflections in the epigraph of this chapter also point to the diversity of perspectives on what constitutes community, particularly as people are drawn together along various (and occasionally competing) lines such as faith, national affiliation, hobbies, sexual orientation, gender, and occupation. For Parpia, his sense of belonging was contingent on learning about life in the United States from American students and, to this day, his community includes those both inside and outside of his ethnic group. Nasar, on the other hand, describes the importance of having a culturally specific site for "like-minded" people who can find solace in shared language, worship, and nationality. So what then drives communities to form and how have notions of community changed through the immigration experience?

Narrators' stories shed light on both questions and demonstrate that the processes of forging new friendships and forms of community are often an ·outlet for creative expression and cultural reinvigoration. At the same time, any examination of community must account not only for coalescences, but also for fissures and fractures that result in diversely aligned groups. Shifts in immigration policies, geopolitical events, and worldwide movements have impacted the evolution of these immigrant communities in the Pacific Northwest. For instance, narrators who came to the United States in the 1940s and 1950s arrived when the area was largely unpopulated by other

South Asians. They quickly engaged in building new institutions and had to learn to connect with non–South Asians. In contrast, recent arrivals find themselves able to choose from a complex and specialized web of organizations ranging from identity-based groups such as the Seattle Maharashtra Mandal, which brings together people who embrace Marathi language and culture, to The Citizen's Foundation, which is focused on promoting education in Pakistan. While the experience of creating connections and institutions seems to repeat itself across generations, the notion of a singular community becomes difficult to map as more South Asians arrive in the region. However, the growth of public spaces like houses of worship, community centers, and entertainment venues offers a way to trace how the mosaics of South Asian communities living in the Pacific Northwest are pieced together today.

A PLACE OF THEIR OWN: SOUTH ASIANS MAKE A HOME IN THE PACIFIC NORTHWEST

From the days of the early Sikh settlers through the contemporary moment of transnational migration, community building has meant more than creating ethnic enclaves or reproducing life from the homeland; instead, South Asians have adapted their traditions while also inventing new institutions and organizations that have become part of social and civic life in the Pacific Northwest. These spaces and events range from informal potlucks rotating at different families' homes to large-scale cultural celebrations that attract thousands of people and link immigrants and long-time residents together. At the same time, existing institutions such as the University of Washington, the Boeing Company, and Microsoft have been galvanizers for South Asian communities as they provided both a reason for immigration and important networks once immigrants arrived. Each has also been transformed by the South Asian students and workers that have helped build up their reputations as leaders of education, innovation, and industry.

While institutions have been transformed by South Asians, so too have the towns and cities of the Pacific Northwest. S. Mitra Kalita's account of the Indians living in northern New Jersey highlights how community formation is a diffuse process, particularly when immigrant communities shift from urban ghettos to spread across increasingly disconnected suburbs.[2] Rather than live in particular sections of a city, as early East Asian immigrants did in the International District of Seattle or the Chinatowns of Portland or Vancouver, more recently-arrived South Asians have congregated in the outlying areas of major American cities partly for economic reasons and partly because of their participation in industries that are more likely to be located in suburban office parks. For instance, Microsoft's company headquarters are in Redmond, Washington, which is about fifteen miles east of Seattle across Lake Washington. Traveling to the "east side" of Seattle, as the Washington cities of Bellevue, Redmond, Kirkland, and Bothell are often known, reveals a geographical orientation of the South Asian community around religious centers like temples and mosques, ethnic grocery stores, and other commercial amenities. Situated at the intersection of NE 8th Street and 156th Avenue NE in Bellevue, the Crossroads Mall is an area where *salwaar kameez*–clad young women pushing babies in carriages stroll busily up and down the main roadway. These women pass older couples out for their daily constitutionals around the parking lots that link together commercial areas. While predominantly a shopping area, the two-mile stretch from Crossroads Mall to the heart of the Microsoft campus is dotted by apartment complexes that largely house recent arrivals from across South Asia. Snippets of conversations in Urdu, Bengali, Telugu, and Tamil are as likely to be overheard in the mall's food court as those in English and the sounds of Bollywood music blare on car stereos waiting at the string of endless lights between immigrants' homes and offices.

Further down the road, the city of Bellevue blurs into Redmond and large strip malls punctuate the forested landscape. At the heart of this commercial district are grocery stores and restaurants and clothing shops that cater to South Asians. Apna Bazaar, a full-service Indian grocery and video store, is one example: tucked in a strip of businesses dominated on one end by the superstore chain Fred Meyer and the neon-yellow-and-red sign depicting the famous mouse of Chuck-E-Cheese, Apna Bazaar draws a steady stream of customers still wearing the badges marking them as employees of various technology firms. People can stop by to pick up rice and spices before moving next door to the extensive dinner buffet at the Spice Route restaurant, or heading further north to Totem Lake Cinemas to catch the latest Bollywood blockbuster; these shops contain the seeds of community life. Bulletin boards are peppered with advertisements from enterprising women offering their services as nannies who speak Hindi or Tamil in addition to English, cooks specializing in food from all parts of the subcontinent, clas-

sical dance and music teachers, and seamstresses whose skills include hem-
ming *lehengas* and making sari blouses, as well as the smiling faces of South
Asian realtors, doctors, dentists, and travel and insurance agents plastered
on countless business cards. Interspersed are advertisements for lectures
on South Asia history, celebrations of religious festivals, numerous music
and dance recitals, fundraisers for charities, and many other public events.

A similar scene unfolds in south King County, just outside Seattle's city
limits. There, Punjabi bhangra exercise classes are in high demand and the
dosa cafes have been replaced by restaurants specializing in *chaat* and *dahi
vadas*. Entire strip malls are dedicated to South Asian businesses and are
within close proximity to several large *gurdwaras* where Sikhs worship.
South Asians may not be well-represented in Seattle's International District,
but their presence is more than notable in the suburban hills and valleys
across the water on the east side and south of the city. A far cry from the
daily markets of urban centers in Sri Lanka, or the open-air bazaars in India
or Pakistan, strip malls are an American adaptation where cheaper rents,
greater availability of space, and local demand have created new spaces
for community interaction. Thus, these shops, entertainment venues, and
houses of worship are integral to South Asians' ability to maintain a sense of
identity and culture in what would otherwise be foreign territory. They have
also changed the cities and suburbs of the Pacific Northwest by introducing
new foods, fashions, films, and events that engage a much broader audience.

CO-CURRICULAR COMMUNITIES: STUDENTS' IMPACT ON PACIFIC NORTHWEST CAMPUSES

For many South Asian immigrants, community building and networking
began on university campuses as newly arrived students strove both to create
cultural groups and to find ways of reaching out beyond other South Asians.
Often places where students from various backgrounds are thrown together
for the first time in their lives, university campuses have long been rich sites
for bringing together new constellations of individuals and strengthening
bonds between people of similar backgrounds. American universities have
been active in helping international students merge into the wider social
space of the campus through dedicated international student offices, campus events, and student-led clubs that promote cross-cultural exchange. The
University of Washington has been a key facilitator in bringing young South

FIG 6.1 Jeff Siddiqui with University of Washington's Foundation for International Understanding through Students (FIUTS) colleagues Jim Leonard and Jeff Crollard, Seattle, 1978. Photo courtesy of Jeff Siddiqui.

Asian students to the region since the first decades of the twentieth century. Intended to connect international and local students, a chapter of the Cosmopolitan Club was founded at the University of Washington in 1907, and other institutions such as the Hindustan Club and the Hindoo Students' Ashram were also established specifically for South Asians.

For the South Asian students who arrived in the 1940s and 1950s, the University of Washington was a place where students had the chance to befriend professors and other members of the wider Seattle South Asian community. Padmini Vasishth recounts the support of faculty and student organizations in bringing people together through the University of Washington:

> My husband and I were the only Indian married couple on campus . . . Irene [Joshi] used to come, her mother used to come, and Dr. Bailey, [Mrs. Bogardus], Mrs. Sweeney used to come. They were all members of this foreign students committee. We also had a Dr. Mularky; he was a doctor. First Christmas we had was at his

house, because he had invited [some twenty] foreign students. It
was fun. He looked after us so graciously, he and his wife. They had
a huge tree, gave us all little gifts of chocolates, I don't remember
what it was. [There was a big meal with all the trimmings, and we
sang carols.] He had a big fire and it was like old times—what we
had imagined Christmas was like. Then they took us back to our
apartments and we felt at home, comfortable. That was our first
Christmas.

Key advisors and university liaisons introduced Vasishth to American
rituals and helped her connect with other international students. She was
able to catch a glimpse into American life by participating in what might
otherwise be unfamiliar customs and holidays in a safe and welcoming space.

The home has been a vital component in building a sense of community, as many informal gatherings at South Asian students' homes provided
spaces for new experiences and to maintain certain traditions. Sat Kapahi
was living in the University District, the residential and commercial neighborhood around the University of Washington, when he was a graduate

FIG 6.2   Padmini Vasishth, Irene and Raj Joshi, and Asgar Ahmedi at a summer
picnic at Golden Gardens Park, Seattle, Washington, 1957. Photo courtesy of Raj Joshi.

student. Because there were few opportunities for South Asians to meet one another on campus, they would use apartments and group houses to gather: "We would go to each other's houses. There were at least three, four couples that became quite close to each other. We would go to each other's house and have a party." At a time when South Asians were few in number and events and cultural organizations were not well established, the private home represented a protected space where immigrants could come together to make food and celebrate festivals without worry about blending into larger American society.[3] The home became a space for socializing and also reinforced the sense of an intentional family that sustained individuals living away from their kin and old friends.

The immigrant home as a meeting space also fostered intergenerational communities. Vasishth recalls how important her own position as part of a married couple was in supporting other "young boys and girls" from South Asia who came after she and her husband arrived:

We were only about twenty-odd Indian students, and we were the only married [couple]. There were other young boys and girls who were there, but none of them was yet married. They were going out, dating, this and that. We had an association, Indian Students Association—about twenty-odd people, around that figure. We would [gather] at least once a month and we would have our parties and go out for picnics. We organized that everyone got involved, even those Indians who were not [at UW]—like Sat Kapahi, he and his wife were not students of the university. [He worked for Boeing.] We met them through our association. And then there is Inder Dewan, he was also not a student. He was also at Boeing. They would come. So we all would go and have these mountaineering [outings] in different parks here. Make our menu, sort out things, what each person has to do. And of course, Irene [Joshi] was so helpful. She would say, "Now we have these plates, we have this, I'll make this." Her mother also; they both used to come and help us. Sometimes we wouldn't have the utensils, then this church— you know, they were associated with some church—we would get then some utensils [from the church] to do our cooking and all. It was great fun. We were a community by ourselves. We could just ring up any of them and they would be there and we would not feel homesick. It was like growing up together. We had a very nice time.

Vasishth's assertion that "we were a community by ourselves" points out how important it was that earlier immigrants could come together with others of a similar background. The group allowed "older" South Asians to support "newer" arrivals, thereby growing and sustaining the community as other members moved out of the area. Though centered on the University of Washington, the group expanded much farther out to include South Asians living in the region.

At the same time that building South Asian networks was important, narrators were keenly aware of the need to integrate and participate in the wider American milieu. While making friends with other South Asians was affirming for many, Kris Gupta found it vital to also mingle with individuals from various backgrounds. While in school, he recalls:

> I stayed at the international house, so there were quite a bit of
> local people you met anyway. My roommate was this American
> guy—very focused. Seemed to me he worked sixteen-hour days
> and wanted to graduate, and he was being drafted. We ended up
> [being] close friends. It may be funny, but he'll show up at 10:00,
> just drop the pants and get in bed. Five minutes later, he was asleep.
> And in the morning, he would put them on, and he was ready to
> go. So it kind of gave you [an idea] how life works here. He was, as
> I said, very intense. He was in ROTC, was going to be an officer,
> finishing his master's. So it kind of gave you [the idea]—hey, this
> is the tempo, this is what you need to accomplish, this is what you
> need to fight. Then, as far as meeting students, there were student
> dances, or you just happen to meet somebody. There wasn't a very
> big group. But right around the university, there were some Indians
> who lived in the houses—people who had come long before. So you
> could always stop by, just drift in there on weekends, and some-
> body was always there and food was there, you could cook. But we
> didn't make any special effort to strictly meet Indians. It was just
> very, very open.

Gupta's experience with living with an American student who was part of the military provided him with exposure to parts of life in the United States to which he otherwise may not have had access. In his mind, this exposure helped him adjust to working and schooling in the United States.

FIG 6.3   Asgar Ahmedi pictured in the University of Denver yearbook *The Kynewis-bok*, with members of the Alpha Kappa Psi fraternity, 1954. Photo courtesy of the Ahmedi family.

For others, such understanding came through joining American social clubs. Thinking back to his time in school in Denver in the early 1950s, Asgar Ahmedi recalls:

> I was the first Indian to be initiated into a business fraternity called Alpha Kappa Psi. I lived in the house. My president, he says, "Asgar, this is why we made you a member—we want to get to know you. You have to live with us." My only objection to them was, "I don't know how to take a bath in a bathtub. You don't have a shower." [Laughs.] But I said I'll come and live there for a while. And this was true, you know? But it was an interesting experience there. Every Wednesday we have a meeting, go and get drunk, drink beer.

Gupta and Ahmedi both found that living with Americans offered them insight into how life worked in the United States. Though they were also invested in connecting with others who came from a similar background, both Ahmedi and Gupta pushed themselves out of their comfort zones in order to learn more about the people and culture around them.

Immigrants who came in the 1960s and 1970s also found campus organizations to be crucial in helping them establish a sense of place after arriving in the Pacific Northwest. By the late 1960s, South Asians began to enter the United States in unprecedented numbers and across the country new organizations and services emerged that eased these immigrants' entry into American life. Prem Kumar came to Moscow, Idaho, for his graduate studies in English at the University of Idaho and was pleasantly surprised to be so warmly welcomed by the university's international student office, which ran a "big brother" and "big sister" program: "So my 'brother' was an Indian. An Indian student who had been there for a couple of years. So it made things a little bit easier. He was there to receive me and help me out with whatever I needed." Even with the help of a university-assigned mentor, Kumar recalls the loneliness and frustration of his early days as a graduate student, especially when it came to things like figuring out how to cook Indian food or navigating the American educational system. As an English graduate student, Kumar was also expected to teach classes which required extensive knowledge of American cultural touchstones: "I tried to learn as much and as fast as I could by reading books about American history, American society, culture. Also watched lots of TV. That helped me to pick up the accent because that was essential." While engaged in the task of instructing American students in the early 1970s, Kumar had to present himself as an authority within his field. Scrambling to absorb as much as he could, Kumar turned to radio, films, friends, and professors to reformulate his knowledge base and worked hard to "try to brush up on my accent and my vocabulary, all of those things." While embedded in a welcoming university community, Kumar still found it difficult to quickly acclimate to American norms, particularly after leaving behind his own family, friends, and country.

GROWING PAINS: CULTURAL, SOCIAL, AND POLITICAL GROUPS PROLIFERATE

While the university was an important place for immigrants to meet others, the growth of industries in the region also contributed to the spread of various community organizations. As aeronautics and other technical fields became increasingly essential to the development of newly independent nations in South Asia, students came to Seattle to study aviation technology and to gain valuable work experience in the field. The University of Washington emerged in this era as a leader of science and technical training and attracted aspiring engineering students. Rather than return to their countries of origin, many of these students found jobs at the Boeing Company and went on to work in design, engineering, and business operations.

Others came to the region specifically to work with Boeing and contributed to the foundation of several important South Asian institutions. Santosh Wahi, who was not a student or worker when she moved to Seattle in 1973, but rather a young wife who moved with her husband when he took a position with Boeing, wanted to find other South Asians who were also raising families in a new cultural environment. Wahi started a Hindi language school to help children of immigrants learn about and retain facets of Indian language and culture. Wahi remarks: "You know, in those days, there weren't very many people. And so whomever you met became your friends. Now, there's so many people from India that, you know, probably there's a lot of selection and they're selective about who and who not [to be friends with]. At that time, it was whoever." She held the language classes in a public library, which helped her meet families in the area that wanted their children to learn Hindi.

After her daughters entered the Washington State public school system, Wahi became an active volunteer in area schools, both through the parent-teacher association and as a self-styled ambassador giving lectures on South Asian history and culture. Remarkably similar to Padmini Vasishth's description of South Asian community life in the 1950s, nearly twenty-five years earlier, Wahi's decision to act as a cultural liaison and preservationist points to the ways in which South Asian women mobilized their roles as mothers and wives to help create intergenerational community spaces in public and private.[4] At the same time, Wahi and her husband were also involved with the India Association of Western Washington (IAWW). One of the largest South Asian groups in the area, the IAWW has been an important point of connection for Seattle Indians. Several narrators chronicled in this book have been involved in the organization by serving on the board and as members. The association plans annual Diwali events, runs programs for senior citizens, and organizes a youth camp. Wahi and her husband, who was also a past president of IAWW, led local efforts to reach out to Indian senior citizens, who are often left out of mainstream South Asian organizations. Wahi notes that it can be a difficult adjustment for seniors who come at a later stage in life to join their children who are established in the United States: "They don't know what to do with themselves. Or they feel lost not being able to meet with other seniors or get some senior help." By focusing on family-related issues, IAWW attempts to serve the needs of a changing and intergenerational community.

However, the focus on family, Indian cultural events, and religious festivals does not necessarily meet the needs of all Indians. For many, the IAWW serves an important function by providing opportunities to meet others; for others, it represents the homogenization of Indian culture and overemphasizes middle-class Indian experiences in America, rather than focusing on more diverse concerns. When asked about whether she participates in cultural organizations like IAWW, Amy Laly, who arrived in Portland and then moved to Seattle in the 1960s, responds:

> I don't see myself as part of any community, frankly. If you say, "Do I think of myself as an Indian?" Of course, I'm an Indian! But I'm also an american, with a small "a." Not a big "A." A small "a." I refuse to think of myself as anything other than a person who belongs to the world. In the sense that I think we should be concerned about every citizen in the world. Not just what's between our borders or our ethnicities or our family groups.

At first glance, Laly's position may seem to contradict the ways in which South Asians have constructed their identities as family-oriented immigrants who want to blend into American society while maintaining a distinct sense of culture; however, for Laly, her experience of going to college in the United States in the 1960s and growing up in a community of activists has forever shaped her worldview to look beyond ethnic or national affiliations. Laly's years participating in the various student and activist movements of the era were crucial to her identity and community affiliations. As for her own views on community today, Laly notes that she is not an active participant in South Asian–specific organizations unless they coincide with her other interests, such as Chaya Seattle, which focuses on women's rights, and Tasveer, which is an independent South Asian film organization.

Chaya, in particular, has become an important organization that brings together South Asians who share a progressive worldview. The Seattle-area

FIG 6.4   Amy Laly and friends protest the apartheid regime in South Africa outside the Seattle home of the consular officer of South Africa, 1985, Seattle, Washington. Photo courtesy of Amy Laly.

group is dedicated to ending domestic violence and works with communities coming from Afghanistan, Bangladesh, Bhutan, India, Myanmar, Nepal, Pakistan, Sri Lanka, and Tibet. For Laly and others, Chaya represents the sort of identity-based work that serves an important community function while connecting like-minded South Asians and non–South Asians. Though primarily started to serve South Asian women in crisis and to raise awareness about domestic violence, Chaya has been a key force in bringing to light gender justice issues in the Pacific Northwest and particularly in the greater Seattle area.[5] Chaya provides direct services to clients and also mobilizes around issues of violence, immigration, health, and well-being. An important piece of the larger constellation of South Asian organizations in the Pacific Northwest, Chaya also attends to some of the most exigent community needs. Dedicated to changing ideas and values that are sometimes couched as "cultural," Chaya works to address not only the positive, but often the darker and more challenging aspects of South Asian family life. An explicitly feminist organization, Chaya fills a vital role in the region by tackling head-on issues of family and gender violence, which the larger or more conventional South Asian organizations cannot or choose not to address.

Like Chaya, Trikone-Northwest is an organization that serves a less visible population of South Asians. It brings together members and allies of
the lesbian, gay, bisexual, and transgendered community, or, as their mission states: "differently-oriented South Asians and their family, friends and
community."[6] Both groups seek to promote new social and political outlets
for South Asians who are interested in changing norms and conceptions
about family, gender, sexuality, and culture. Though dealing with sensitive
topics, both Trikone and Chaya are visible community institutions that are
supported to varying degrees by more mainstream South Asian communities. For instance, a small but significant proportion of direct contributions
to Chaya come from work-place giving programs, such as the Microsoft
Employee Giving Campaign, where employers match a portion of employees' charitable donations. The existence and support for Chaya and Trikone
demonstrate the diversity of South Asians and their needs.

Another community organization with a strong activist focus in the
region is One America, which was previously known as Hate Free Zone. Its
founder and former president, Pramila Jayapal, is a South Asian who echoes
Amy Laly's desire to create community spaces with explicitly progressive
political agendas, rather than primarily identity-based groups. She notes
that while there has been a surge of political mobilization among younger
generations of South Asians, particularly under President Barack Obama's
administration, there is much work to be done to promote progressive policies and legislation that address issues of relevance to South Asians:

> There have been cultural organizations like Indian cultural orga-
> nizations, and there's Chaya. And there's One America, though
> we don't focus specifically on South Asians. But there aren't a lot
> of organizations that are focusing on South Asians, in a social
> justice, organizing, policy, advocacy way. I have noticed interest-
> ingly that there are many more Indians becoming involved with
> the Obama campaign. And I think that has to do with, you know,
> they are also the young generation of . . . well, young generation in
> general, but of South Asians. There are a lot of tech-savvy people,
> very into the Internet, very into the, you know, mobile kind of way
> of communicating. Obama has a lot of appeal for them, there's a lot
> of excitement around him. So you know there's South Asians for
> Obama. There are all these political things that I am getting invited

to now that are South Asians for a [particular] political candidate. My question is whether that results in concrete policy change or whether at this stage in the political development of the community, it's still . . . and obviously, this is a generalization, but for some people, I think it's still at the stage of we want to be seen with a candidate, an elected official. And that's prestigious. But it isn't to the stage of saying, "here's where we want to see change. Here are our demands. Here's our strategy for how to accomplish that as a community." You know, those are two different things. And I don't think we've gotten to the other one.

For both Jayapal and Laly, being a part of South Asian communities comes with a sense of social responsibility to address wider issues like immigration, family violence, and racism in the United States. Since the terrorist attacks of September 11, 2001, the intersection of identity and politics is especially urgent and complex for many South Asians, particularly those who are Muslim or Sikh, as they have been the subject of direct and indirect attacks and are indiscriminately associated with terrorism.[7] Jamal Rahman, who migrated from Bangladesh and is a Sufi interfaith minister in Seattle, articulates the tensions of being an open and practicing Muslim today. When asked about the backlash against Muslims, he replies:

You know, I think after 9/11, and I was not like this before, but circumstances make me think that, I am a Muslim first of all. Then I am a South Asian. And third I am an American. And I think that would reverse if conditions change here. But right now, given the environment, that's how I feel. You know, in practical terms.

He notes that even simple things that he took for granted before, such as boarding a plane or getting a visa to travel internationally, are difficult. He decided to become a U.S. citizen after September 11 partly because he realized how precarious his status was as a Muslim immigrant. Najma Rizvi, another Bangladeshi immigrant, also experienced difficulties after she retired when she was applying for social security benefits in a climate filled with suspicion of all Muslims. Even though she had become a citizen several decades prior and lived and worked almost her entire life in the United States, she was asked to provide an alien registration number in order to process her application for benefits. Suspecting that she was singled out because of her identifiably Islamic name, she ruefully notes: "Here I have given all my life here. And then this when I'm retiring? This is the way I'm being treated? I would tell you that. . . . That was really very disappointing."

Though the effects of political crisis such as September 11 have been challenging for South Asians, they have also provided an opportunity to open new dialogues among communities that might not have otherwise done so. As an interfaith minister, Rahman finds that people of other faiths have grown interested in learning more about Islamic principles and values. Muslims of different backgrounds have also had to come together and build communities across national identities. However, struggles remain for Muslim South Asians as they continue to be challenged by racial profiling and stereotyping. The killing of Osama Bin Laden, the most widely recognized figure behind the September 11 attacks, in Pakistan, and the failed bombing attempt in Times Square by a Pakistani American, Faisal Shahzad, have further exacerbated the problem. Newspaper reports following the Shahzad incident have noted that Pakistanis no longer view the United States as a welcoming place and visa applications from Pakistani students have dropped significantly because of the fears of racism and repression in the United States.[8]

Considering these political issues facing South Asians, local community leaders such as Prem Kumar have dedicated themselves to increasing the political presence of South Asians in the region and nationally. Kumar remarks:

> When I moved into the area, of course my first interest was in the area of culture. Social organizations which would give us an opportunity to help the children learn about their heritage, their parents' culture. So I got involved in those types of organizations. Mainly, the India Association of Western Washington. . . . And then, sometime around 1995, some of us felt a need for the community to get involved in the political process of the country because most Indians who had come during the time frame that I did were fairly settled by this time and successful. They had children and families and were not going to go back to India, but were not involved in that political process. So we felt that you need to do that, to educate yourself [about] what are your rights and responsibilities as new

citizens of this country. So we started an organization, Indian American Political Advocacy Council. And for the first four or five years, we tried to involve the community, for them to get educated and accept their responsibility. At the same time, we networked with the government agencies, organizations, and political affiliations at the local level, city, county, state, as well as at the national level. We networked with congressmen and -women, senators, governors. Those type of things. That made people more aware and motivated to get involved.

Jayapal's and Kumar's work to increase the presence of South Asians in the political process stems from a desire to see South Asian perspectives more fully integrated into the mainstream of American consciousness. These efforts contradict Vijay Prashad's assertion that South Asians readily accept the notion that the United States "simply wants their labor, but does not care too much for their lives"[9] by retreating into cultural spaces rather than actively mobilizing for social or political change. While South Asians fall across the spectrum of political affiliation and there may not be agreement about the best political positions to take, there is a growing presence of South Asians in national- and regional-level politics. Kumar's insistence on figuring out "what are your rights and responsibilities as new citizens of this country" refutes the notion that South Asians are a passive group sitting quietly in the corners of democracy. On multiple levels, political and social activism has been an important feature in the establishment of South Asian communities in the Pacific Northwest.

CULTURAL BRIDGES: THE IMPORTANCE OF MUSIC, FILM, AND THE ARTS

In addition to social and political groups, South Asians have been active in establishing arts and cultural organizations in the region. Expressions of high culture in the form of classical music, dance, theater, and art, as well as popular culture like films and songs are central components of diasporic expression and offer a way to stay connected to the subcontinent.[10] Popular cinema, like Bollywood, has a far wider reach than Bombay (where the heart of the Hindi film industry is located). Finding audiences around the world, ranging from Indonesia to Afghanistan, and increasingly in western nations,

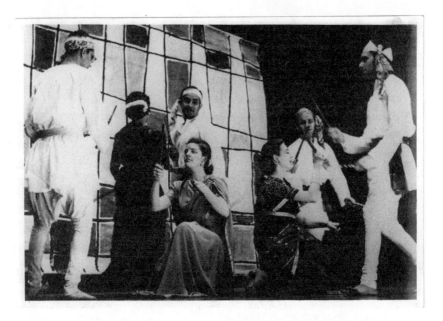

FIG 6.5 Asgar Ahmedi, Irene Joshi, and several foreign students promoting Indian culture and dance forms such as dandiya raas, a Gujarati folk dance pictured here, Washington State, 1955. Photo courtesy of Raj Joshi.

Bollywood has offered immigrants and nationals all over the globe a glimpse into fantastical representations of India and Indian culture. Links such as these are of particular importance for members of the South Asian diaspora living far from their home nations.[11]

Watching the latest Amitabh Bachan movie or, more recently, Sharukh Khan or Kareena Kapoor film has brought South Asian families together, offering a cultural reference point that crosses national boundaries. Watching films is seen as a family-friendly activity because, until very recently, overt displays of sex or physical affection were conspicuously absent in Bollywood films. Alok Mathur, who came to Seattle in 1978, played an important role in creating spaces for South Asians to come together to watch films in an era before widely circulated DVDs and online streaming films were available:

We found the auditorium over in the Bank of America building in downtown Seattle and they had an auditorium on the ground floor. So we would rent that and sometimes we would screen movies over there. It was different at that time, because each film had about five big rolls. So we would go to the airport and pick up the film from there and bring it over to the theater. Screen it and return it the same night because it had to go someplace else, was screening in some other city. . . . We would have about easily 150 . . . 150–200 people would come if it was a good movie.

Even though Mathur was not a self-proclaimed film connoisseur and the process of bringing Indian films to Seattle was arduous, screening films served a greater purpose of drawing local Indian communities together. Today, Bollywood films are widely available, from the online movie site Netflix to numerous South Asian grocery stores. Bollywood songs have taken on new life in the diaspora and can be found on hip-hop tracks—even the popular television series *So You Think You Can Dance* featured a Bollywood dance portion of its competition. Younger generations of South Asians have also claimed Bollywood for themselves through dance nights featuring Hindi film music, which are immensely popular in urban nightclubs across the United States. In Seattle and Portland, clubs often host Bollywood-themed nights with titles such as "I Heart Shiva" or "BollyQ" that draw large South Asian and non–South Asian crowds.

While Bollywood is just one galvanizing cultural genre, South Asian classical music societies have also had a lasting impact on the music scene in the Pacific Northwest. Shanta Gangolli and her husband Ramesh Gangolli have been driving forces behind the formation of the group Ragamala. Though Ramesh Gangolli is a professor emeritus of mathematics, his status as adjunct professor of music at the University of Washington was crucial to the foundation of the organization. Shanta Gangolli recalls:

My husband is very fond of Indian classical music. So he started, about twenty-three years ago, a music nonprofit organization to promote Indian classical music in Seattle. It's called Ragamala. And at one time, we had a very good membership and a lot of attendance. We had about eight to ten programs every year by visiting Indian artists from India. And we used to get NEA [National Endowment of the Arts] grants and King County grants. But now all that money has gone and there are a lot more Indian groups that have come up. So people have different, other interests.

Despite Gangolli's humble framing of the group, Ragamala continues to draw large audiences to hear musicians from all over South Asia perform. Regular performances and concerts continue to be held primarily on the University of Washington campus. While started over two decades ago, Ragamala continues thanks to the work of later generations of immigrants interested in bridging Indian classical music and more contemporary forms. While significant to South Asian communities, the organization has also collaborated with key Seattle arts and cultural institutions like Town Hall Seattle, the Seattle Center, and the Seattle Art Museum to stage events with broad appeal. Along with live performances, Ragamala also runs an online journal, *Ragavani*, which publishes articles on South Asian music and dance.

While Ragamala focuses primarily on Hindustani music, the growth of South Asian communities since the 1980s has brought a large number of music and dance aficionados from across the subcontinent to the Pacific Northwest. Several musical organizations and schools that teach Carnatic music and *bharatnatyam* dance[12] have emerged and organizations like Rasika and Abhinaya Fine Arts bring well-known performers to the region on a regular basis. Several musical events developed in India have traveled to the United States with the immigrant community, such as the Saint Tyagaraja music festival. The annual event, which takes place in the birthplace of the revered composer Saint Tyagaraja, draws thousands of people to Thiruvaiyaru in South India to celebrate the composer's life and work. The popularity of this festival has spread to the United States and a similar celebration has been held in Cleveland, Ohio, since 1978. The success of the Cleveland event, which attracts musicians and audiences from across North America and India, has spawned several other such festivals around the United States. The celebration in the Pacific Northwest began in 1991 when a group of individuals in Corvallis, Oregon, organized events similar to the Cleveland festival. Since then, the festival rotates among Corvallis, Portland, and Seattle and brings together music lovers from across the region.

In addition to sponsoring musical and dance performances, South Asian communities have continued to expand and promote arts and cultural events. Owais Jafrey, a retired librarian and poet who settled in Seattle in 1976, founded a poetry and writing organization that holds regular readings and events. Jafrey notes that while the organization is named the Urdu Literary Society, it has a much wider reach: "We have poets from all other languages. Punjabi, Hindi, like that. We have poetry recitals called *mus-*

hairas, or *kavi sammelans*. And people [who speak] different languages, from Hindi, and Punjabi, they participate in them." These gatherings draw up to 200 people per event and simulate the feeling of poetic symposiums held in Pakistan and North India. Instead of taking place in the open-air courtyards of Islamic institutions, as is often the case in South Asia, these *mushairas* tend to be held in high school auditoriums and community centers. The *mushairas* and *kavi sammelans* provide a space for the singing of *ghazals* and recitation of classical verses and original poetry. Pratidhwani is another arts organization dedicated to promulgating South Asian culture through dance, music, and drama performances. Members of Pratidhwani stage regular multilingual plays around the Seattle area and host performers from other parts of the country. The organization acts as a conduit for contemporary theater and music from South Asia, while also facilitating new productions in the diaspora. Both the Urdu Literary Society and Pratidhwani are important venues for creative expression for area South Asian artists, writers, and dramatists.

Tasveer is another grassroots community group dedicated to promoting independent film and avant-garde performances. Tasveer hosts an annual Independent South Asian Film Festival in Seattle, where pieces from Afghanistan, Bangladesh, Bhutan, India, Maldives, Nepal, Pakistan, Sri Lanka, and Tibet, as well as the South Asian diaspora in other parts of the world, are showcased. Explicitly interested in supporting independent filmmakers and arts, the group sponsors an annual festival highlighting local South Asian women artists, directors, and business owners. The pinnacle of the festival is the staging of a South Asian version of the *Vagina Monologues* called *Yoni Ki Baat*.[13] An emotional and powerful event, *Yoni Ki Baat* is directed by a volunteer and features a mix of original writing and scripted pieces exploring issues of violence, sexuality, relationships, and identity. Always evocative and occasionally controversial, *Yoni Ki Baat* draws a wide audience of South Asians and non–South Asians of all backgrounds.

Though separate in mission and scope, many South Asian organizations come together regularly, along with other local institutions, to cosponsor a variety of events. In 2004, several key individuals and local organizations including the Seattle Asian Art Museum, the University of Washington, and Seattle University held a film retrospective of Indian film star Waheeda Rehman. The event not only offered the Seattle South Asian community an opportunity to watch Rehman's famous cinematic performances but also introduced Rehman and her work to non–South Asians. In 2007, Chaya, Tasveer, the University of Washington, and the Seattle Public Library hosted several community-wide events around the visit of acclaimed Bengali-American author Jhumpa Lahiri. By contributing to and supporting events ranging from town hall meetings with authors to film screenings to readings of stories, such as those from Lahiri's book *Unaccustomed Earth*, which are partly set in Seattle, South Asian organizations have been instrumental in building the cultural, artistic, and literary terrain of the Pacific Northwest. Such events not only celebrate South Asian works but also allow local South Asian communities to actively build the cultural institutions of the Pacific Northwest.

However, South Asian influence in the arts is not limited to culturally specific organizations; Bharti Kirchner, a Seattle-based cookbook and fiction author, has stayed connected with both South Asian and more broadly based organizations to hone her own writing craft:

I am involved with IAWW—India Association of Western Washington. I have been a member for a long time. Also, I've helped PPI, People for Progress in India. It's an organization staffed totally by volunteers from here who help in India. So I helped them out. But over a period of time, I have also been involved in the Pacific Northwest Writers Association. And this is a big writer's organization. I have been involved with them from the very beginning, from the time I had begun to write. I had volunteered for them—helped them with their summer conference. And also Artist's Trust; this is an artist's organization. I have volunteered for them for many years. And also over a period of time, I have been involved with a journalist organization and they put up their big summit here in 1999 called "Unity." I was a volunteer for them, helped them out with the summit. Another organization I have worked with is APAWLI. It stands for Asian Pacific American Women's Leadership Institute. They had their summit here in 2000, and I was a volunteer for them. So I have worked with many different organizations that have nothing to do with India or Indians, but on broader community-based issues. I have always been interested in helping out or contributing to these other organizations because I feel that as an Indian, living in the Pacific Northwest, I should help local and regional organizations, but also I have a commitment . . . I have an interest in the much bigger [picture], you know, in the kinds of international [issues].

For Kirchner, being part of regional and national networks of writers has been an essential part of her practice of writing, which centers on food, travel, and cultural encounters. In particular, she has written several novels in which protagonists travel across various geographic locations—from Northern India to San Francisco and Seattle—and echo her own life histories. Similarly, Amy Laly, who is a Seattle-based documentary filmmaker in addition to being a retired Boeing employee, has been a longtime supporter of the Seattle International Film Festival (SIFF). Reflecting on the festival's origins in 1976, Laly recalls: "There was a young punk [from Calcutta] by the name of Rajiv Gupta. He ran the film series at the University of Washington. And he would bring Satyajit Ray movies and he would bring, you know, all these very artsy movies to the University of Washington." That series of film screenings allowed Laly and others to connect with other film enthusiasts, including two founding members of the SIFF. Today, the festival is one of North America's top film festivals and draws over 150,000 attendees annually for a nearly month-long celebration of independent film. While both Laly and Kirchner have benefitted from their involvement in Pacific Northwest–based film and writing organizations, those institutions too have undoubtedly expanded as a result of their and other South Asians' participation.

KEEPING THE FAITH: THE FOUNDATION OF SPIRITUAL AND RELIGIOUS INSTITUTIONS

In addition to cultural and arts organizations, South Asian communities have carved out spaces dedicated to religious and spiritual practices. One of the first South Asian religious institutions established in Seattle was the Vedanta Society of Western Washington, a branch of the larger international Vedanta Society. Founded in 1938 by Swami Vividishananda, the Western Washington wing has provided South Asians and non–South Asians alike a space to explore Hindu philosophy and to participate in religious celebrations for the past seventy years. South Asian religious organizations have grown in number since then and represent a diverse array of faiths in the

FIG 6.6   Swami Vivdishanada (*right*) and Swami Aseshanda, Seattle, Washington, 1938. Both men went on to found the Vedanta societies in Seattle and Portland, respectively. Photo courtesy of Vedanta Society of Western Washington and the Wing Luke Museum of the Asian Pacific American Experience, 2003.200.075.

region. As of 2010, there are several churches that cater to predominantly South Asian congregations, eight Hindu temples, fourteen Sikh *gurdwaras*, twenty-three mosques, and over twenty Buddhist temples between Washington, Oregon, and Idaho.[14] While categorized as sites of worship, these establishments offer an opportunity for broader community formation and cultural engagement. These groups blur religious and cultural lines by sponsoring events that correspond to religious festivals and other cultural holidays in South Asia.

In her study of the Indian Orthodox Syrian Christian Church in the American Midwest, Sheba George shows the important role that religious institutions play in creating linkages among newly arrived immigrants from South India.[15] The Church offers immigrants a sense of continuity with the rituals that defined their community life in India and has become an important mediating institution for families in America, especially when women move into the workforce and men are forced to redefine their roles at home and in society. Similarly, Aparna Rayaprol's study of a South Indian community outside of Pittsburgh, Pennsylvania, finds that the local Hindu temple serves as a semi-private space where Indian women are able to not only connect with one another but also become leaders in a social space that is seen as culturally appropriate.[16] As a new immigrant from Pakistan living in Seattle in the 1970s, Owais Jafrey used to meet other Muslim students in a church space near the University of Washington as a way to stay connected to a faith-based community. Because there were virtually no spaces for Muslims to worship together in that area, he obtained permission to hold services in the church basement: "There were several students who were studying, who were Muslims, drawn from the Arab world and from Pakistan and India. And we used to go and pray there. The Friday congregation of prayers . . . I used to skip my lunch and used that time [to pray] instead of having lunch." Likewise, informal sites of worship offered Zakir Parpia and his family a chance to connect with people from their cultural background in Spokane, Washington, in the 1980s, and then in the Seattle area after moving there in 1989:

> There was a little a mosque there [in Spokane]. And there were maybe fifteen Indian families. And they were not necessarily Muslim. So we met to socialize and things like that, and maybe sometimes for Eid and sometimes for Diwali [festivals]. So it really didn't matter because there was no regular prayer at Friday, or at least I didn't do it. After we came to Seattle in [19]89, there is a large community here of Ismailis. And we ran into a few of them and found that we thoroughly enjoyed [socializing with them]. Most of them are from East Africa and a few from India/Pakistan. They're mostly people who moved from India to East Africa and then when Idi Amin persecuted them, they moved to Vancouver, B.C., and then came down to Seattle.

For Jafrey, the lack of a formal place of worship led him to seek out public meeting spaces to bring together others seeking religious community, whereas Parpia found that coming together with other Ismailis actually offered more of a social outlet than a strictly religious one. Nonetheless, for both narrators, the ability to connect with others of a similar faith was an important part of establishing roots in the area.

Today, there are a variety of institutions that bridge new and old traditions and serve both religious and broader community interests. For Dev Manhas, creating a space for Hindus to worship and gather was important to him personally, but it was also a marker of the permanence of the South Asian community in the region:

> There was not much here, as opposed to East Coast. We didn't have any temple and stuff here. [Before 2002, we used to celebrate our festivals in our homes and in churches and community halls, which we rented.] Now we have more than one temple [in the greater Seattle area where we celebrate those festivals]. A community temple. Both I and Asha have been very, very involved in that and made big donations to the temple, just for that same reason: to have a place where the community can meet, it can pray together, talk, socialize. And also, you know, as a community getting older, if there are any deaths and stuff, at least some priest will be there to do something. That wasn't there before.

For Manhas, a temple serves the function of facilitating community gatherings, but it also ensures the continuation of certain rituals and rites that would otherwise be lost in America, particularly as older generations of Hindus living in the area age. Manhas recalls the inauguration of the Hindu Temple and Cultural Center in Bothell, Washington, as an important step toward fulfilling that legacy: "On the opening day in November 18, 2002, I mean the first day, there was no room for parking. There, I think about fifteen hundred to maybe eighteen hundred, or maybe two thousand people walked through the temple." With free food catered by a local restaurant and literally thousands of people in attendance, the opening of the temple alone shows how great the hunger is for South Asian community spaces.

This blurring between religious and cultural space has also resulted in new syncretic traditions as South Asians increasingly use the public space of religious institutions to develop community cohesion. While the worship of specific deities and legends in India is distinctly local, the Hindu temples in the diaspora tend to be broader in their rituals, icons, and practices. For example, the Hindu Temple and Cultural Center in Bothell celebrates major holidays like Dussera or Janmashtami by incorporating a variety of rituals from different regions in South Asia and from the Hindu diaspora. The array of idols in the temple represents a variety of sculptural styles and the adornment of the idols is similarly pan-Hindu. Rizwan Nasar is an active member of the Muslim Association of Puget Sound, which maintains a mosque and community space used by Muslims from different parts of the world. He notes that this geographic diversity has led to religious practices that are hybridized and in flux: "It's not really Pakistani or Indian culture or it's not really . . . because, you know, when we come from India or Pakistan, we bring our own baggage. We bring our own culture. We bring our own form of religion." He notes that particular festivals have become central to Islamic practice in the Pacific Northwest partly as a result of needing to find common ground among Muslims coming from places such as Egypt, Saudi Arabia, and other parts of the Middle East, as well as South and Southeast Asian nations like Indonesia and Malaysia. Even though these new forms can have the effect of homogenizing religious practices, they are also attempts to create new kinds of communities of people living in diaspora that transcend national borders.

STAYING CONNECTED: CHANGING TECHNOLOGY, DEVELOPMENT, AND SOCIAL ORGANIZATIONS

While South Asian immigrants have been deeply committed to building communities in various forms across the Pacific Northwest, as populations continue to grow and telecommunications in both the subcontinent and North America rapidly expand, they are also able to stay in contact with communities in their countries of origin. In his essay on "imagined communities," Benedict Anderson famously argued that the spread of print capitalism and early media technologies allowed people in far-flung locations to feel connected to one another and fostered a sense of nationalism.[17] More recent changes in the forms of communication available, such as email, video chatting, and social media tools, have opened up opportunities for immigrants in the United States to remain abreast of organizations, social movements, and politics in South Asia.[18] The growth of virtual communities and the increased mobility between South Asia and the United States have further transformed immigrants' daily relationships with their homelands.

This sense of connection is a marked change from previous moments of the South Asian immigrant history. In earlier years, immigrants reported a sense of dislocation and disconnection from their home countries. Sat Kapahi recalls:

> I felt very cut off, because I'd be looking in the paper—where is the news about India? Maybe once in two weeks, there'd be a little article in there. So in those days, [Indian stories on] TV and news

were not that common. Now, you know, you can switch to any channel and be watching a channel from Indian news or all that. At that time it wasn't [common]. So that part seemed very difficult. I seemed to be totally cut off.

Kapahi's feeling of isolation is a far cry from that of more recent immigrants, who inhabit a media-saturated world where webcams, SMS messaging, and relatively easy flights to and from the subcontinent keep them in much closer communication with home. For instance, when talking about his parents' final years in Sri Lanka, Prasanna Samarawickrama notes:

> I didn't live with them in their later years. And, you know, it also brings a different perspective of life for them, not living within their proximity. I knew that but we both tried to manage it. And they did come here once before they got sick. But we tried to manage that through phone calls and more frequent travel. I'd try to do even shorter visits but more frequently. So I was never so far away that they had to wait a whole year to see me.

In the span of thirty years between Kapahi's arrival in the United States in 1952 and Samarawickrama's in 1982, the sense of ease and accessibility between "here" and "there" was fundamentally transformed.

The effort to stay connected to South Asia has also created new communities in the Pacific Northwest that are interested in deepening links in both locations. In particular, South Asians have been extremely active in the promotion of development projects, fundraising efforts, and other modes of giving back economically to their homelands. In the mid-1970s, Santosh Wahi, her husband Pran Wahi, and a few others came together to found People for Progress in India (PPI), which links communities in Seattle with projects in India. Wahi remembers some of PPI's early efforts:

> A lot of people pledge money every month—how much they'll give for the year or whatever to take on some projects in India. We don't just dole out money. We want to give the money so people can become self-sufficient. For instance, there is one of our projects. Probably one of our first or second projects. The first was in a hospital. But the other project was in a village where we gave them

money to buy buffalos or cows to nurse the children. Give them milk and lots of things are made from milk. And gave them sewing machines so they can make clothes and clothe themselves. After a few years, the village gave us the money back and we wondered why they were giving it back to us. And they said that, "Now the cows have, their calves have grown. And the machines, we have sewn a lot of clothes and we have benefited, profited by sewing for others for profit and embroidering. So, please take this money and give it to another village to start off."

While PPI has focused on giving loans to people living in villages in India, it and other similar organizations have been vital outlets for South Asians to foster a commitment to addressing the problems of the nations that they left behind. An article published in the *Seattle Times* about Pakistanis' efforts to contribute to the development of their homelands notes that

Pakistanis in the U.S. sent back more than $1.7 billion last year. The Citizens Foundation, based in Karachi, Pakistan's economic hub, receives as much as half of its budget from Pakistanis abroad and relies on overseas chapters such as TCF-Seattle for overseas fundraising. The organization tackles some of the stark educational inequalities there by building and maintaining well-funded schools in Pakistan's poorest communities. Now the largest educator of children in Pakistan other than the government, TCF serves 80,000 students in 600 schools.[19]

South Asians in diaspora have made a considerable impact across the subcontinent by sending monetary remittances to family members and raising funds for a number of causes and organizations. In Seattle alone, there are over fifty organizations working in South Asia on issues such as microfinance, gender equity, health, education, technology, and urban planning.[20] These organizations link South Asians in the Pacific Northwest to development projects through fundraising, as noted above in the case of The Citizen's Foundation or PPI, and also through commitments made by individuals to go abroad and work in the region. A symposium hosted by the University of Washington South Asia Center in May 2010 and again in 2011 brought together South Asians from multiple generations to think about how the diaspora relates to the subcontinent through development projects and how that relationship has shifted over time. In a session composed of first-generation immigrants from India and Pakistan, the question of why the diaspora ought to give back to South Asia came up as a repeated theme. Rao Remala, who participated in the session as a representative of his private foundation,[21] spoke about how he felt when visiting the small town in South India where he grew up. After living away for many years, he was struck by the immense changes that have transformed India, but he was also deeply moved by the ways in which ailments with simple cures continue to wreak havoc on the lives of the poor. For example, routine eye surgery could immensely increase the quality of life for someone afflicted with cataracts; however, few people in rural areas have access to procedures that are almost taken for granted in western nations. These observations spurred Remala's awareness about how little it would take to considerably improve even one person's life in an economically depressed area like his hometown, leading him to establish a foundation that works toward increasing the accessibility of basic services and education.

For South Asians such as Remala, being away from their homelands has increased their political and social awareness of the conditions of the countries left behind. Newer nonprofit organizations like Children's Rights and You (CRY) and Asha Seattle, the local branch of Asha for Education, are working in India to promote small-scale development projects similar to the work of PPI. Starting from the mid-1990s, these organizations have grown in number and are increasingly run by younger generations of South Asians. Many of the younger generation participants are recent arrivals from South Asia and come to work in the region's booming technology industries on temporary work visas. Often unsure if they will be able to stay in the United States permanently because of their visa status, these immigrants have a decidedly homeward-facing orientation in their community work. While CRY and Asha serve an important social function of connecting like-minded South Asians locally, as other groups have done in the past, they are also plugged into virtual and geographically dispersed networks that cross national boundaries. These groups have benefitted tremendously from financial support from local industries. For example, Microsoft matches employee charitable contributions up to $12,000 per employee annually. A substantial portion of those funds goes to organizations operating in the greater Seattle region—including groups like those mentioned above who are linked transnationally. Considering that Microsoft currently has several thousand employees of South Asian origin, many of whom are engaged in South Asia–specific projects, much of this charitable giving has gone to support the growth of these sorts of economic and social development efforts.

Both as a representative of Microsoft and on his own accord, Akhtar Badshah has worked extensively with a number of South Asia–focused and domestic organizations ranging from local arts councils to academic departments at the University of Washington. When asked about the need for individuals who have left their home countries to give back to them, Badshah comments:

> I believe that whether you've left or not left, everybody has an obligation to give back. And I actually don't necessarily believe that Indians who have left have to give back to India. You should give back to where you want to give back. You should give back to where you live, as much as you give back to where you come from. So I fully believe that every individual has to give back. Without giving back we're just not creating a virtual cycle of development and growth.

For Badshah, the impulse to give back is an essential piece of giving people a sense of place—whether that place is near or far. Though we are only able to sample the tip of the iceberg of community organizations and efforts in the region, there is no doubt, for South Asians in the Pacific Northwest, maintaining vibrant and deep connections in the United States and across the seas is not only a matter of personal desire, but also a social and moral imperative.

CONCLUSIONS

As narrators' and others' stories reveal, the process of forming communities and establishing a home in a new place is by no means uniform. While maintaining cultural or religious traditions is important for ethnic groups to preserve a sense of group cohesion, regional, religious, caste, gender, class, and generational differences always complicate how communities are formed and mediated. Debates over nation and identity, the passage of values across generations and from home countries to the United States, and the re-creation of religious and spiritual practices emerge across these accounts of community building. Today, South Asians are definitional to the Pacific Northwest, as they have become an important part of the region's immigration history, industry innovations, community development, and cultural expression. At the same time, South Asians have been impacted by life within the rich culture and environment of the lush forests, looming mountains, and icy emerald waters that characterize the region. Even though they remain connected across the world and carry with them the long legacies of colonialism, war, displacement, and multiple migration, there is no doubt that they are very much a part of the history and the future of the Pacific Northwest and the United States.

EPILOGUE: MEDITATIONS ON METHODOLOGIES

M ORE than a century after the first Sikh migrants set foot on the west-ern shores of Canada and wound their way down the coast, South Asian communities in the Pacific Northwest thrive in the rich inheritance of that first arrival. South Asians created new institutions and organiza-tions in the region, even during the "barred zone" period of Asian immigra-tion, and communities quickly expanded following the Immigration and Nationality Act of 1965. The development of the aerospace and software industries in the region has led to a third wave of migration that continues into the twenty-first century. These immigrants' stories of arrivals, depar-tures, adjustments, and displacements make up a previously unexplored history of South Asian settlement and community formation in the Pacific Northwest. Personal stories, told through the medium of oral histories, form the backbone of this archive.

Some of the oral histories speak of the extraordinary successes that nar-rators found in their professional lives. These tales are the stuff of legends: from working on teams to launch early space shuttle missions to being the very first South Asian to work at the technology giant Microsoft. Other nar-rators candidly relate the hardships of being one of very few people of color or a foreigner working in a particular industry. Some of the women narrators faced both race and gender discrimination in the workplace. Although work and education drive the plot of these stories, the other significant story line is the importance of personal relationships and the creation of friendship networks and families. However, South Asian immigration to the Pacific Northwest has also been about the public ways in which immigrants have set down roots in the region and established strong and visible organizations designed to preserve cultural customs and traditions, while creating space for new causes and activities.

Although these stories and the insights into regional and community histories they provide are important in their own right, it is also necessary to consider why oral histories are foundational to this book, the strengths and limitations of using oral history in conjunction with other methodologies, and what others might derive from this project. Writing about evolving communities is a challenging task, especially when the authors are also a part of the same histories. As authors, we were consistently urged to tell a positive story that extolled South Asians' achievements and questioned about why we chose to include particular individuals or events rather than others. This interest and concern over the construction of a book project reflects the stakes that individuals have in the production of what they may claim as their community's history. It also signals the sometimes difficult terrain that we have had to navigate in order to interpret and situate these oral histories in the context of competing narratives and our own interdisciplinary training as feminist scholars who seek to showcase the stories of those whose voices are often left out of the historical record. We therefore take a closer look at the methodologies underlying this book in order to reflect on our own work and offer other scholars a road map to undertake similar studies of community formation and immigration in the future.

SITUATING THE STORIES: ORAL HISTORY AND INTERDISCIPLINARY RESEARCH

Although several themes weave across the narrators' stories, these same stories also reveal the heterogeneity of experiences within the various South Asian communities profiled in this text. For example, some South Asians arrived as relatively privileged students and workers, while others fled political strife in their homelands and came as refugees. Such differences among South Asians are as important as the commonalities between them. The stories recounted here attest to the complicated and layered relationships that individuals have to their home countries, their adopted countries, larger South Asian communities, intimate family networks, and public and private events that shape their lives. In order to tease apart the various strands that make up each individual's life story and to contextualize them in other representations about South Asians in the Pacific Northwest and the United

States, we have employed an interdisciplinary approach. We have drawn on oral history, contemporary news and academic accounts, other historical documents, and even fictional accounts, interested in not only historical events that shape these communities but how events are interpreted, re-imagined, and related to and by others. Although personal narratives and fictional stories are distinct genres, both are forms of storytelling and reveal how memory, point of view, and imagination create a living archive of experiences. Thus, this text is driven by specific insights about life in the Pacific Northwest from a variety of perspectives and contributes to a nuanced mapping of the region's history and social geography that centers personal stories.

Oral history as a method to build up dynamic and living archives is useful for capturing these stories while also offering narrators the chance to reflexively engage with their own representations. Oral histories differ from standard interviews because they often cover a wider variety of topics over a longer period of time than what might be addressed in a qualitative interview. The oral historians of the South Asian Oral History Project (SAOHP), Amy Bhatt and Julie Kersson, asked narrators to answer a series of questions about his or her life history, but otherwise allowed the narrators to shape the direction of the interviews. The interview format captured personal reflections through interviews lasting between one and a half to over two hours; in some cases, narrators spoke with the oral historians several times to tell different pieces of their stories. Since the content of each oral history is also driven by individual memories, the stories do not abide by stricter qualitative models of research which strive for generalizability or accuracy. Instead, each story remains a unique blend of public events and private interpretation.

Thus, oral history is a counterpoint to the sweeping narratives of the extraordinary events that make up "History" with a capital "H," or the official and conventional accounting of events. Often official histories are given weight because they are presumed to be accurate, shaping our understandings of the past through a single perspective. Personal stories solicited through oral history, however, offer a glimpse into not only personal reflections on major events but also more intimate moments. This telling of stories has a gendered element as well. Arguing in favor of foregrounding the voices of women through oral history, Jennifer Scanlon writes that "recording women's voices and then telling their stories has, arguably, been empowering for all involved, for the woman telling her own story, the woman recording and then retelling this story, and then the reader, who vicariously experiences it."[1] In that way, oral histories allow for women's perspectives on events to shine through. For instance, when Najma Rizvi recounts the turmoil of the Bangladesh Civil War in 1971, it is colored by her memories of becoming a young widow and her efforts to make sense of personal tragedy in the wake of national upheaval. The two events together, one intensely private and the other shared by millions, led her to move permanently to the United States. Oral history takes seriously the personal and the public moments that texture representations of history and complicates binaries that relegate some stories to a less important register while highlighting others. Likewise, Amy Laly's story of her father's work in the Indian Railway system during the period immediately following the Partition of India and Pakistan is told through the eyes of a child who did not witness the bloodshed first hand, but learned about it through her father's haunted memories. These are the sorts of insights that oral histories offer. Rather than seek to replace the authoritative versions generated by historians, it is a chance to record informal accounts through narrators' memories, emotions, and interpretations.

The focus on personal stories therefore allows the reader to see not only how individuals responded to key historical events but also how they were part of history in the making. For instance, Pramila Jayapal's founding of Hate Free Zone (now One America) in response to the attacks of September 11, 2001, reflects a larger concern among immigrant communities in the wake of American tragedy. Similarly, Rizwan Nasar, whose extended family was affected by the devastating earthquakes that destroyed parts of northwest Pakistan in 2005, came together with other Pakistanis living in the Puget Sound area to raise almost $20 million in relief funds and partnered with local organizations to build 500 homes in the affected regions. Both of these leaders' articulations of their efforts are embedded in their experiences of living as immigrants while still maintaining close ties to various communities around the world. Oral history offers an important understanding of how individual decisions sparked by tragedy and disaster, as in both of these cases, have the potential to mobilize local communities to tackle national and even international issues.

While many narrators are writers, poets, filmmakers, musicians, artists, or activists who comment on public events, their intimate reflections and life stories offer personal insights into historical moments. Whether they spoke of their involvement in landmark events like the 1962 Seattle World Fair or the early Apollo space shuttle launches, increasing the scope of services and products created by Boeing or Microsoft, or crafting faith-based community responses to national events, these moments are recounted through their particular perspective and location in the Pacific Northwest. The event itself, while important, is not the focus of the oral history; rather, each person's interpretation of and implication in the event shows how South Asians are integrated into the rich historical tapestry of the Pacific Northwest.

Moreover, the public hosting of each narrator's full transcripts, along with audio and video recordings, at the University of Washington Libraries, means that others can build on the work started in this book.[2] This is another advantage of using oral history as part of a multi-modal methodology for archiving community histories. The online availability of the narrator-crafted and -edited interviews means that future scholars, researchers, and community members can access these stories as the narrators intended them to be heard. By asking narrators to recount experiences across a wide swath of time—from their early childhoods through their lives in the contemporary moment—oral history allows the narrator to travel a nonlinear path that does not have to follow a conventional form of story-telling. As folk tales, epics, novels, narrative poems, and other forms of cultural production have shown, different accounts of history are possible through the medium of song or story. Indeed, the story itself takes shape through the telling; it is not necessarily intended to reach an expected conclusion, or even known beforehand.

Of course, using self-generated histories in order to map the past also raises questions about selective recall and representation. Alice Yang Murray, a professor and oral historian who has documented the histories of Japanese Americans interned during World War Two, reflects on her interviews with Japanese American activists in San Francisco.[3] Despite her efforts to elicit stories that had not been told in mainstream accounts of internment, she found that narrators also had critical stakes in the public telling of *particular* stories. She writes,

> Understanding how particular contexts could impact memories and representations forced me to re-examine my views on oral history and the relevancy of post-modern theory. I no longer took it for

granted that I could discover the "definitive facts" of someone's life from an interview. Instead, I would need to analyze the constructions and interpretations of the past as influenced by the dynamics of our interview and the larger historical context. At the same time, I realized that oral histories were no less "reliable" than other historical sources. All sources, whether newspapers, archival documents, personal letters or oral histories, should be contextualized.[4]

Murray makes the argument that we cannot stop with the solicitation of oral history alone; such stories ought to be read as narratives like any other, not just as pure representations of some true experience or event.[5] Interpretation is a key element in oral history and we offer one perspective on how these individual stories might be analyzed and situated in larger social, political, and cultural contexts.

At the same time, it is important to note that while oral history has a number of advantages, relying on specific voices and experiences also creates challenges. In their recent work on how oral history shapes public memory, Hamilton and Shopes make the case that oral history can have several drawbacks. They note:

Oral history, driven by the passion for the personal story, assumes that every individual's experience can indeed be made into a purposeful story, and so, like autobiography, it tends to offer linear, causal explanations of individuals as the inevitable products of their past experiences. This approach tends to occlude the social and cultural processes that have shaped subjectivity and that are central concerns of historians of memory.[6]

Hamilton and Shopes argue that narrators tend to privilege particular themes and narratives at the expense of other explanations that reveal a more complicated understanding of personal identities or even historical events. Even in the SAOHP, there is a strong emphasis on the success of the community and a focus on individuals whose stories are emblematic of the American dream, or the notion that individuals who work will become successful, rather than on those who have encountered significant discrimination or disadvantage. The fact that some South Asians, such as those belonging to the increasingly wealthy Indian American segment, are among the most economically successful immigrant groups in the United States[7] glosses over the difficulties that many others experience. Instead, because these narratives of success and economic prosperity emerge from census data, public media, and personal narratives, a reader is led to assume that hard work, family values, and cultural attributes are the primary reasons behind South Asian achievements.

However, carefully crafted immigration, educational, and labor policies between countries like India and the United States have also ensured the migration of the highly educated and middle class and must also be considered vital factors behind certain immigrant successes. For instance, a *New York Times* article paints a dark portrait of Bangladeshis scraping by in Queens.[8] These immigrants do not survive on the fruits of the information technology industries or as professionals, but on the minimum wage provide by factory jobs. Their story, too, is one of perseverance, hard work, and sacrifice, but it does not get as much coverage as the success of high-profile South Asian entrepreneurs and business leaders such as Sabeer Bhatia, the founder of Hotmail, or Indra Nooyi, the CEO of PepsiCo. While stories complicate understandings of race, class, religious, linguistic, and gender politics in South Asian communities, relying on personal narratives may not necessarily highlight the structural aspects of economic or social success and must also be read critically.

Furthermore, there are many silences and gaps in any history that relies on oral sources. Narrators must weigh the risks of disclosing details about themselves in such a public way for posterity's sake. In choosing *not* to share a particular story or deciding to reframe an experience in a more positive light, or even refusing to participate in the project at all, narrators—and potential narrators—are always gauging how much to reveal. While each narrator volunteered to be a part of the SAOHP, the fact that the archive would be available to a large audience was a serious issue to consider for many. The public nature of the archive also means that there were those who decided not to participate in the project at all, for various reasons, including fear about what others might think. For example, individuals who have survived personal traumas were reluctant to fully disclose details about their experiences, while others feared offending members of their community in the region with their account of particular events. Their voices are conspicuously absent and would have added depth and counter-points to the stories presented. Thus, while oral histories themselves offer a rich source of information to be mined in the future, the silences and absences within this archive must also be considered carefully when thinking about how communities are represented.

Other challenges to oral history are the reliance on spoken word as the medium through which stories are told and the emphasis placed on personal experience. Each narrator had the opportunity to review his or her typed transcript after the oral history was completed. Some narrators experienced a sense of discomfort after reading the printed representations of their oral interviews. Even though oral history can be an organic way of collecting information because of the open-ended questions and semi-formal format of the interviews, each narrator still engaged in some form of self-editing and self-monitoring during the interview itself and then afterward. While some narrators had never told their life stories in a single sitting before, others are well-versed at the art of giving interviews and were clearly comfortable with offering a carefully crafted version of their life history. Oral historians use the term "narrators" rather than "study participants" or "interviewees" to describe their subjects in order to highlight the sense of story-telling, rather than objective data collecting, that oral history engenders. This focus on narration also underscores how experience itself is a dialectic concept that shapes public representations. Feminist historian Joan Scott's critical understanding of the idea of experience has been useful to us as we worked to situate narrators' stories within larger frameworks of histories, identities, and discourse. She writes that "it is not individuals who have experience, but subjects who are constituted through experience. Experience in this definition then becomes not the origin of our explanation, not the authoritative (because seen or felt) evidence that grounds what is known, but rather that which we seek to explain, that about which knowledge is produced."[9] In the case of this and any history project, experience is always a contested term and must be viewed as a form of knowledge production through which identities and memories are produced and reproduced.

Recognizing the constructed nature of experience, narrators were given the opportunity to further revise their own transcripts, mainly for accuracy and other issues related to editing. Following Valerie Yow's critical principles of interviewing, we strove to use the oral histories in a way that places "the individual's well-being at the center of decisions, not as a second consideration where searching for truth is first."[10] Many asked that their language be corrected to fit with a standardized form of English and made additions and deletions to their transcripts. Going beyond editing, some narrators chose to seal portions of their interview until a predetermined date in the future and in several cases, narrators re-crafted their interview to editorialize on their lives after confronting the written transcript. Nonetheless, allowing narrators to revisit the text of their interviews is an attempt to honor the voice and comfort of each narrator, while recognizing the constructed nature of any representative act.

The resulting transcripts are therefore a record of the actual meeting for the oral history interview as well as the revisions, edits, and clarifications made by each narrator. In the process of adapting sections of individual interviews for the book, we also edited the oral histories for clarity and flow, while seeking to maintain the integrity of the final transcript. In doing so, we use the various versions of stories offered by narrators without assuming that the end product generated through the interview process alone is what matters when creating an account of community memories.

The question of how to create accurate yet diverse representations, however, remains. One concern is that the oral histories featured here were all conducted in English and thus exclude possible narrators that are not English proficient. English is arguably one of the most important languages in South Asia because of the long history of British colonization in the region.[11] Among South Asians living in the United States and other parts of the world, English is the key to communicating effectively with non–South Asians. Furthermore, proficiency in English has been one of the reasons that South Asians continue to be perceived as easily adaptable, particularly in western countries where English is the lingua franca. All of these reasons informed the choice to use English to compile an archive that was created with the hope of reaching a global audience. Therefore, the oral historians who made contact with each narrator and conducted the interviews for the SAOHP were primarily English speakers. Amy Bhatt, for instance, is also conversant in Gujarati and Hindi, but Julie Kerssen, who conducted interviews in the first phase of the project, does not have facility in any South Asian languages. Both were trained as oral historians, however, and were integral in shaping the interviews overall.

However, the prioritization of English comes at the cost of a richer array of stories. By virtue of having grown up or having spent substantial portions of their lives in South Asia or in South Asian communities, narrators also spoke at least one other language that they might consider their "mother tongue" such as Marathi, Sinhalese, Tamil, Telugu, Bangla, and Urdu. It is possible that narrators may have offered a different account of their experiences in their native languages. Considering the often affective ties that people have to language, in some cases using English meant that narrators were asked to present a version of their life story in a language that might not be the one in which they feel most comfortable expressing their intimate thoughts and feelings. Several of these narrators also engage in rich cultural production such as publishing topical articles for Marathi magazines, writing poetry in Urdu or fiction in Punjabi, or singing in Bengali; therefore these interviews in English must also be read as a particular kind of representation that might not be the same if narrators had the opportunity to use different languages.

Finally, another challenge presented by oral history projects can be the reliance on personal networks to select narrators and the biases that inevitably result. In the case of the SAOHP, there are three overt issues: the majority of narrators profiled live in Seattle or the greater Puget Sound area; the majority of narrators are of Indian origin; and the narrators' economic status is skewed toward the upper middle classes. In order to recommend narrators, the University of Washington Libraries convened an advisory board composed of South Asian community leaders and interested participants from the University of Washington. The advisory board developed criteria for narrator selection including community involvement and presence, diverse life histories, and potential interest in participating. While some advisory board members saw narrator diversity as tantamount to selection, others hoped to profile the most prestigious aspects of South Asian communities.

Since the selection process required some level of personal connection to potential narrators, this method of selection was a type of snowball sampling, where one contact leads to more down the line. The advisory board of the SAOHP was also most representative of the Indian American communities in the Seattle region, which further entrenched the overrepresentation of Indian narrators in the project and the focus on the Seattle metro area. However the postcolonial histories of South Asian nations also play a role: for instance, some narrators had been born in modern-day Pakistan or India, but moved with their families following Partition. Others were forced to flee their homes as a result of war; in the case of Bangladesh, they were Pakistani subjects until the war for independence ended in 1971 and made them citizens of a new country. While there certainly are more Indian narrators in the SAOHP than narrators from other nations, the relationship between where narrators were born, their regional community affiliations, and where they claim citizenship is often quite complicated.

The narrators selected also had to be proficient and comfortable enough with English to give an interview in it, which generally implied that they had access to English-medium education in their home countries as well as some education in the United States. Narrowing the selection criteria on linguistic grounds meant that the project lost some class and community diversity by not having as many perspectives from individuals who might not have English language skills as well developed as those of South Asian professionals. The overall demographics of South Asians in the United States are also heavily slanted toward individuals with at least some level of formal education: for example, over 50 percent of Bangladeshi immigrants over the age of twenty-five are estimated to have bachelor's degrees, compared to less than 25 percent of the native-born American population. The number of bachelor's degrees jumps to 65 percent when one looks at the number of college-educated Indian immigrants. Furthermore, Indians are estimated to be the ethnic group with the highest median household income in America, as well as the second fastest-growing demographic, after Chinese immigrants.

As mentioned before, these indicators are not simply proof of the "success story" of South Asians; they are the result of carefully crafted immigration policies that have promoted the immigration of specific students and workers from the subcontinent. While several stories told by narrators recount humble beginnings, the opportunity to come to the United States in the first place was usually possible because of a certain degree of familial support and access to educational and professional networks that eased the transition to life abroad.

Immigration policy and personal networks have played substantial roles in shaping the presence of South Asians in the Pacific Northwest more broadly, and those changes are reflected in the organization of the SAOHP itself: The project was divided into three phases that correspond roughly to key moments in South Asian immigration history to the United States. The first phase of narrators arrived between the 1940s and 1950s, when more stringent laws barring Asian immigration were still in effect. The second phase of the project tracks the histories of narrators who came between 1965 and 1980. The passage of the Immigration and Nationality

Act of 1965 bookended one side of this period and resulted in immigration preference categories privileging students and educated professionals from South Asia. On the other end, the 1980s ushered in new regulations that made family reunification easier for immigrants who were settled in the United States. The third phase picks up in the 1980s and 1990s, as more immigrants came to work in a wide variety of fields. Though the project was intended to track these distinct phases of migration, there are difficulties in neatly categorizing when individuals immigrated: some came as students and then returned to their home or other countries before settling in the United States, whereas some spent years in different parts of the country before arriving in the Pacific Northwest, and others came directly to the Pacific Northwest and have never left. The varied routes of immigration further complicate how the SAOHP has been constructed as an archive, but also point to the importance of considering the confluence of public policy and individual paths.

Today, the community has continued to expand and change dramatically with the arrival of new waves of immigrants. While the SAOHP (and this book) ends with the arrival of narrators in the 1990s, the decades since then have witnessed new iterations of immigration restrictions in the wake of September 11, 2001, and debates over "border control" have been re-ignited on a national scale. There have also been expansions in immigration opportunities; the increase in the number of temporary worker visas, known as the H-1B visa, issued annually to immigrants coming specifically from India has contributed to new immigration patterns since the 1990s. The H-1B visa is often used to bring in highly skilled and educated workers to the United States for short periods of time. Because of the Pacific Northwest's high concentration of technology, engineering, and medical industries, there is a large market for H-1B visa holders in the region. These immigrants are carving out a new relationship to the area as they move between the United States, their home countries, and other parts of the world with increasing frequency. While they are a large and visible presence, they make up a different constituency that is not as rooted in the region as older immigrants and is more tied to jobs and transnational networks.[12] For that reason, this book ends just before the newer waves of immigration in the 2000s began, as those stories are still unfolding.

FINAL INTERVENTIONS AND OBSERVATIONS

Through this project, we hope to have demonstrated the usefulness of bringing together personal narratives and contextualizing historical moments
to further improve understandings of South Asian diasporas and community formation. We have worked to show the methodological importance
of reading oral histories alongside other representations of South Asian
immigrant life in order to add to the rich bodies of work emerging from
academic, journalistic, and creative registers about these communities.
When examined through a longer historical lens, these representations also
intervene in theoretical discussions related to Asian American studies more
broadly. Until relatively recently, South Asians have occupied either a silent
or a curiously undifferentiated location within the broader field of Asian
American Studies. South Asians have categorically been seen as outside of
the U.S.-based formulations of "Asian America" partly because of differences in cultural assertions, physiology, and colonial histories. As a result,
many early academic reflections on Asian American studies did not include
South Asian voices, though more recent examinations have reversed that
trend.[13] Yet since the early twentieth century, as we demonstrated in our
discussion of the early history of Sikh migration to the Pacific Northwest,
South Asians have played an important role in the formation of American
immigration policy and must be recognized as a vital part of Asian American history more broadly.

Thus, this attempt to think about the overlaps and differences that make
up South Asian communities in the Pacific Northwest and the personal
stories documented here contribute a vibrancy to historical understandings
of both region and cultural formations that other accounts alone cannot.
Diaspora studies have been largely concerned with how communities form
in light of displacement, changing connections to the homeland, family, and
kinship networks, nationalism, and new forms of cultural production. The
Jewish experience of expulsion from the kingdom of Judah or the Atlantic
slave trade that created the African diaspora are often used as reference
points for thinking about the condition of diaspora more generally. The
South Asian communities living around the world, in some ways, follow
these depictions of diaspora; at the same time, they also make up immigrant communities that no longer expect to return "home," but instead work

to create new cultures and institutions while maintaining connections to the birthplace of their ancestors. In that way, we have attempted to bridge the gap between diaspora and immigration studies by focusing on both the identity and cultural aspects of community formation and the historical and material contexts that give rise to immigration and use both terms "diasporic" and "immigrant" throughout this book.

As these living histories demonstrate, the experience of creating communities in a new country is continually mediated through gender, class, race, nationality, and other markers of difference. These narratives shed light on the spectacular as well as mundane ways in which diaspora and immigration are not just temporary conditions, but a lived and dynamic experience fraught with contradictions. Our job as interlocutors has not been to verify the truth or authenticity of these stories; rather, it is to think creatively and critically about how people construct images of themselves and the worlds that they have encountered, attempt to assimilate while maintaining ties to their traditions, and reinvent their ideas about homeland, family, and national identity. Ultimately, this has been a story about how South Asians have been changed by the immigration process; it is also a tale of how their arrival, settlement, and rootedness have forever changed the Pacific Northwest.

APPENDIX 1

INTERVIEWS IN THE SOUTH ASIAN ORAL HISTORY PROJECT

All the interviews listed below are part of the South Asian Oral History Project at the University of Washington Libraries in Seattle, Washington. These interviews can be accessed through University of Washington Libraries Digital Collections at http://content.lib.washington.edu/saohcweb.

Ahmedi, Asgar. Interview by Julie Kerssen, February 4, 2005.

Badshah, Dr. Akhtar. Interview by Amy Bhatt, February 13, 2008.

Gangolli, Shanta. Interview by Julie Kerssen, April 1, 2005.

Gaur, Dr. Lakshmi. Interview by Amy Bhatt, April 10, 2008.

Gnanapragasam, Dr. Nirmala. Interview by Amy Bhatt, September 4, 2008.

Gupta, Kris. Interview by Julie Kerssen, April 26, 2005.

Hossain, Dr. Mohammad Zahid. Interview by Amy Bhatt, October 2, 2008.

Jafrey, Owais. Interview by Amy Bhatt, October 31, 2007.

Jayapal, Pramila. Interview by Amy Bhatt, July 21, 2008.

Joshi, Rajnikant (Raj). Interview by Julie Kerssen, December 29, 2004.

Kapahi, Sat. Interview by Julie Kerssen, March 23, 2005.

Keskar, Dr. Dinesh. Interview by Amy Bhatt, September 10, 2009.

Kirchner, Bharti. Interview by Amy Bhatt, March 7, 2008.

Kode, Dr. Shaila. Interview by Amy Bhatt, February 8, 2008.

Kumar, Dr. Prem. Interview by Amy Bhatt, July 27, 2007.

Laly, Amy. Interview by Amy Bhatt, September 20, 2007.

Manhas, Dr. Dev. R. Interview by Amy Bhatt, August 15, 2007.

Manhas, Rajinder Singh. Interview by Amy Bhatt, June 18, 2007.

Mathur, Alok. Interview by Amy Bhatt, July 24, 2008.

Nasar, Syed Rizwan. Interview by Amy Bhatt, May 21, 2008.

Parpia, Zakir. Interview by Amy Bhatt, November 15, 2007.

Rahman, Jamal. Interview by Amy Bhatt, July 28, 2008.

Remala, Rao V. Interview by Amy Bhatt, March 20, 2008.

Rizvi, Dr. Najma. Interview by Amy Bhatt, August 30, 2007.

Samarawickrama, Prasanna Manjula. Interview by Amy Bhatt, September 23, 2008.

Siddiqui, Jafar (Jeff) Hussain. Interview by Amy Bhatt, June 29, 2007.

Sokkappa, Dr. Balraj. Interview by Julie Kerssen, January 14, 2005.

Vashee, Vijay. Interview by Amy Bhatt, October 27, 2009.

Vasishth, Dr. Padmini. Interview by Julie Kerssen, December 28, 2005.

Wahi, Santosh. Interview by Amy Bhatt, November 20, 2007.

APPENDIX 2

NARRATOR BIOGRAPHIES

ASGAR AHMEDI was born in 1928 in the town of Vohemar on the island of Madagascar. His family was originally from Kutiania, a small town near Mumbai, India. His grandfather and father came to Madagascar in the early 1920s and began an export business, but when Asgar Ahmedi was young, he was sent by his family to India to complete his early schooling. In 1950, he came to the United States to pursue higher education. He was granted admission to the Colorado School of Mines, but transferred to the University of Colorado, Denver. He graduated in 1954 with a bachelor's degree and then moved to Seattle in 1955 to pursue his master's degree at the University of Washington. During this time, he began working as a chemist in a steel factory. Soon after, Mr. Ahmedi began an import-export business and in 1962, with a partner, he ran a booth at the Seattle World's Fair. In 1963, he owned an Indian handicrafts shop in the Seattle Center, and went on to have shops throughout Washington State, including in the Tri-Cities area, Tacoma, and Seattle. Mr. Ahmedi passed away in June 2008 and is survived by his wife, four daughters, Sara, Rabab, Zarina, and Yasmin, and stepdaughter, Habiba.

AKHTAR BADSHAH was born in Mumbai, India, in 1955. He came to the United States in 1981 as a doctoral student at the Massachusetts Institute of Technology. While completing his degree, he taught in the Aga Khan Program for Islamic Architecture and was research faculty in the Design for the Islamic Societies program. After years of working and living in New York and New Jersey, he and his family moved to the Seattle area in 1998. He was CEO and president of Digital Partners Foundation, a Seattle-area nonprofit organization whose mission is to utilize the digital economy to benefit the poor. His work included the development of the Digital Partners Social Venture Fund, designed to support the expansion of IT-based anti-poverty efforts around the world, and the Digital Partners Social Enterprise Laboratory (SEL), an initiative that provides mentorship and seed money to entrepreneurs whose vision and business models use information communication technology to empower the poor and their underserved communities. Today, Akhtar Badshah is the director of community affairs for Microsoft. He is also a board member of United Way King County, the Global Knowledge Partnership, and Youth Employment Summit Inc. and serves on the advisory boards of several organizations, including the World Affairs Council in Seattle; Santa Clara University Center for Science, Technology, and Society; the University of Washington South Asia Center; and the University of Washington Business School. He has co-edited *Connected for Development: Information Kiosks for Sustainability* and *Technology at the Margins: How IT Meets the Needs of Emerging Markets* and authored *Our Urban Future: New Paradigms for Equity and Sustainability*, as well as several articles in international journals on information communication technology for development, megacities and sustainability, housing, and urban development. He lives in the Bellevue, Washington, area with his wife, Alka, and has three sons, Anish, Aseem, and Akash.

SHANTA GANGOLLI was born in 1934 in Mumbai, India. She completed her bachelor's degree in economics with a subfield of statistics. She met her husband, Ramesh, while studying in college. They got married in 1958, when she had been working as a stenotypist for a Japanese firm in India. The same year, Ramesh won a scholarship to study at the Massachusetts Institute of Technology and they moved to Boston together. In 1960, after having her first son, she gained admission to Boston University, where she studied education for the hearing impaired. After she and her family moved to Seattle in 1962, she worked for the Speech and Hearing Center and eventually began working with the Seattle School District in various schools, teaching sign language and providing other services to hearing-impaired students. She and Ramesh were the original founders of Ragamala, a Seattle-area classical Indian music society. She lives in Seattle with her husband and has three sons.

LAKSHMI GAUR was born in 1954 in Jeypore, India. Her family moved to Hyderabad in the mid-1960s, where she completed much of her early schooling. She lived in an extended family which included her father, a sister, grandmother, and other relatives. After finishing her high school education, Lakshmi Gaur earned her bachelor's degree from Amrit Kapadia Navjeevan Women's College and her master's degree from Andhra University. She went on to enroll in a doctoral program in physical anthropology and human genetics at Punjab University. While completing her Ph.D., she was awarded a Fulbright fellowship that gave her the opportunity to come to the United States to continue her studies in Charleston, South Carolina. She later moved to Seattle. She has received research fellowships at the Max Planck Institute in Tübingen, Germany, and has published numerous papers in noted scientific journals. She currently works at the Puget Sound Blood Bank in Seattle and is also an affiliate associate professor in the Department of Laboratory Medicine at the University of Washington School of Medicine. Dr. Gaur is a former president of the Indian Association of Western Washington and serves on its board. She lives in Redmond, Washington, and has two sons, Prashant and Sharat.

NIRMALA GNANAPRAGASAM was born in 1961 in Colombo, Sri Lanka, where she completed her early studies. She obtained her bachelor's degree in civil engineering with top honors from the University of Moratuwa, Sri Lanka, in 1985. After getting married, she came to Chicago for further studies in 1985. She earned her master of science degree in 1988 and her Ph.D. in 1993 from Northwestern University. She joined Seattle University as an assistant professor in 1993. She teaches courses in fundamental engineering and geotechnical engineering. She has been the department's design coordinator for Seattle University's year-long, industrially-sponsored design project program. She is a registered professional engineer in Washington State and is active in engineering education research, consulting, and K-12 math education. She is also an accomplished musician and plays the *veenai*. She lives in Shoreline, Washington, with her husband, Kirthikumar, and has two sons, Danushan and Logan.

KRIS GUPTA was born in 1930 in Kashmir, India. He came to the United States in 1951 to attend the University of Washington, where he earned an undergraduate degree in civil engineering. After he finished his degree in 1954, he worked for the Department of Transportation for a short time before receiving his master's degree in transportation and traffic engineering from the University of California, Berkeley. He returned to India briefly and taught at the Punjab Engineering College in Chandigarh. He settled permanently in the United States in 1961 and rejoined the Washington State Department of Transportation. Just before retiring from the DOT, he was recruited to work on a five-year, $250-million research program in Washington, D.C., called the Strategic Highway Research Program. After the project wrapped up, he continued traveling around the country as a transportation expert and consultant. Since retiring, he volunteers for the AARP and other local organizations. He lives in Olympia, Washington, with his wife and has two daughters, Rashi and Pooja.

MOHAMMAD ZAHID HOSSAIN was born in Khulna, Bangladesh, and was the eldest of eight children. After completing his high school education in Khulna, he moved to Dhaka to pursue his bachelor's and master's degrees in biochemistry from Dhaka University. After graduating, he worked as a lecturer at Dhaka University before winning the prestigious East-West Center Scholarship to study in the United States. With this scholarship, he came to the University of Hawaii, Manoa, in 1984 to work on his Ph.D. in biochemistry. After finishing his doctoral degree, he moved to Winnipeg, Canada, to work as a university researcher. He then moved to Seattle with his family to work at the Pacific Northwest Research Institute. In 2004 he joined the Fred Hutchinson Cancer Research Center. He now works in regulatory affairs. In his spare time, he writes short stories and is involved in regional Bangladeshi and Bengali cultural communities. He currently lives in Bellevue, Washington, with his wife, Suram, and has two children, Semonti and Prottush.

OWAIS JAFREY was born in 1938 in Bulandshahr, India. After moving to Pakistan as a young man, Mr. Jafrey began working for the United States Information Service based in Pakistan. He also completed his master's degree in English with a certificate in library science from Punjab University. After his marriage in 1968, he moved to Seattle to begin working for the University of Washington while completing his degree in library science. In 1986, he took a position with Skagit Valley Community College, where he was the college's first librarian. He worked there for about twenty years before retiring in 2007. He is an avid reader of literature and particularly enjoys poetry. An accomplished poet himself, he was one of the founders of the Urdu Literary Society, which works to bring together poets from all over the world. He has been instrumental in convening lovers of Urdu poetry and music for events in the Seattle area. He lives in Shoreline, Washington, with his wife, Musarrat, and has two sons, Suhail and Ifran.

PRAMILA JAYAPAL was born in 1965 in Chennai, India, and grew up between Indonesia, Singapore, and India. She came to the United States in 1982 to attend Georgetown University, where she earned a bachelor's degree in English and economics. She went on to earn a master's degree in business administration from Northwestern University's Kellogg School of Management. From 1991 to 1995, she served as director of the Fund for Technology Transfer at the Program for Appropriate Technology in Health (PATH). In 1995, she was awarded a two-year fellowship from the Institute of Current World Affairs to live in villages and towns across India and write about her perspectives on modern Indian society in the context of development and social justice. Ms. Jayapal has provided consulting assistance to several international and domestic nonprofit social justice organizations and is the author of *Pilgrimage to India: A Woman Revisits Her Homeland*. She is a former board chair of Chaya, a nonprofit organization serving South Asian women and families in crisis, and is also a board trustee of the Institute of Current World Affairs. Today, she is an activist, writer, and founder of the Hate Free Zone Campaign of Washington (now called One America), a grassroots nonprofit organization that was created in November 2001 in response to the backlash against immigrant communities of color in the wake of 9/11. Prior to her experience in the social justice arena, she worked for several years in the private sector. She lives in Seattle, Washington with her husband, Steve, and has one son, Janak.

RAJNIKANT (RAJ) JOSHI was born in 1932 in Gwalior, India, and was raised in Allahabad, where his father was a university professor. He completed his early schooling there before moving to Washington, D.C., in 1946 when his father came to work for the United Nations Food and Agriculture program. As a young teenager, Mr. Joshi attended high school in Washington, D.C. Even though his parents moved on to a posting in Rome, Italy in 1951, he moved to Pullman, Washington, to attend Washington State University. He went on to the University of Washington to get his master's degree in geography in 1956 and a second master's degree in urban planning in 1960. While in Seattle, he met and married his wife, Irene. Irene went on to become the University of Washington's first South Asian studies librarian from 1970 to 2000. Throughout his career, Mr. Joshi worked in the urban planning field, first for local and state government and then as a consultant. At the age of forty-nine, Mr. Joshi joined the Peace Corps and spent a tour in the Philippines. He also spent fifteen years as a reservist for the Federal Emergency Management Agency, which took him to disaster sites around the country. He lives in Seattle, Washington, and has two daughters, Manisha and Elizabeth.

SAT KAPAHI was born near Lahore, Pakistan, where he completed his early schooling before his family left for India following Partition. The family settled in Mehrauli,

near Delhi, India. In 1952, Sat Kapahi arrived at the University of Louisiana for graduate school. Soon after finishing his degree, he moved to Seattle to take a job with the
Boeing Company in 1955, the same year that the first 707 airplane was delivered to
Pan-American Airlines. He was among the first Indians to be hired by Boeing. He spent
many years of his career as a field service engineer and traveled abroad on assignments,
eventually retiring from Boeing in 1991. He was involved with the classical music society, Ragamala, and since retiring has taken up playing the piano. He lives in Redmond,
Washington, and has two sons and one daughter.

DINESH KESKAR was born in 1954 in Rajkot, India. He grew up in Amaravati, in the
state of Maharashtra, where he completed his schooling. He received his bachelor's
degree in mechanical engineering from Visvesvaraya Regional College of Engineering,
where he was a Gold Medalist. He came to the United States in 1975 to attend the University of Cincinnati and completed his master's and doctorate degrees in aerospace
engineering. At the University of Cincinnati, he studied under famed American astronaut Dr. Neil Armstrong. After finishing his degree, he worked as a research associate in the Flight Dynamics and Control Division at NASA's Langley Research Center.
In 1980, he moved to Seattle to join the Boeing Company, where he has held senior
positions in engineering, marketing, and sales. Today he holds the dual positions of
vice president of Boeing International and president of Boeing India. In this role, he is
responsible for sales efforts in India and Nepal, including oversight of the Boeing India
office. He received his master's degree in business administration from City University
in Seattle in 1987 and attended the Berkeley Executive Program at the University of
California, Berkley, in 1994. Dr. Keskar has served on several national boards, including
the directors of the American Society of Engineers of Indian Origin, the Federation of
Indian Chambers of Commerce and Industry's civil aviation committee, the U.S.-India
Business Council and the International Society of Transport Aircraft Trading. He is
also a Fellow of the Royal Aeronautical Society and an Associate Fellow of the Ameri-
can Institute of Aeronautics and Astronautics. Today, he splits his time between Delhi,
India, and Renton, Washington, where he lives with his wife, Medha. He has one son,
Mahesh.

BHARTI KIRCHNER was born in 1940 in Kalimpong, near the Himalaya Mountains
in Northern India. She did most of her schooling in Calcutta and came to St. Louis,
Missouri, in 1962 as a graduate student, later teaching for two years at Southern Illinois
University. She lived and worked in Chicago before moving to San Francisco to work in
the burgeoning software industry in the late 1960s. She met and married her husband
there and they lived in Iran, Holland, and France before moving to Seattle in 1984. Mrs.
Kirchner gave up life as a software engineer and entered the publishing world in 1992.
Since then, she has written four novels, *Shiva Dancing, Darjeeling, Sharmila's Book*, and
Pastries: A Novel of Desserts and Discoveries, and four cookbooks—along with numerous articles and essays on food, travel, fitness, and lifestyle. A celebrated author and
speaker, she has won two Seattle Arts Commission literature grants and an Artist Trust
GAP grant. She lives in Seattle with her husband, Tom.

SHAILA KODE was born in 1947 and grew up in Belgaum, India. Her family moved to Mumbai in 1966, where she studied at Grant Medical College. She lived with her family in Goregaon while she fulfilled her father's dream of her becoming a doctor. Afterward, she spent two years as a physician in a rural primary health center in Ratanagari, until she moved to the Seattle area in 1974. After passing her Educational Commission for Foreign Medical Graduates (ECFMG) exams, she completed her medical residency at New York Methodist Hospital in Brooklyn. After finishing her residency, Dr. Kode joined the United States Army and moved back to the Pacific Northwest to work at the Madigan Army Medical Center, first on active duty and then as a civilian. She continues to work as a physician at both Madigan and Group Health Cooperative in Seattle, Washington. In her spare time, Dr. Kode is very involved with regional Marathi organizations and writes magazine articles in Marathi. She lives in Newcastle, Washington, and has three children, Tarul, Minal, and Vishal.

PREM KUMAR was born in 1945 and grew up in a small town in Punjab, India, where he received his early education. After he completed his master's degree in English at Punjab University, he came to the University of Idaho in 1970. In 1978, he earned a doctorate in English at Washington State University. He taught English and humanities at Washington State University, the University of Miami, and Colorado State University until 1986, when he joined the Boeing Company as a technical editor, thinking that it would be a temporary assignment. However, over twenty years later, he is still working at Boeing. In 1994, Dr. Kumar cofounded the Indian American Political Advocacy Council (IAPAC), which is an organization intended to give greater attention to the concerns of the Indian subcontinent within mainstream American politics. In 2000, Dr. Kumar set up the Indian American Education Foundation (IAEF) as a grassroots, voluntary effort to help educate the mainstream American public about the Indian American community. The IAEF's mission is to raise awareness about the plight of children in India with disabilities, to campaign against discrimination toward and segregation of the disabled, and to increase educational opportunities for marginalized populations. Dr. Kumar lives in Kirkland, Washington, with his wife, Swarn, and has one daughter, Rashmi.

AMY LALY was born in Jhansi, India, in 1947. Shortly after the partition of India, she moved to Mumbai with her parents and three siblings. She started her undergraduate education at the University of Bombay and then migrated to the United States to complete her education. She came to Portland, Oregon, in 1966 to attend Portland State University and completed her master's degree in business administration. She moved to Seattle from Portland and after working at the Bon Marche and United Way of King County, she joined the Boeing Company and worked there for over twenty-five years until her retirement. Starting with her student days in Portland and through her time in Seattle, Amy Laly was closely involved with the civil rights and women's rights movements. She remains an avid and passionate champion of social justice. She also has a deep interest in Indian cinema and music. She is often called upon by local organizations to speak on the histories and nuances of Indian film. She has long been involved with the Seattle International Film Festival and the Langston Hughes African American Film Festival. She is also an accomplished documentary filmmaker and made two films in the 1990s: *Ballad of the Causeway* and *Jala Do—Torch the Pyre*. She resides in Seattle, Washington.

DEV R. MANHAS was born in 1937, grew up in the state of Jammu-Kashmir, and received his MBBS degree from Government Medical College Amritsar (Punjab). He came to the University of Washington in 1967 to complete his medical residency and subsequently specialized as a cardio-thoracic surgeon. He has been practicing in the Seattle area since his arrival and retired in March 2007 as a well-respected physician in his field. He is affiliated with the University of Washington Medical School as an adjunct professor, as well as with Swedish Hospital, and he is a member of several professional organizations. Dr. Manhas is one of the founding members of the Indian American Political Advocacy Council (IAPAC), a nonprofit organization registered in Washington State in 1994 to mobilize the Indian American community to participate in the American political process. Since 1999, Dr. Manhas has been associated with the Hindu Temple and Cultural Center, Bothell, as a board member, and he was instrumental in finalizing the fundraising efforts and inauguration of the temple. Dr. Manhas lives on Mercer Island, Washington, with his wife, Asha. He has a son, Subeer, and two daughters, Davita and Angeli.

RAJINDER (RAJ) SINGH MANHAS was born in 1948 in the Punjab province of India. He grew up in a very large and close-knit joint family, just after the partition of India and Pakistan. He spent his childhood and completed his schooling in that area before moving to Chandigarh to join the Punjab Engineering College, where he majored in aeronautical engineering. He came to Seattle in 1973 to study at the University of Washington. After completing his master's degree in industrial engineering, he began a successful career in the banking industry and worked over the next seventeen years at Security Pacific Bank Northwest and Rainier National Bank. In 1993, Raj Manhas switched career paths and joined the public sector and became director of facilities maintenance and development for the Seattle Department of Parks and Recreation. He went on to serve as the deputy superintendent of the Seattle Water Department and eventually as the director of field operations for Seattle Public Utilities. He joined Seattle Public Schools in 2001 as chief operating officer. He was appointed interim superintendent and later superintendent in 2003. He retired from his position in July 2007. He lives in Lake Forest Park, Washington, with his wife, Asha, and has one son, Amitoz, and one daughter, Simran.

ALOK MATHUR was born in 1952 in Delhi, India. After he finished his schooling in Delhi, he worked for Escorts Motorcycle Company. In 1977, he migrated to the United States along with his brother and parents. A year later, he moved from Washington, D.C., to Seattle to work for the Boeing Company. In 1987, Mr. Mathur earned a master's of business administration from City College in Seattle. After his degree, he switched jobs within Boeing to work in the Customer Engineering Department. Mr. Mathur has been very active with the Indian Association of Western Washington and was president of the organization in the mid-1980s. He and his wife have also been involved with the Indo-American Friendship Forum and the construction of the Hindu Temple and Cultural Center in Bothell, Washington. In his spare time, he enjoys biking, swimming, and traveling. He lives in Federal Way, Washington, with his wife, Anjali, and has three sons, Sulabh, Salil, and Shikher.

SYED RIZWAN NASAR was born in 1966 in Karachi, Pakistan, where he lived with his parents and seven siblings and completed his early schooling. He began his bachelor's degree at the University of Karachi, but then moved to East Lansing, Michigan, to attend Michigan State University in 1985. After completing his bachelor's degree in advertising, he earned a master's degree in business administration and went into marketing and communications. He worked for McCann-Erikson and was one of the orchestrators of Coca-Cola's marketing campaign in South Asia. Today, Mr. Nasar consults with various companies, including Microsoft. He also runs a production company that makes television commercials, documentaries, and short movies. He is a board member of the Pakistan Association of Greater Seattle and has been involved in the Pakistani community for numerous years. He was one of the leaders in relief efforts after Pakistan suffered an earthquake in 2005. He is the editor of the local Pakistani newspaper *Pakbaan*. In his spare time Rizwan Nasar enjoys the great outdoors, sings, listens to music, and, if time permits, produces and directs movies. He lives in Sammamish, Washington, with his wife, Shahina, and has a daughter, Anushey.

ZAKIR PARPIA was born in 1948 in Mumbai, India. After completing his bachelor's degree in engineering and working in the construction industry in India, he came to Pullman, Washington, to pursue his master's degree in civil engineering from Washington State University, where he graduated magna cum laude. After starting his own company in Spokane, Washington, he, his wife, and their children moved to western Washington in 1989. Today he is the founder and president of Himalaya Homes, Inc. In his time as a builder, Mr. Parpia has earned the respect of his peers in the building trade, as evidenced by the numerous awards he has received, such as Builder of the Year for Washington State in 1986 and Builder of the Year for King and Snohomish Counties in 1992. Most recently he was honored for his years of service by being inducted into the first class of the Master Builder's Hall of Fame. His long record of community involvement includes numerous offices held in state and national building organizations and he served as president of the Master Builders Association for King and Snohomish Counties in 1997. He lives in Kirkland, Washington, with his wife, Chitra, and has three children, Zarina, Aliza, and Raheem.

JAMAL RAHMAN was born in 1950 in Chapai Nawabganj, Bangladesh. His father was a diplomat for East Pakistan and later Bangladesh; as a result, Mr. Rahman grew up traveling the world. He came to Eugene, Oregon, in 1970 to study at the University of Oregon and completed a master's degree at the University of California, Berkeley, in politics, economics, and sociology before deciding to live in Egypt and France, where he devoted himself to studies of Sufism. After a brief stint in Canada, he returned to the

Seattle area. In 1990, he decided to pursue his passion for interfaith community building. Today, Mr. Rahman is co-minister at Interfaith Community Church in Seattle, co-
host of Interfaith Talk Radio, and adjunct faculty at Seattle University. He is the author
of *The Fragrance of Faith: The Enlightened Heart of Islam,* and a co-author of *Out of
Darkness into Light: Spiritual Guidance in the Qu'ran with Reflections from Jewish and
Christian Sources.* He lives in Seattle, Washington.

RAO REMALA was born in 1949 in Talagada deevi Kothapalem, a small village in the
state of Andhra Pradesh, India, where he lived with his parents and four brothers and
two sisters. He finished high school in a neighboring village and graduated with highest honors from REC Warangal College, India, in 1972. He earned a master's degree
in computer science from IIT Kanpur and was a Ph.D. candidate at the University of
Washington. While in India, he worked at DCM data products and for Hindu Computers Limited, which developed India's first microcomputer in 1978. Mr. Remala came to
Seattle in 1981 to join Microsoft and was amongst the company's first fifty hires. He
was also the first Indian hired and wrote the very first line of code of Windows (then
called Interface Manager). He architected, developed, and managed such Microsoft
flagship products as Basic, Cobol Compiler, Windows 1.0, Windows 2.0, OLE 1.0, OLE
2.0, Office 95, and Office 97 and held a range of positions in his twenty-three-year-
long career there. He retired from Microsoft in 2004. Since retirement, he travels the
world and funds a few charitable projects, including a foundation named after his family, which is building an eye hospital in his village in Andhra Pradesh. He lives Medina,
Washington, with his wife, Satya, and has two daughters, Srilakshmi and Srilata.

NAJMA RIZVI was born in Dhaka, Bangladesh, in 1938. She came to the United States
with her husband in 1959 as a student at Cornell University and completed her master's
degree in geography at the University of Florida. She moved to Bangladesh to teach and
live there until returning to the United States in 1969 as a permanent resident. After
immigrating, Dr. Rizvi went on to complete her Ph.D. in anthropology from the University of California, Los Angeles. She has extensive teaching and research experience
promoting cross-cultural understanding both in the United States and abroad. Her
research has focused on hunger, malnutrition, and infectious disease in Third World
countries and she has worked as a consultant to various organizations such as UNI-
CEF and the International Center for Diarrheal Diseases Research in Bangladesh. Her
research findings have been published in professional journals and books, and she has
presented papers in international meetings, seminars, and workshops. She moved to
Seattle in 1995 to teach in the Pacific Northwest. She splits her time between Los Angeles and Bangladesh since retiring from North Seattle Community College in 2007. She
has two children, Nahid and Navin.

PRASANNA MANJULA SAMARAWICKRAMA was born in 1964 in Colombo, Sri
Lanka, and spent most of his childhood in the region. While attending high school, he
won a scholarship through the American Field Service program to attend a year of high
school in the United States. He then spent a year living in Oregon. After returning to Sri

Lanka, he attended Ananda College in Colombo and majored in physics. After college, he joined Air Lanka as a flight attendant. While working for the national airline for five years, he traveled much of the world. After saving enough to return to the United States for college, he moved to the West Coast and attended Southern Oregon State University and then Oregon State University to work on his Ph.D. in nuclear physics. Just prior to finishing his degree, he was hired by Microsoft and moved to Washington State. He has been with Microsoft since then and is a principle group program manager working on Windows Mobile. Prasanna Samarawickrama lives in Woodinville, Washington, with his wife, Anne, and has two sons, Tyler and Kyle.

JAFAR (JEFF) HUSSAIN SIDDIQUI was born in Peshawar in the Northwest Frontier Province of Pakistan shortly after the partition of India and Pakistan. Growing up in a military family, he lived in various parts of Pakistan and completed his university education in engineering at Sind University in Jamshoro. After receiving his degree, he decided to apply to schools in the United States to pursue his master's degree in engineering. He arrived at the University of Washington in 1974 and earned his master's degree in industrial engineering. While at the University of Washington, Mr. Siddiqui was involved with student politics and worked with organizations like the Foundation for International Understanding through Students (FIUTS), the Commission for International Students, and the Pakistan Student Association. After graduating, he moved to England to work with the Coca-Cola Company, where he put together a recycling program that was replicated all over the United Kingdom and parts of Europe. One of his energy-conservation projects won the Queen's Commendation Certificate. He returned to the United States and married his long-distance sweetheart, Kathy Albia. He is also involved with various interfaith and community organizations and speaks on issues of importance to the Muslim community and for other social justice causes. He is currently a successful real estate agent. He lives in Lynnwood, Washington, with his wife, Kathy, and has two children, Heather and Arman.

BALRAJ SOKKAPPA was born in 1930 in Madurai, India. He grew up on a hospital compound run by American missionaries, where his father was the treasurer of the American mission. Although he was interested in medicine, he was admitted to the engineering track at the University of Madras, where he completed his college education. After graduating, he taught in the same engineering college where he received his degree. In 1954, he applied for graduate school in the United States. He came initially to Ohio State University, but then transferred to the University of California, Berkeley, where he completed his master's degree in electrical engineering. Soon after completing his degree, Dr. Sokkappa took a job with Seattle City Light and moved to Washington State, where he completed his Ph.D. in electrical engineering at the University of Washington. Dr. Sokkappa moved to Boston briefly to work for the MITRE Corporation, where he worked on Air Force transport systems. He went on to another lab affiliated with the Massachusetts Institute of Technology and worked on the Apollo space project resulting in the 1969 lunar landing. After that, he worked for the Federal Aviation Administration through MITRE and traveled to various countries around the world. In 1978, he was selected to be a Congressional Fellow through the Institute of Electrical and Electronics Engineers. After retiring in 2000, he and his wife moved back to the Pacific Northwest. He lives in Sequim, Washington, and has a son and a daughter.

VIJAY VASHEE was born in 1950 in Bulawayo, Zimbabwe. His family is originally from Gujarat, India, but had been living in Africa since his grandfather migrated there and he grew up in a large community of Gujarati merchants and settlers. He completed his early schooling in Zimbabwe before moving to India in 1969 to attend the Indian Institute of Technology, Mumbai, to study electrical engineering. After completing his degree, he came to the United States in 1974 to attend Cornell University, where he earned his master's degree in biomedical engineering. Mr. Vashee enrolled in the University of Chicago and pursued a master's degree in business administration before moving on to work for Abbott Labs Diagnostic Division in 1977. Soon after that, he moved to Portland, Oregon. After spending a few years in Portland, he was recruited by the Microsoft Corporation in 1982 and worked on MS DOS (Microsoft Disk Operating System). During his time at Microsoft, he worked on several top projects and drove the acquisition and development of the PowerPoint division. Vijay Vashee continues to be a major influence in the technology industry as an investor, and he co-founded the Seattle chapter of The Indus Entrepreneurs. Today, he and his wife regularly contribute funds and time to several national and Seattle-area charitable organizations. He lives with his wife, Sita, in Mercer Island, Washington, and has three sons, Ajay, Nilesh, Nikhil.

PADMINI VASISHTH was born in 1928 in Lahore, Pakistan, where her family lived until the partition of India and Pakistan. They moved to Simla in East Punjab, and then settled in Delhi. She met her husband, Ramesh, while studying chemistry at Punjab University, where she completed her master's degree. After working for the Indian Institute of Science in Bangalore and then as a research scholar for Central Chemical Labs in Hyderabad, she and Ramesh moved to Canada in 1954, where they lived for a year and a half before moving to the Seattle. They joined the University of Washington, where they were both graduate students, and Padmini Vasishth completed her master's degree in organic chemistry in 1960. After graduating, her husband took a job with Reichhold and they traveled the world on assignments, settling in Canada briefly. After that, she and Ramesh formed their own company, Aditi, where they specialized in stabilizing wood. In 1985, Ramesh was invited to the University of Mississippi as a research scientist. She joined him there and went back to school, eventually earning her Ph.D. from the University of Mississippi in Wood Science and Technology in 1993. Dr. Vasishth splits her time between Redmond, Washington, and India, and has a son, Karan, and a daughter, Chandini.

SANTOSH WAHI was born in Northern India in the 1940s and was the daughter of an Indian diplomat. Because of her father's postings, she had lived in Delhi, Holland, and New York City by the time she graduated college. She studied chemistry and earned her bachelor's and master's degrees from the Birla Institute of Technology and Institute of Sciences before moving to New York City with her family in 1968. She eventually went back to India, where she met and married her husband, Pran Wahi, in 1970. After getting married, the Wahis moved first to Boston and then to the Pacific Northwest in 1973. Santosh Wahi became involved with the fledgling Indian community, teaching children Hindi and Indian history for twenty years. She shared her culture in local public schools, volunteered at the Seattle Asian Art Museum, and coordinated events that promoted Indian traditions. She also works in area hospitals, courts, and school systems as a language interpreter. She and her husband are longtime members of and contributors to the India Association of Western Washington and People for Progress in India. She lives in Mercer Island, Washington, with her husband and has two daughters, Charu and Anshu.

NOTES

PREFACE

1. Richa Nagar and Amanda Lock Swarr, "Introduction: Theorizing Transnational Feminist Praxis" in *Critical Transnational Feminist Praxis*, ed. Swarr and Nagar (Albany, NY: SUNY Press, 2009), 14.

INTRODUCTION: SITUATING STORIES

1. We use the term Pacific Northwest to refer to the states of Washington, Oregon, and Idaho, although during the time of the actual interviews, the narrators were all located in the greater Seattle area. The stories they tell of their journeys to Seattle also involve other locations in the Pacific Northwest, such as university towns in Oregon, Washington, and Idaho. Several of our narrators have connections to Canada and the proximity of Vancouver, just two hours from Seattle, makes British Columbia an important site as well in our conceptualization of the region. Thus, while our project is primarily circumscribed to the greater Seattle region, the Pacific Northwest as a site of imagination crosses the boundaries between Canada and the United States.

2. In general "South Asia" refers to those countries primarily located on the Indian subcontinent: India, Pakistan, Bangladesh, Nepal, Sri Lanka, Bhutan, and the Maldives. Though these countries have different religious, cultural, linguistic, political, economic, and social histories, South Asia has been solidified as a category in the study of international relations and the field of "area studies" more broadly in the United States. Scholars such as Tani Barlow in "Founding Positions," *Postcolonial Studies* 3, no. 1 (1999): 19–29 argue that current formations of area studies evoked in American universities have legacies in Cold War–era attempts to increase knowledge about particular regions to promote U.S. military and economic interests. Nalini Natarajan, in "South Asian Area Studies in Transatlantic Dialogue," *Comparative Studies of South Asia, Africa and the Middle East* 27, no. 3 (2007): 591–600, builds on this point and argues that the influx of South Asian professionals and intellectuals to North America in the 1960s worked to further solidify the category as both a regional marker and a wider imaginary that includes a broad range of actors associated with the culture and history of the

region. Thus, the legacies of colonialism and still-shifting national boundaries (as well as lingering territorial disputes and historical linkages that complicate clear boundaries between nation-states) make the classification of South Asian countries under a single umbrella possible.

At the same time, the South Asian communities residing in the United States are internally variegated and continue to be differentiated thanks to contemporary events and geopolitics. Therefore, we use the term "South Asian" to represent the geographic region, but also as a political marker of a pan-ethnicity, which binds together a diversity of people. The oral histories profiled in this book require us to carefully use the term as a marker of new community constellations that are not only rooted in South Asia but also reconfigured in particular ways in North America.

3 Oral history projects use the term narrator, rather than interview subject or participant, because the narrator is an equal participant in the interview and is telling his or her story through his or her own reflections.

4 For an extensive history of this early migration, see Joan Jensen's *Passage from India: Asian Indian Americans in North America* (New Haven, CT: Yale University Press, 1988).

5 The narrators' fluency in English is both a product of colonial and postcolonial state policies and a marker of class and education. We discuss these confluences in chapter 3.

6 Oral histories have been a crucial tool in documenting the formation of Asian American communities. See Eric C. Wat's *The Making of a Gay Asian Community: An Oral History of Pre-AIDS Los Angeles* (Lanham, MD: Rowman and Littlefield Publishers, 2002) and Kenneth Kaname Takemoto, Paul Howard Takemoto, and Alice Takemoto's *Nisei Memories: My Parents Talk about the War Years* (Seattle: University of Washington Press, 2006).

7 Sandhya Shukla's *India Abroad: Diasporic Cultures of Postwar America and England* (Princeton, NJ: Princeton University Press, 2002); Sunaina Maira's *Desis in the House: Indian American Youth Culture in New York City* (Philadelphia, PA: Temple University Press, 2002); and S. Mitra Kalita's *Suburban Sahibs: Three Immigrant Families and Their Passage from India to America* (New Brunswick, NJ: Rutgers University Press, 2003) represent just a small sample of the growing archive of ethnographic and journalistic accounts of South Asians living in the United States.

8 Dan Ouellette, "South Asians' Growing American Clout," *Adweek*, http://teens. adweek.com/aw/content_display/special-reports/other-reports/e3i5e732e045deaa-ba3b04b8fd2ebbf81aa; Allied Media Corporation, "South Asian Demographics," http://www.allied-media.com/southasian/south%20asian%20demographics.html (accessed May 24, 2010).

9   This survey information is available online through the nonprofit Northwest Heritage Resources, http://www.northwestheritageresources.org/Essays/Indian_ American_essay.pdf (accessed June 4, 2010).

10 Allied Media Corporation, "South Asian Demographics."

11 "Midnight's children" is a phrase derived from Salman Rushdie's acclaimed 1981 novel by the same name. The term is used broadly to refer to the generation of Indians/Pakistanis brought up in the immediate post-independence era. See Salman Rushdie, *Midnight's Children* (New York: Knopf, 1981).

12 Among South Asians, questions of nation are always mediated by linguistic, regional, and caste markers. So an individual might identify as Indian or Pakistani and as Goan Christian or Baluchi simultaneously. The sources used here demonstrate the ambivalent nature of national identification, particularly when individuals must reinvent themselves in a new location, in which case the nation-state becomes the primary site of affiliation for individuals who are transformed into immigrants. Because of these intersecting axes, we focus on the importance of regional forces in the creation of this particular pan-South Asian community.

13 For information about the history of the Bengali Language Movement, also known as the Language Movement, see Umar Badruddin, *Language Movement in East Bengal* (Dhaka: Jatiya Grontha Prakashan, 2000). The movement played a major role in the buildup to the Bangladesh Liberation War, which led to the creation of the Bangladesh nation in 1971. India was central in this struggle and fought against what was then known as "West Pakistan" for the liberation and conversion of "East Pakistan" into Bangladesh.

1. "FINDING TRACES OF OUR EXISTENCE HERE"

1   University of Washington Libraries, "New, Thinking, Agile, and Patriotic: 'Hindu' Students at the University of Washington, 1908–1915," http://www.lib.washington. edu/exhibits/southasianstudents/index.html (accessed May 27, 2010).

2   Kartar Dhillon, "The Parrot's Beak," in *Growing Up Asian American: Stories of Childhood, Adolescence and Coming of Age in America, from the 1800s to the 1900s, by 32 Asian American writers*, ed. Maria Hong (New York: Avon Books, 1993), 275–84.

3   The term "Indian" used before 1947 refers to people from South Asia and encompasses modern day India, Pakistan, and Bangladesh.

4   Indians were paid $2.00 per hour while the white workers' wages were $2.22 per hour.

5   The Indian immigrants were often referred to as "Hindus" or "Hindoos" in the

local press although the men were of diverse religious persuasions. The word "Hindu" is often spelled "Hindoo" in early-twentieth-century documents. When we quote such sources we keep the spelling used in the source for historical accuracy; otherwise, we use the more contemporary and standard spelling, "Hindu." We must note here, however, that Hindoo/Hindu is only sometimes in early documents referring to a particular faith; more often it is synonymous with Indian without any concern for the diversity of religious beliefs in India.

6   For detailed accounts of the Bellingham riots, see Joan M. Jensen, *Passage from India: Asian Indian Immigrants in North America* (New Haven, CT: Yale University Press, 1988) and the film *Present in All That We Do*, Seattle Civil Rights and Labor History Project, University of Washington, http://depts.washington.edu/civilr/bham_history.htm (accessed June 15, 2011).

7   The University of California at Berkeley provides an excellent online exhibit that documents the history of South Asians in California. See "Echoes of Freedom: South Asian Pioneers in California, 1899–1965," Center for South Asia Studies, University of California at Berkeley, http://www.lib.berkeley.edu/SSEAL/echoes/echoemls.html (accessed May 27, 2010).

8   There are notable exceptions, however; for examples of pre–World War Two histories of South Asian immigration, see Joan M. Jensen's *A Passage from India: Asian Indian Immigrants in North America* (New Haven, CT: Yale University Press, 1988) and Harold A. Gould's *Sikhs, Swamis, Students, and Spies: The India Lobby in the United States, 1900–1946* (Thousand Oaks, CA: Sage, 2006). Notable among the studies that focus on post-1965 immigration are Rajini Srikanth's *The World Next Door: South Asian Literature and the Idea of America* (Philadelphia: Temple University Press, 2005), Priya Agarwal's *Passage from India: Post 1965 Indian Immigrants and Their Children* (New Delhi: Yuvati, 1991), and S. Bhatia's *American Karma: Race, Culture, and Identity in the Indian Diaspora* (New York: New York University Press, 2007).

9   See Will Irwin's piece in *Colliers* and Herman Scheffhauer's "Tide of Turbans" in *The Forum*, June 1910. University of Western Washington, Woodring College of Education, "Asian American Curriculum and Research Project," http://www.wce.wwu.edu/Resources/AACR/documents.shtml.

10 For a discussion of how South Asians became emblematic of anti-immigrant sentiment along the West Coast and across the nation, see Erika Lee and Judy Yung, *Angel Island: Immigrant Gateway to America* (New York: Oxford University Press, 2010): 145–71.

11 Jensen, *Passage from India*, 15.

12 "The 1907 Bellingham Riots in Historical Context," Seattle Civil Rights and Labor History Project, University of Washington, http://depts.washington.edu/civilr/bham_history.htm (accessed June 15, 2011).

13 Ibid.

14 The contours of this debate can be found in the primary documents available in the online archive of the Woodring College of Education. See Asian American Curriculum and Research Project, Woodring College of Education, Western Washington University, Bellingham, http://www.wce.wwu.edu/Resources/AACR/documents.shtml (accessed May 27, 2010).

15 In the racial discourse at the time, Indians were viewed as being of Aryan stock and so more akin to European immigrants than immigrants from East Asia. However, the decision in *United States v. Bhagat Singh Thind* case (1923) negated the Aryan theory of ethnicity put forth by Thind to make his claim for U.S. citizenship. The Supreme Court noted that Thind was not white as was understood in the popular discourse (as opposed to social scientific discourse) of the time and denied his claim for U.S. citizenship.

16 See online documents of the Woodring College of Education at Western Washington University, http://www.wce.wwu.edu/Resources/AACR/documents/bellingham/main/1.htm.

17 From the online documents of Woodring College of Education at Western Washington University, http://www.wce.wwu.edu/Resources/AACR/documents/east-indian-1907-10-12-colliers/main/1.htm (accessed May 27, 2010).

18 From the Woodring College of Education online archive, "East Indian Documents—Everett," http://www.wce.wwu.edu/Resources/AACR/documents/east-indian-everett/index.htm (accessed May 27, 2010).

19 "100 Years after Riot Coverage: Our Apology," *Bellingham Herald*, September 2, 2007, http://www.bellinghamherald.com/315/v-print/story/169787.html (accessed June 20, 2010).

20 "Gadar," which means revolution, is spelled variously as "Ghadr," "Ghadar," or "Gadar." We use "Gadar" as our preferred spelling and abide by alternative spellings when citing outside sources.

21 For an overview of Indian students who studied at the University of Washington, see the online exhibit "New, Thinking, Agile, and Patriotic: 'Hindu' Students at the University of Washington, 1908–1915," http://www.lib.washington.edu/exhibits/southAsianStudents/index.html.

22 Jensen, *Passage from India*, 21.

23 Though less extensive, the agricultural and working-class communities have also left records of their experiences. Ved Prakash Vatuk and Sylvia Vatuk have gathered the folk songs (many of which were in Punjabi) of Indian farming communities in California. These songs were regularly performed as a way to bring the community together to fight British colonialism in South Asia and racism in America. See Ved Prakash and Sylvia Vatuk, "Protest Songs of East Indians on

the West Coast, U.S.A," in *Thieves in My House: Four Studies in Indian Folklore of Protest and Change* (Varanasi: Vishwavidyalaya Prakashan, 1969), 63–80.

24 Maia Ramnath, "Two Revolutions: The Ghadar Movement and India's Radical Diaspora, 1913–1918," *Radical History Review* 92 (Spring 2005): 7–30.

25 Ibid., 9.

26 Ibid., 8.

27 For a detailed discussion of the student radicals and activists, especially Har Dayal and Taraknath Das, see Harold Gould, *Sikhs, Swamis, Students, and Spies* (Thousand Oaks, CA: Sage, 2006).

28 See Kartar Dhillon, "The Parrot's Beak," in *Growing Up Asian American*, ed. Maria Hong (New York: Avon Books, 1993), 275–84; Kartar Dhillon, "Astoria Revisited and Autobiographical Notes," http://www.sikhpioneers.org/P1astoria.html; Kartar Dhillon and Ayesha Gill, "Witness to the Gadar Era," http://www.sikhpioneers. org/p5witne.htm; Satyadeva Parivrajak, *A Glimpse of America*, unpublished translation by Raj Joshi; *Free Hindusthan*, in "New, Thinking, Agile, and Patriotic."

29 This raises the question of whether early South Asian students were part of the South Asian diaspora or temporary sojourners. We suggest here that the distinction between sojourner and immigrant or diasporic subject relies too much on individual choice and does not recognize that individual choice is circumscribed by social, political, and legal definitions of immigrants and citizens. So rather than distinguish between sojourner and diasporic subject, we examine the writings of these early South Asians as documents that articulate the lived experience of dislocation. In those writings we see the emergence of diasporic subjectivity determined not by states but by individuals and the communities which they create.

30 University of Washington, "New, Thinking, Agile, and Patriotic."

31 We are very grateful to Raj Joshi, one of our narrators and the spouse of Irene Joshi, who began this oral history project, for sharing with us his translation of this book.

32 Satyadeva's narrative is not chronological and there is occasional confusion about dates and places. Some of this confusion is part of the narrative itself and some results because only portions of the text have been translated. The other chapters of the narrative are summarized by the translator.

33 Satyadeva's narrative contains other stories about his travels, but both the text's translator and we have chosen to keep our discussion to the matters involving the Pacific Northwest.

34 Robert W. Rydell, John E. Findling, and Kimberly Pelle, *Fair America: World's Fairs in the United States* (Washington, D.C.: Smithsonian Institution Press, 2000).

35 Ibid., 9.

36 For a detailed discussion of the deployment of racial subjectivities in the AYPE, see Robert Rydell's chapter "The Expositions in Portland and Seattle" in *All the World's a Fair: Visions of Empire at American International Expositions, 1876–1916* (Chicago: University of Chicago Press, 1984), 184–207.

37 Satyadeva Parivrajak, *Glimpse of America*, 12.

38 Ibid., 17.

39 Ibid., 18.

40 Nard Jones, *Seattle* (Garden City, NY: Doubleday, 1972), 313.

41 Satyadeva, *Glimpse of America*, 22.

42 Ibid.

43 The Swadeshi movement was a broad political resistance movement that swept the Indian subcontinent in the first decade of the twentieth century. In response to Lord Curzon's plan to divide the province of Bengal (a move that anticipates the 1947 partition of the region), Indian nationalists launched a movement to boycott British goods and to use only Indian-made or "swadeshi" products. Their plan was to cripple the British economy through the boycott and to build up Indian self-reliance. Gandhi's later political strategy of embracing "Khaddar" or Indian handloom fabric that he produced himself was a continuation of this political philosophy.

44 The Anusilan Samiti, or the "self-culture association," was an anti-British movement started in Bengal that became the primary revolutionary group in the area in the beginning of the twentieth century. The organization advocated armed revolt against British imperialism.

45 Tapan K. Mukherjee, *Taraknath Das: Life and Letters of a Revolutionary in Exile* (Calcutta: National Council for Education, Jadavpur University, 1997).

46 Ibid., 6.

47 Ibid.

48 The Vedanta Society was founded in New York by Swami Vivekananda in 1894 and has spawned several organizations and groups dedicated to the study and practice of the Vedic texts known as the Upanishads. The Vedanta Society promotes the teachings of Sri Ramakrishna Paramhama, an Indian saint and mystic.

49 Bhagat Singh Thind challenged U.S. immigration and naturalization laws that prevented Asians from obtaining citizenship. Following the Ozawa decision of 1922, in which the Supreme Court had ruled that the white race was synonymous with people identified as Caucasian, Thind applied for citizenship in Oregon. He

claimed that social scientists of the time had accepted that Indians were Aryans who originated in the Caucasus Mountains region and not akin to the people originating from East Asia. Therefore, as Caucasian, Indians should be considered white and eligible for citizenship. The government repudiated the social science argument and insisted that the "white" race should be interpreted according to how common people understood the term. The Supreme Court unanimously supported the government interpretation in the Thind case and ruled against his application for citizenship. For a history of the naturalization and citizenship debates, see Jensen, *Passage from India*, 246–69.

50 Mukherjee, *Taraknath Das*, 40.

51 *Hindusthan* is a reference to India, as defined by the British Empire in the early twentieth century. See *Free Hindusthan* in "New, Thinking, Agile, and Patriotic."

52 *Free Hindusthan.*

53 Ibid.

54 For more information on Das and his political activities, see Mukherjee's *Taraknath Das* and Gould's *Sikhs, Swamis, Students, and Spies*.

55 Jogesh C. Misrow, "East Indian Immigration on the Pacific Coast" (master's thesis, Stanford, CA, May 1915), 31.

56 Ibid., 32.

57 Ibid., 64.

58 Ibid., 37–38.

59 We examine Kartar Dhillon's memoirs, including an essay titled "Parrot's Beak," an article called "Astoria Revisited and Autobiographical Notes," and an interview she gave to Dr. Ayesha Gill.

60 According to Huping Ling, in 1901–1911, of the 5,800 South Asians to enter the United States, 109 were women. *Voices of the Heart: Asian American Women on Immigration, Work, and Family* (Kirksville, MO: Truman State University Press, 2007), xxxi.

61 The life of this community in California is richly documented in the collections of the University of California at Berkeley.

62 Erika S. Andersen, *Turbans* (Different Drum Productions, 2000).

63 In *Strangers from a Different Shore*, Takaki notes that in 1914 in California, women represented 0.24 percent of the Asian Indian population of 5,000. The reasons for this population disparity were many, according to Takaki, including the farmers' financial inability to transport wives and children from India and the Immigration Law of 1917 which prevented Indian men from bringing their wives to the United

States. Takaki notes that in 1909, the Immigration Commission surveyed 464 Indians and showed that of this group, 21 were widowed, 228 were single, and 215 were married and had left behind families in India (308–9). Ronald Takaki, *Strangers from a Different Shore: A History of Asian America* (New York: Penguin, 1991).

64 "Astoria Revisited and Autobiographical Notes," http://www.sikhpioneers.org/P1astoria.html (accessed February 10, 2009).

65 Ibid.

66 "Dr. Bhagat Singh Thind," http://bhagatsinghthind.com/hindooalley.html (accessed June 5, 2010).

67 Dhillon,"Parrot's Beak," 275–83.

68 Ibid., 282.

69 Kartar Dhillon and Ayesha Gill, "Witness to the Gadar Era," http://www.sikhpioneers.org/p5witne.htm.

70 For a detailed discussion of the origins of the Punjabi-Mexican community and the evolution of this community in present-day California, see Karen B. Leonard's *Making Ethnic Choices: California's Punjabi-Mexican Americans* (Philadelphia: Temple University Press, 1992)

2. ROOTS AND ROUTES

1 Minal Hajratwala, *Leaving India: My Family's Journey from Five Villages to Five Continents* (Boston: Houghton-Mifflin Harcourt, 2009).

2 The British Raj refers to the period between 1858 and 1947 during which the majority of the Indian subcontinent was under British colonial rule. The Raj included modern-day India, Pakistan, and Bangladesh and extended to Burma, Somaliland, and Singapore at various points in time. The countries of Nepal and Bhutan were recognized as independent states after fighting separate wars with Britain and, along with Sri Lanka (then Ceylon), were not considered part of the Raj. Sri Lanka was under the control of Britain from the early nineteenth century and after fighting for independence in the early twentieth century, it became the Democratic Republic of Ceylon in October 1947. The island was renamed Sri Lanka in 1972. Likewise, the Maldives was a British protectorate until it was granted independent status in 1965.

3 For a longer history of the partition of India and Pakistan, see Urvashi Butalia, *The Other Side of Silence: Voices from the Partition of India* (Durham, NC: Duke University Press, 1998); Mushirul Hasan, *India's Partition: Process, Strategy and Mobilization* (New Delhi: Oxford University Press, 2001); and Gyanendra Pandey, *Remembering Partition: Violence, Nationalism and History in India* (Cambridge: Cambridge University Press, 2002).

4   For a longer discussion of the creation of the NRI category, see Sareeta Amrute, "The 'New' Nonresidents of India: A Short History of the NRI," in *A New India? Critical Reflections on a Long Twentieth Century*, ed. Anthony D'Costa (London: Anthem Press, 2010), 127–50.

5   See Binod Khadria, *The Migration of Knowledge Workers: Second Generation Effects of India's Brain Drain* (Thousand Oaks, CA: Sage Publications, 1999). Khadria argues that South Asian nations started to rely on the remittances sent by foreign workers back to family members residing in their home countries, leading to a false sense of economic security even when national economies stagnated.

6   Burki and Swamy argue that South Asians disproportionately entered into new industries in the United States such as aerospace, electronics, and computers and worked in new services sectors such as software development and health care. They note, "since the new industries and services constitute the growth sector of the U.S. economy, it seems legitimate to conclude that without the scarce skills provided by the immigrants, the two sectors may not have grown as rapidly." Shahid Javed Burki and Subramaniam Swamy, "South Asian Migration to the United States: Demand and Supply Factors," *Economic and Political Weekly*, March 21, 1987, 513.

7   Sandipan Deb describes the role of pioneers such as Ashok Jhunjhunwala in the growth and development of the Indian state-run telecommunications company (Bharat Sanchar Nigam Ltd [BSNL]) in his book *The IITians: The Story of a Remarkable Indian Institution and How Its Alumni Are Reshaping the World* (New Delhi: Viking/Penguin, 2003). Other accounts credit technology titans such as Sam Pitroda, an entrepreneur and engineer who had migrated to the United States in the 1960s and then returned to India, for revolutionizing the telecommunication industry in India.

8   Mira Kamdar's memoir *Motiba's Tattoos* captures her father's experience with an American diet when he was a newly arrived student in the Pacific Northwest in 1949. A practicing Jain who was raised on strictly vegetarian cuisine, the young Prabhakar (Pete) Kamdar often had to make do with a vegetable or cheese sandwich as his regular dinner during the period in which America, as Kamdar writes, "was solid meat-and-potatoes country. It was a time of culinary innocence so profound that a new dish called 'pizza' had to be explained to the general public." Mira Kamdar, *Motiba's Tattoos: A Granddaughter's Journey into Her Indian Family's Past* (New York: Public Affairs, 2000), 131.

9   As Krishnendu Ray has noted in *The Migrant's Table: Meals and Memories in Bengali-American Households* (Philadelphia: University of Pennsylvania Press, 2004), food is a distinctive marker of ethnic identity for Indian immigrant groups. His study of the Bengali-American community reveals that *probashi* (immigrant) Bengali-Americans use rice and fish served during dinner as a means of demon-

strating that they are distinct *within* Indian American immigrant groups and to preserve a sense of cultural continuity against the broader non-Indian cultures in which they live. While many immigrants may think of food habits as traditional and unchanging, Ray carefully documents how migration within Bengal, changes in economic situations, and generational differences amongst immigrants all contribute to the transformation of eating and cooking practices. As Arjun Appadurai has suggested, something akin to a national cuisine has evolved in postcolonial India that is fostered by cookbooks written for and by middle-class housewives (see Arjun Appadurai, "How to Make a National Cuisine: Cookbooks in Contemporary India," *Comparative Studies in Society and History* 30 (1988): 3–24). The amalgamation of food cultures has unfolded in part because migration within and outside of South Asia has brought people into close contact with other ethnic groups, which has changed the idea of regional or ethnic-specific food traditions.

3. CREATING PROFESSIONAL CLASSES

1   See Nigel Crook, *The Transmission of Knowledge in South Asia: Essays on Education, Religion, History, and Politics* (Delhi: Oxford University Press, 1996); Philip G. Altbach, Denzil Saldanha, and Jeanne Drysdale Weiler, *Education in South Asia: A Select Annotated Bibliography* (New York: Garland, 1987); Craig Jeffrey, Patricia Jeffery, and Roger Jeffery, *Degrees without Freedom? Education, Masculinities, and Unemployment in North India* (Stanford, CA: Stanford University Press, 2008); Fauzia Shamim, "Trends, Issues and Challenges in English Language Education in Pakistan," *Asia Pacific Journal of Education* 28, no. 3 (2008): 235–49; and Syeda Rumnaz Imam, "English as a Global Language and the Question of Nation-building Education in Bangladesh," *Comparative Education* 41, no. 4 (2005): 471–86.

2   Thomas Babington Macaulay, "Minute on Indian Education, February 2, 1835," in *Postcolonialisms: Anthology of Cultural Theory and Criticism*, ed. Gaurav Desai and Surpiya Nair (New Brunswick, NJ: Rutgers University Press, 2005), 123.

3   Ibid., 124.

4   Ibid., 130.

5   Jawaharlal Nehru, *The Essential Writings of Jawaharlal Nehru*, vol. 2, ed. S. Gopal and Uma Iyengar (New Delhi: Oxford University Press, 2003), 516–17.

6   Ibid., 516.

7   Ibid., 516.

8   For a discussion of bilingual education in India, see Viniti Vaish, *Biliteracy and Globalization: English Language Education in India* (Clevedon, UK: Multilingual Matters, 2008).

9   Syeda Rumnaz Imam, "English as a Global Language and the Question of Nation

Building Education in Bangladesh," *Comparative Education* 41, no. 4 (2005): 471–86.

10 Ibid., 484.

11 According to Discovery Bangladesh, a government tourism website, there are eleven government universities and approximately twenty private universities in the country, which has a population of 158,570,535 people, http://www.discovery-bangladesh.com/meetbangladesh/education.html (accessed June 12, 2010).

12 Nehru, *Essential Writings*, 528–29.

13 See Sandeepan Deb, *The IITians: The Story of a Remarkable Indian Institution and How Its Alumni are Reshaping the World* (New Delhi: Penguin/Viking, 2004) for a history of the founding of the IITs.

14 Sangeeta Kamat, Ali Mir, Biju Mathew, "Producing Hi-tech: Globalization, the State and Migrant Subjects," *Globalisation, Societies, and Education* 2, no. 1 (2004): 5–23.

15 See Ahsan Abdullah, "Pakistan since Independence: A Historical Analysis," *Muslim World* 93 (2003): 351–72.

16 Amna Latif, "A Critical Analysis of School Enrollment and Literacy Rates of Girls and Women in Pakistan," *Educational Studies* 45 (2009): 424–39.

17 The first Asian student to receive a degree at an American university was Yung Wing of China, who graduated from Yale in 1854, according to Teresa Brawner Bevis and Christopher J. Lucas, *International Students in American Colleges and Universities: A History* (New York: Palgrave/Macmillan, 2007), 42.

18 Even during the period of aggressive exclusion of South Asians during the first decades of the twentieth century, students and those from wealthy families in India were readily admitted to the United States, and the stringent application of immigration restrictions affected Indian laborers disproportionately. See Erika Lee and Judy Yung, *Angel Island: Immigrant Gateway to America* (Oxford: Oxford University Press, 2010), 145–76.

19 Bevis and Lucas, *International Students*, 79.

20 Ibid., 114–15.

21 Ibid., 107.

22 William W. Hoffa, *A History of US Study Abroad: Beginnings to 1965* (Carlisle, PA: Forum on Education Abroad, 2000).

23 Bevis and Lucas, *International Students*, 118. Because the subcontinent had just been decolonized at this time, it is not clear if the numbers here refer to postcolonial India or to India and Pakistan.

24 According to Hazen and Albers, the State Department issued 65,000 international student visas in 1971 and 315,000 international student visas in 2000. In 2003, that number was 586,323. Helen Hazen and Heike Albers, "Visitor or Immigrant? International Students in the US," *Population, Space and Place* 12 (2006): 201–16. This boom in student arrivals followed very specific patterns: in 1969–1970, following the Immigration and Nationality Act, India had the second-largest number of foreign students at American universities (11,327); the only other South Asian nation in the top twenty-five nations sending students to the United States was Pakistan, with 1,576 (Bevis and Lucas, *International Students*, 165). In 2011, American universities have seen an 11 percent rise in foreign student enrollment; India has the second-largest number of students enrolled, and the total enrollment of Indian students at American universities has increased by 8 percent since 2007. "Admissions Offers for Foreign Students at U.S. Graduate Schools Climbs at a Faster Pace," *Chronicle of Higher Education*, August 16, 2011.

25 University of Washington Libraries, "New, Thinking, Agile, and Patriotic: 'Hindu' Students at the University of Washington, 1908–1915," http://www.lib.washington. edu/exhibits/southAsianStudents/index.html.

26 Bevis and Lucas, *International Students*, 166.

27 Of the 623,805 international students that came to the United States in 2007–2008, 94,563 came from India. The other South Asian nations with the highest number of students were Nepal, with 8,936 students in 2007–2008, and Pakistan, with 5,345 students that year. Institute for International Education, "Open Doors Online Report on International Education Exchange," http://www.opendoors. iienetwork.org/ (accessed June 12, 2010). In 2008, the University of Washington enrolled 2,970 students (on F visas), 1,125 exchange scholars (on J visas), and 555 H1-B workers in specialty occupations across its three campuses in Seattle, Bothell, and Tacoma. Of this total international student and scholar presence at the UW campuses, India had 198 students and 115 scholars (on the H and J visas). India, the only South Asian nation listed in the UW statistics on international students and scholars, ranked fourth for nation of origin behind China, Korea, and Taiwan. See University of Washington, "International Quick Stats," http://depts. washington.edu/reptreq/reports/quick-stats.pdf.

28 For a history of the Cosmopolitan Clubs, see Bevis and Lucas, *International Students*, 81–84.

4. ALL IN A DAY'S WORK

1 Vijay Prashad, *The Karma of Brown Folk* (Minneapolis: University of Minnesota Press, 2000).

2 See Sharmila Rudrappa, "Braceros and Techno-braceros: Guest Workers in the

United States and the Commodification of Low-wage and High-wage Labour," in *Transnational South Asians: the Making of a Neo-diaspora*, ed. Susan Koshy and R. Radhakrishnan (New York: Oxford University Press, 2008), 291–324, for a longer discussion of the overlap between the Bracero Program initiated in the 1950s and the H-1B program.

3 Margaret L. Usdansky and Thomas J. Espenshade, *The H-1B Visa Debate in Historical Perspective: The Evolution of U.S. Policy toward Foreign-Born Workers* (San Diego, CA: Center for Comparative Immigration Studies, 2000), 1–13.

4 U.S. Citizenship and Immigration Services, "H-1B Specialty Occupations, DOD Cooperative Research and Development Project Workers, and Fashion Models," Department of Homeland Security, http://www.uscis.gov/portal/site/uscis/menu-item.eb1d4c2a3e5b9ac89243c6a7543f6d1a/?vgnextoid=73566811264a3210VgnVCM1 00000b92ca60aRCRD&vgnextchannel=73566811264a3210VgnVCM100000b92ca6 0aRCRD.

5 H-1B visa holders can sponsor their spouses and biological children under the age of twenty-one to accompany them to the United States on the H-4 family reunification visa. However, an H-4 visa holder's immigration status is dependent on the H-1B visa holder; if that person loses her job or returns to her home country, the H-4 visa holders would lose their immigration status.

6 The Family Reunification Act was not intended to open new channels of labor migration, as Chandan Reddy notes in "Asian Diasporas, Neoliberalism, and Family: Reviewing the Case for Homosexual Asylum in the Context of Family Rights," *Social Text* 23, no. 3–4 (2005): 101–120. Reddy argues that "while immigrants are recruited by the persistence of entry-level jobs in the services, industrial, and informal sectors of New York, the federal government continues to recruit such workers through the language and networks of family reunification. The effect of creating economic pull factors that recruit immigrants to the United States while using bureaucratic categories like 'family reunification' to code that migration as essentially produced by the petitioning activity of resident immigrants living in the United States is to enable the appeasement of capital's need for immigrant workers" (p. 109). Though writing about New York City, Reddy's point that the distinction between family-based and labor migration is somewhat overstated holds true more broadly.

7 The term "middle class" is more of a political signifier than a self-evident, definable demographic category. As Bhatt, Murty, and Ramamurthy have argued, "the middle class is an idea, an assemblage, that was inherited with other colonial baggage and came to be inhabited by those who saw their role as the shapers of national historical destiny and national modernity." Amy Bhatt, Murty Madhavi, and Ramamurthy Priti, "Hegemonic Developments: The New Indian Middle Class, Gendered Subalterns, and Diasporic Returnees in the Event of Neoliberalism,"

Signs 36, no. 1 (2010): 128. Middle class as a category is often used to flatten individual differences and access to different resources and sources of power in South Asia. For immigrants to the United States, this attachment to a middle-class identity is not surprising because it is this very cultural capital that has facilitated their adjustment in a country where they are marked as racial, ethnic, and often religious outsiders.

8   Herbert J. Gans, "First Generation Decline: Downward Mobility among Refugees and Immigrants," *Ethnic and Racial Studies* 32, no. 9 (2009): 1658.

9   Bharti Kirchner, *Shiva Dancing* (New York: Dutton, 1998).

10 Bharti Kirchner, *Pastries: A Novel of Desserts and Discoveries* (New York: St. Martin's Press, 2003).

11 Pramila Jayapal, *Pilgrimage: One Woman's Return to a Changing India* (Seattle, WA: Seal Press, 2000).

12 Akshaya Mukul, "36% of Scientists at NASA Are Indians: Govt Survey," *Times of India*, March 11, 2008, http://timesofindia.indiatimes.com/articleshow/2853178.cms (accessed June 7, 2010).

5. FALLING FROM THE TREE

1   McClintock et al. argue that "home" is often conceived as a set of material, communal, and emotional securities which is revered as a stable site, free of dissonance between desire and place. They argue that instead of valorizing the home as a space untouched by the difficulties of "public" life, building or losing home is a recurring theme of modernity and must be read as a site of contention and reinvention. This compelling argument has implications for our project, in which home as a site of conflict and cultural reinvention, and particularly women's roles within the home, take on great significance in our narrators' stories. See Anne McClintock, Aamir Mufti, Ella Shohat, and Social Text Collective, eds., *Dangerous Liaisons: Gender, Nation, and Postcolonial Perspectives* (Minneapolis: University of Minnesota Press, 1997).

2   Writing about Indian immigrant communities living in the United States, Anannya Bhattacharjee argues, "The site for preservation of India, its culture, and its tradition is the family—the domestic space in which the figure of the woman stands. On the other hand, the site for economic/political advancement in the United States is the workplace, the legislature—the public space in which the figure of the man stands. This binary continues to work even for women who work outside the home, as the home still remains a place to affirm one's Indian-ness and the Indian woman is expected to be responsible for maintaining this Indian home in diaspora by remaining true to her Indian womanhood." Her observation holds

true in the stories related by the narrators profiled in this book. While the family is a contested space, it is often the responsibility of women to ensure that the proper customs are followed and passed on to the next generation. "The Habit of Ex-Nomination: Nation, Woman, and the Indian Immigrant Bourgeoisie," *Public Culture* 5, no. 1 (1992): 31. For additional studies on the South Asian immigrant family and cultural preservation, see also Avatar Brah, *Cartographies of Diaspora: Contesting Identities* (New York: Routledge, 1996); Shamita Das Dasgupta, ed., *A Patchwork Shawl: Chronicles of South Asian Women in America* (New Brunswick, NJ: Rutgers University Press, 1998); Sangeeta Gupta, ed., *Emerging Voices: South Asian American Women Redefine Self, Family, and Community* (Walnut Creek, CA: AltaMira Press, 1999).

3   The term "care work," or reproductive labor, is often used to describe the work done to reproduce the daily conditions of life within the family. It involves work that is often unpaid and associated with the household, such as cooking, cleaning, and taking care of others. See also Evelyn Nakano Glenn, *Forced to Care: Coercion and Caregiving in America* (Cambridge, MA: Harvard University Press, 2010); Paula England, "Emerging Theories in Care Work," *Annual Review of Sociology* 31, no. 1 (2005): 381–99; Nancy Folbre, *The Invisible Heart: Economics and Family Values* (New York: New Press, 2001); Nancy Folbre, *The Economics of the Family* (Cheltenham, UK: E. Elgar Publications, 1996).

4   Ramah McKay, "US in Focus: Family Reunification," Migration Information Source, 2003, http://www.migrationinformation.org/Feature/display.cfm?ID=122 (accessed May 12, 2010).

5   The critical acclaim of the movie *Monsoon Wedding* by Mira Nair in the United States (the film was nominated for a Golden Globe Award in 2001) speaks to the fascination with the elaborate and colorful Hindu wedding rituals that are reenacted both in South Asia and abroad. The film follows a Punjabi family as they prepare for the wedding of Aditi, the daughter of the family patriarch, Lalit. Aditi's marriage is arranged by her father and she agrees to the wedding even though she is having an affair with her married ex-boss. The spectacle of the elaborate wedding with lavish clothes, sparkling jewelry, sexy dance numbers, and beauti-ful decorations has come to represent what marriage looks like for South Asians, particularly those from India. However, the film also alludes to the darker aspects of marriage and family life: Aditi is a willing but very confused bride who doesn't know how to balance her desires with her parents', while her cousin Ria struggles with the dark secret of abuse. The film has received such wide public acclaim in part because it breaks with the easy façade that marriage is a panacea and reveals it to be a much more complicated relationship. At the same time, the film was wildly popular among diasporic audiences who relished the portrayal of marriage, family, and love that are presumed to define the South Asian community.

6   *India Abroad*, matrimonial advertisements, December 25, 2009, A53.

7   Ibid., A54.

8   In her book, *Speaking the Unspeakable: Marital Violence against South Asian Immigrants in the United States* (New Brunswick, NJ: Rutgers University Press, 2000), Margaret Abraham argues that domestic violence is a difficult subject for the South Asian community to address. She notes that "domestic patriarchy has been assumed by the mainstream immigrant community and has not been an issue for public discussion. While women were responsible for the home, men still assumed greater power and control within it. To talk of marital violence within the community was to shatter the social construction of the community's image, challenge domestic patriarchy, and threaten the moral solidarity of community—a moral solidarity frequently reflected in the rhetoric of the collective and religious practices of the community" (12).

9   Ibid.

10 The North Carolina–based organization Kiran reports that in the United States, roughly 31 percent of women experience domestic violence at some point in their lifetime. According to Kiran and other organizations, as a group, South Asian women living in the United States report a similar rate of violence. As of 2011, there are approximately forty organizations dedicated to ending family violence in South Asian communities. See Kiran, http://kiraninc.org/sadvorganizations.aspx (accessed June 22, 2010).

11 According to Chaya's informational materials, the organization responded to 1,100 calls on its helpline in 2009 and served an average of twenty survivors every month. Chaya notes that 38 percent of its clients are recent immigrants and 53 percent of them have children.

12 Mira Kamdar, *Motiba's Tattoos: A Granddaughter's Journey into Her Indian Family's Past* (New York: Public Affairs, 2000), 226.

13 Ibid., 227.

14 "Mama-ji" or "mama" is a term for maternal uncle in several Indian languages, including Marathi, which Shaila Kode speaks.

6. SEEDS TAKE ROOT

1   The importance of community institutions has been documented in several studies and collections examining South Asian community formation in the West. See Crispin Bates, *Community, Empire, and Migration: South Asians in Diaspora* (New York: Palgrave, 2001); Sangeeta Gupta, ed., *Emerging Voices: South Asian American Women Redefine Self, Family, and Community* (Walnut Creek: AltaMira Press, 1999); Nirmal Puwar and Parvati Raghuram, eds., *South Asian Women in the*

Diaspora (New York: Berg, 2003); Aparna Rayaprol, *Negotiating Identities: Women in the Indian Diaspora* (New York: Oxford University Press, 1997).

2   While S. Mitra Kalita's book is focused on the growth of the Indian community in New Jersey, many of her observations map onto the growth of the South Asian community in the Pacific Northwest. She notes: "In the 1970s and 1980s, Indians were widely scattered; often there would be only one or two Indian families—who might also be the only people of color—in an entire neighborhood or town." However, by the 2000s, towns and cities across the United States had been transformed by the presence of large South Asian communities. See S. Mitra Kalita, *Suburban Sahibs: Three Immigrant Families and Their Passage from India to America* (New Brunswick, NJ: Rutgers University Press, 2003), 11.

3   Sara Ahmed et al. note the importance of home in fashioning immigrant imaginaries: "Being at home and the work of home-building is intimately bound up with the *idea* of home: the idea of a place (or places) in the past, and of *this* place in the future. Making home is about *creating* both pasts and futures through inhabiting the grounds of the present." See Sara Ahmed, Claudia Castaneda, Anne-Marie Fortier, and Mimi Sheller, "Introduction: Uprootings/Regroundings: Questions of Home and Migration," in *Uprootings/Regroundings: Questions of Home and Migration*, edited by Sara Ahmed, Claudia Castaneda, Anne-Marie Fortier, and Mimi Sheller (New York: Berg Publishers, 2003), 9.

4   Writing about the Indian community, Ananya Bhattacharjee argues that "the home still remains a place to affirm one's Indian-ness, and the Indian woman is expected to be responsible for maintaining this Indian home in diaspora by remaining true to her Indian womanhood." See "The Habit of Ex-Nomination: Nation, Woman, and the Indian Immigrant Bourgeoisie," *Public Culture* 5, no. 1 (1992): 32.

5   In 2011, Chaya merged with the Asian and Pacific Islander Women and Family Safety Center to provide services to a larger group of women and also to enable both organizations to be economically sustainable in a time of government cutbacks.

6   Trikone-Northwest, "About Us," http://trikonenw.org/ (accessed June 8, 2010).

7   Though Sikhs were not involved in the attacks of September 11, 2001, their traditional turbans have led them to be confused with Muslims originating from parts of the Middle East who wear similar garb and have been associated with the event. Days after September 11, a Sikh gas station owner was shot and killed in Arizona by a white American man who was taken into custody shouting "I am a patriot." Since then, there have been several attacks in various parts of the country.

8   Tara Bahrampour and Pamela Constable, "For Many Pakistanis, U.S. No Longer Land of Opportunity," *Seattle Times*, May 24, 2010, http://seattletimes.nwsource.com/html/nationworld/2011945451_uspak25.html (accessed May 26, 2010).

9   Vijay Prashad, *The Karma of Brown Folk* (Minneapolis: University of Minnesota Press, 2000), xi.

10   Thomas Turino and James Lea, *Identity and the Arts in Diaspora Communities* (Warren, MI: Harmonie Park Press, 2004), 4.

11   Rajinder Dudrah argues that "an ethnic mediascape, such as Bollywood, offers an audiovisual site where ideas of the homeland can be translated and negotiated in the places of diasporic settlement . . . the diasporic imaginary becomes part of the everyday of diasporic subjects, as the sounds and images of mediascapes are integrated into the routines and rituals of daily life, as well as the struggles for settlement and belonging." See "Queer as Desis: Secret Politics of Gender and Sexuality in Bollywood Films in Diasporic Urban Ethnoscapes," in *Global Bollywood: Travels of Hindi Song and Dance*, eds. Sangita Gopal and Sujata Moorti (Minneapolis: University of Minnesota Press, 2008): 291.

12   These art forms, although supported by a predominantly South Indian upper caste community in India, have become an important site of community mobilization and gathering across the South Indian immigrant community in North America. For an analysis of the postcolonial politics of nationalism in the institutions and practices of Carnatic music, see Amanda J. Weidman, *Singing the Classical, Voicing the Modern: The Postcolonial Politics of Music in South India* (Durham, NC: Duke University Press, 2006).

13   *The Vagina Monologues* is a production that was first staged by Eve Ensler in 1996. It has subsequently been staged around the world, often as part of efforts to raise awareness about violence against women. In 2003, the South Asian Sisters, an organization of women in the San Francisco area, came together to create a script and performance based on *The Vagina Monologues*. Today, the performance is known as *Yoni Ki Baat* and has been performed all over the United States, continuing to raise money for ending violence.

14   Figures on Hindu and Sikh temples come from Garamchai.com, which is an online portal catering to non-resident Indians living abroad that tracks information about various religious institutions that cater to these communities. See "Hindu Temples in the North West US: For Indians and NRIs in America" at http://www.garamchai.com/. Figures on Washington State mosques come from the University of Washington's Muslim Students Association resource guide. See "Resources," http://www.msauw.org/resources.htm#MOSQUES (accessed January 1, 2009).

15   Sheba Mariam George, *When Women Come First: Gender and Class in Transnational Migration* (Berkeley: University of California Press, 2005).

16   Aparna Rayaprol, *Negotiating Identities: Women in the Indian Diaspora* (New York: Oxford University Press, 1997).

17 Benedict Anderson, *Imagined Communities: Reflections on the Origin and Spread of Nationalism* (New York: Verso, 1991).

18 Arjun Appadurai, *Modernity at Large: Cultural Dimensions of Globalization* (Minneapolis: University of Minnesota Press, 1996).

19 Sarah Stuteville, "Pakistani Immigrants in Seattle Confront a Huge Challenge at Home," *Seattle Times*, August 17, 2009.

20 South Asia Center, University of Washington, "Development, Diaspora and the Next Generation," http://www.uwsouthasiadev.org/ (accessed June 8, 2010).

21 After leaving Microsoft, Rao Remala started the Rao and Satya Remala Foundation, which works on development issues in his home state of Andhra Pradesh.

EPILOGUE

1 Jennifer Scanlon, "Challenging the Imbalances of Power in Feminist Oral History: Developing a Take-and-Give Methodology," *Women Studies International Forum* 16, no. 6 (1993): 639.

2 Please see the appendices for the full bibliography of the oral history interviews cited in the book and biographical information about the narrators.

3 Alice Yang Murray, "Oral History Research, Theory, and Asian American Studies," *Amerasia Journal* 26, no. 1 (2000): 105–18.

4. Ibid., 113.

5 For Murray, this revelation requires taking seriously the insights of post-modern critics who argue that all language is representative and repetitive, and rarely simply reflective of an authentic truth.

6 Paula Hamilton and Linda Shopes, *Oral History and Public Memories* (Philadelphia: Temple University Press, 2008), xi.

7 The *We the People* report published by the U.S. Government's Census Bureau demonstrates the economic advancement of immigrants and U.S.-born members of the South Asian community. See Terrance Reeves and Claudette Bennett, *We the People: Asians in the United States* (Washington, D.C.: U.S Bureau of the Census, 2000), 1–20.

8 David M. Halbfinger, "Our Towns; Bangladeshis Hold Suburban Dream Together, without Buttons," *New York Times*, March 3, 2002, http://www.nytimes.com/2002/03/03/nyregion/our-towns-bangladeshis-hold-suburban-dream-together-without-buttons.html?ref=david_m_halbfinger (accessed June 12, 2010).

9 Joan W. Scott, "The Evidence of Experience," *Critical Inquiry* 17, no. 4 (1991): 780.

10 Valerie Raleigh Yow, *Recording Oral History: A Guide for the Humanities and Social Sciences* (Walnut Creek, CA: AltaMira Press, 2005), 121.

11 The history of English as a legacy of colonialism in South Asia is well documented, and it has often been seen as the language of the public sphere in contrast to indigenous languages, which are aligned with private or intimate spaces. For a detailed discussion about the relationship between English and indigenous languages in India see Bonnie Zare and Nalini Iyer, "Introduction: Problematizing Indian Literary Canons," in *Other Tongues: Rethinking the Language Debates in India*, ed. Nalini Iyer and Bonnie Zare (Amsterdam: Rodopi, 2009), ix–xxxvii.

12 See Amy Bhatt, "At Home in Globalization: Social Reproduction, Transnational Migration and the Circulating Indian Household" (Ph.D. diss., University of Washington, 2011), for a longer look at contemporary communities of South Asian H-1B workers living in the Pacific Northwest.

13 Many anthologies of Asian American literature and other studies that were developed in the 1970s, such as Frank Chin's edited volume *Aiiieeeee!*, did not include South Asians as part of the discussion of "Asian America." Later anthologies since the 1990s like Jessica Hagedorn's *Charlie Chan Is Dead* and Jean Yu-Wen Shen Wu and Thomas Chan's *Asian American Studies Now* include pieces by South Asian writers and academics.

REFERENCES

Abdullah, Ahsan. "Pakistan since Independence: A Historical Analysis." *Muslim World* 9 (2003): 351–72.

Abraham, Margaret. *Speaking the Unspeakable: Marital Violence among South Asian Immigrants in the United States*. New Brunswick, NJ: Rutgers University Press, 2000.

"Admissions Offers for Foreign Students at U.S. Graduate Schools Climbs at a Faster Pace." *Chronicle of Higher Education*, August 16, 2011.

Agarwal, Priya. *Passage from India: Post 1965 Indian Immigrants and Their Children*. New Delhi: Yuvati, 1991.

Ahmed, Sara, Claudia Castaneda, Anne-Marie Fortier, and Mimi Sheller, eds. *Uprootings/Regroundings: Questions of Home and Migration*. New York: Berg Publishers, 2003.

Allied Media Corporation. "South Asian Demographics." http://www.allied-media.com/southasian/south%20asian%20demographics.html.

Altbach, Philip, G. Denzil Saldanha, and Jeanne Drysdale Weiler. *Education in South Asia: A Select Annotated Bibliography*. New York: Garland, 1987.

Amrute, Sareeta. "The 'New' Nonresidents of India: A Short History of the NRI." In *A New India? Critical Reflections on a Long Twentieth Century*, edited by Anthony D'Costa, 127–50. London: Anthem Press, 2010.

Anderson, Benedict. *Imagined Communities: Reflections on the Origin and Spread of Nationalism*. Rev. and extended edition. New York: Verso, 1991.

Anderson, Erika S. *Turbans*. Film. Different Drum Productions, 2000.

Anderson, Wanni A., and Robert G. Lee. "Asian American Displacements." In *Displacements and Diasporas: Asians in the Americas*, edited by Wanni W. Anderson and Robert G. Lee, 3–22. New Brunswick, NJ: Rutgers University Press, 2005.

Appadurai, Arjun. "How to Make a National Cuisine: Cookbooks in Contemporary India." *Comparative Studies in Society and History* 30 (1988): 3–24.

———. *Modernity at Large: Cultural Dimensions of Globalization*. Minneapolis: University of Minnesota Press, 1996.

"Asian American Curriculum and Research Project." University of Western Washington. Woodring College of Education. http://www.wce.wwu.edu/Resources/AACR.

Badruddin, Umar. *Language Movement in East Bengal*. Dhaka: Jatiya Grontha Prakashan, 2000.

Bahrampour, Tara, and Pamela Constable. "For Many Pakistanis, U.S. No Longer Land of Opportunity." *Seattle Times*, May 27, 2010. http://seattletimes.nwsource.com/html/nationworld/2011945451_uspak25.html.

Barlow, Tani. "Founding Positions." *Postcolonial Studies* 3, no. 1 (1999): 19–29.

Bates, Crispin. *Community, Empire, and Migration: South Asians in Diaspora*. New York: Palgrave, 2001.

Bevis, Teresa Brawner, and Christopher J. Lucas. *International Students in American Colleges and Universities: A History*. New York: Palgrave/Macmillan, 2007.

Bhatia, S. *American Karma: Race, Culture, and Identity in the Indian Diaspora*. New York: New York University Press, 2007.

Bhatt, Amy. "At Home in Globalization: Social Reproduction, Transnational Migration and the Circulating Indian Household." Ph.D. diss., University of Washington, 2011.

Bhatt, Amy, Madhavi Murty, and Priti Ramamurthy. "Hegemonic Developments: New Indian Middle Class, Gendered Subalterns, and Diasporic Returnees in the Event of Neoliberalism." *Signs: Journal of Women in Culture and Society* 36, no. 1 (2010): 127–52.

Bhattacharjee, Anannya. "The Habit of Ex-Nomination: Nation, Woman, and the Indian Immigrant Bourgeoisie." *Public Culture* 5, no. 1 (1992): 19–44.

Brah, Avatar. *Cartographies of Diaspora: Contesting Identities*. New York: Routledge, 1996.

Breckenridge, Carol, Sheldon Pollock, Homi K. Bhabha, and Dipesh Chakrabarty, eds. *Cosmopolitanism*. Durham, NC: Duke University Press, 2002.

Burki, Shahid Javed, and Subramanian Swamy. "South Asian Migration to the United States: Demand and Supply Factors." *Economic and Political Weekly*, March 21, 1987, 513–17.

Butalia, Urvashi. *The Other Side of Silence*. Durham, NC: Duke University Press, 1998.

Canadian Broadcasting Corporation. "Tamil Migrants Are Legitimate Refugees: Lawyer." *CBC News*, October 22, 2009.

Crook, Nigel. *The Transmission of Knowledge in South Asia: Essays on Education, Religion, History, and Politics*. Delhi: Oxford University Press, 1996.

Dasgupta, Shamita Das, ed. *A Patchwork Shawl: Chronicles of South Asian Women in America*. New Brunswick, NJ: Rutgers University Press, 1998.

Deb, Sandipan. *The IITians: The Story of a Remarkable Indian Institution and How Its Alumni Are Reshaping the World*. New Delhi: Viking/Penguin, 2003.

Dhillon, Kartar. "Astoria Revisited and Autobiographical Notes." http://www.sikhpioneers.org/P1astoria.html.

———. "The Parrot's Beak." In *Growing Up Asian American: Stories of Childhood, Adolescence and Coming of Age in America, from the 1800s to the 1900s by 32 Asian American Writers*, edited by Amy Tan et al., 275–84. New York: Avon Books, 1993.

Dhillon, Kartar, and Ayesha Gill. "Witness to the Gadar Era." http://www.sikhpioneers.org/p5witne.htm.

Discovery Bangladesh. "Meet Bangladesh." http://www.discoverybangladesh.com/meetbangladesh/education.html.

Dudrah, Rajinder. "Queer as Desis: Secret Politics of Gender and Sexuality in Bollywood Films in Diasporic Urban Ethnoscapes." In *Global Bollywood: Travels of Hindi Song and Dance*, edited by Sangita Gopal and Sujata Moorti, 288–307. Minneapolis: University of Minnesota Press, 2008.

"Echoes of Freedom: South Asian Pioneers in California, 1899–1965." Center for South Asia Studies, University of California at Berkeley. http://www.lib.berkeley.edu/SSEAL/echoes/echoes.html.

England, Paula. "Emerging Theories in Care Work." *Annual Review of Sociology* 31, no. 1 (2005): 381–99.

Fernandes, Leela. *India's New Middle Class: Democratic Politics in an Era of Economic Reform*. Minneapolis: University of Minnesota Press, 2006.

Folbre, Nancy. *The Economics of the Family*. Cheltenham, UK: E. Elgar Publications, 1996.

———. *The Invisible Heart: Economics and Family Values*. New York: New Press, 2001.

Free Hindusthan. In "New, Thinking, Agile, and Patriotic: 'Hindu' Students at the University of Washington 1900–1918." http://www.lib.washington.edu/exhibits/southasianstudents/primary.html.

Gans, Herbert J. "First Generation Decline: Downward Mobility among Refugees and Immigrants." *Ethnic and Racial Studies* 32, no. 9 (2009): 1658–70.

GaramChai. "Hindu Temples in the North West US: For Indians and NRIs in America 2009." http://www.garamchai.com.

George, Sheba Mariam. *When Women Come First: Gender and Class in Transnational Migration*. Berkeley: University of California Press, 2005.

Gibson, Campbell, and Kay Jung. *Historical Census Statistics on Population Totals by Race, 1790 to 1990, and by Hispanic Origin, 1970 to 1990, for the United States, Regions, Divisions, and States*. Washington, D.C.: U.S. Census Bureau, 2002.

Glenn, Evelyn Nakano. *Forced to Care: Coercion and Caregiving in America*. Cambridge, MA: Harvard University Press, 2010.

Gould, Harold A. *Sikhs, Swamis, Students, and Spies: The India Lobby in the United States, 1900–1946*. Thousand Oaks, CA: Sage, 2006.

Gupta, Sangeeta, ed. *Emerging Voices: South Asian Women Redefine Self, Family, and Community*. Walnut Creek, CA: AltaMira Press, 1999.

Hajratwala, Minal. *Leaving India: My Family's Journey from Five Villages to Five Continents*. Boston: Houghton Mifflin/Harcourt, 2009.

Halbfinger, David M. "Our Towns: Bangladeshis Hold Suburban Dream Together, without Buttons." *New York Times*, March 3, 2002. http://topics.nytimes.com/topics/reference/timestopics/people/h/david_m_halbfinger/index.htmlmatch=any&query=bangladeshis&submit.x=4&submit.y=14.

Hamilton, Paula, and Linda Shopes. *Oral History and Public Memories: Critical Perspectives on the Past*. Philadelphia: Temple University Press, 2008.

Hasan, Mushirul. *India's Partition: Process, Strategies, and Mobilization*. New Delhi: Oxford University Press, 2001.

Hazen, Helen, and Heike Albers. "Visitor or Immigrant? International Students in the US." *Population, Space and Place* 12 (2006): 201–16.

Hess, Gary R. "The 'Hindu' in America: Immigration and Naturalization Policies and India, 1917–1946." *Pacific Historical Review* 38, no. 1 (1969): 59–79.

Hoffa, William W. *A History of US Study Abroad: Beginnings to 1965.* [Carlisle, PA]: Forum on Education Abroad, 2000.

Imam, Syeda Rumnaz. "English as a Global Language and the Question of Nation-building Education in Bangladesh." *Comparative Education* 41, no. 4 (2005): 471–86.

Institute for International Education. "Open Doors Online Report on International Education Exchange." http://www.opendoors.iienetwork.org.

Jayapal, Pramila. *Pilgrimage: One Woman's Return to a Changing India.* Seattle: Seal Press, 2000.

Jeffrey, Craig, Patricia Jeffery, and Roger Jeffery. *Degrees without Freedom? Education, Masculinities, and Unemployment in North India.* Stanford, CA: Stanford University Press, 2008.

Jensen, Joan M. *A Passage from India: Asian Indian Immigrants in North America.* New Haven, CT: Yale University Press, 1988.

Jones, Nard. *Seattle.* Garden City, NY: Doubleday, 1972.

Kalita, S. Mitra. *Suburban Sahibs: Three Immigrant Families and Their Passage from India to America.* New Brunswick, NJ: Rutgers University Press, 2003.

Kamat, Sangeeta, Ali Mir, and Biju Mathew. "Producing Hi-Tech: Globalization, the State and Migrant Subjects." *Globalisation, Societies, and Education* 2, no. 1 (2004): 5–23.

Kamdar, Mira. *Motiba's Tattoos: A Grandaughter's Journey into Her Indian Family's Past.* New York: Public Affairs, 2000.

Kazimi, Ali. *Continuous Journey.* Film. Ontario: Peripheral Visions, 2004.

Khadria, Binod. "Migration of Human Capital to the United States." *Economic and Political Weekly*, August 11, 1990. 1784–87, 1789–94.

———. *The Migration of Knowledge Workers: Second Generation Effects of India's Brain Drain.* Thousand Oaks, CA: Sage Publications, 1999.

Khalid, Salim Mansur, and M. Fayyaz Khan. "Pakistan: State of Education." *Muslim World* 96 (2006): 305–22.

Khandelwal, Madhulika S. *Becoming American, Being Indian: An Immigrant Community in New York City.* Ithaca, NY: Cornell University Press, 2002.

Kirchner, Bharti. *Pastries: A Novel of Desserts and Discoveries.* New York: St. Martin's Press, 2003.

———. *Shiva Dancing.* New York: Dutton, 1998.

Lahiri, Jhumpa. *The Namesake.* Boston: Houghton Mifflin, 2003.

Latif, Amna. "A Critical Analysis of School Enrollment and Literacy Rates of Girls and Women in Pakistan." *Educational Studies* 45 (2009): 424–39.

Lee, Erika, and Judy Yung. *Angel Island: Immigrant Gateway to America.* Oxford: Oxford University Press, 2010, 145–76.

Leonard, Karen B. *Making Ethnic Choices: California's Punjabi Mexicans.* Philadelphia: Temple University Press, 1992.

———. *The South Asian Americans.* Westport, CT: Greenwood Press, 1997.

Ling, Huping. *Voices of the Heart: Asian American Women on Immigration, Work, and Family.* Kirksville, MO: Truman State University Press, 2007.Macaulay, Thomas Babington. "Minute on Indian Education, February 2, 1835." In *Postcolonialisms: Anthology of Cultural Theory and Criticism*, edited by Gaurav Desai and Surpiya Nair, 121–31. New Brunswick, NJ: Rutgers University Press, 2005.

Maira, Sunaina. *Desis in the House: Indian American Youth Culture in New York City.* Philadelphia: Temple University Press, 2002.

McClintock, Anne, Aamir Mufti, Ella Shohat, and Social Text Collective, eds. *Dangerous Liaisons: Gender, Nation, and Postcolonial Perspectives.* Minneapolis: University of Minnesota Press, 1997.

McKay, Ramah. "US in Focus: Family Reunification." Migration Information Source, 2003. http://www.migrationinformation.org/Feature/display.cfm?ID=122.

Misrow, Jogesh C. "East Indian Immigration on the Pacific Coast." Master's thesis, Stanford University, 1915.

MPI. "Migration Information Source: Fresh Thought, Authoritative Data, Global Reach." http://www.migrationinformation.org.

Mukherjee, Tapan, K. *Taraknath Das: Life and Letters of a Revolutionary in Exile.* Calcutta: National Council for Education, Jadavpur University, 1997.

Mukul, Akshaya. "36% of Scientists at NASA Are Indians: Govt Survey." *Times of India.* March 11, 2008. http://timesofindia.indiatimes.com/articleshow/2853178.cms.

Murray, Alice Yang. "Oral History Research, Theory, and Asian American Studies." *Amerasia Journal* 26, no. 1 (2000): 105–18.

Muslim Students Association of the University of Washington. "Resources," 2010. http://www.msauw.org/resources.htm#MOSQUES.

Nagar, Richa, and Amanda Lock Swarr. "Introduction: Theorizing Transnational Feminist Praxis." In *Critical Transnational Feminist Praxis*, ed. Amanda Lock Swarr and Richa Nagar. Albany: State University of New York Press, 2009.

Nagel, Joanne. "Constructing Ethnicity: Creating and Recreating Ethnic Identity and Culture." *Social Problems* 41, no. 1 (1994): 152–76.

Nair, Mira. *Mississippi Masala.* Nova Scotia: Black River Productions, 1991.

———. *Monsoon Wedding.* New York: Mirabai Films, 2005.

Natarajan, Nalini. "South Asian Area Studies in Transatlantic Dialogue." *Comparative Studies of South Asia, Africa, and the Middle East* 27, no. 3 (2007): 591–600.

Nehru, Jawaharlal. *The Essential Writings of Jawaharlal Nehru, Volume II*, edited by S. Gopal and Uma Iyengar. New Delhi: Oxford University Press, 2003.

"New, Thinking, Agile, and Patriotic: 'Hindu' Students at the University of Washington, 1908–1915." University of Washington Libraries. http://www.lib.washington.edu/exhibits/southasianstudents/index.html.

"The 1907 Bellingham Riots in Historical Context." Seattle Civil Rights and Labor History Project. University of Washington. http://depts.washington.edu/civilr/bham_history.htm.

"Northwest Heritage Resources." http://www.northwestheritageresources.org/Essays/Indian_American_essay.pdf.

"100 Years after Riot Coverage: Our Apology." *Bellingham Herald*, September 2, 2007. http://www.bellinghamherald.com/315/v-print/story/169787.html.

Oulette, Dan. "South Asians' Growing American Clout." *Adweek*. http://www.adweek.com/aw/content_display/special-reports/other- reports/e3i5e732e045deaaba3b04b8fd2ebbf81aa?pn=1.

Pandey, Gyanendra. *Remembering Partition: Violence, Nationalism, and History in India*. Cambridge: Cambridge University Press, 2002.

Pandurang, Mala. "Conceptualizing *Emigrant* Indian Female Subjectivity: Possible Entry Points." In *South Asian Women in the Diaspora*, edited by Nirmal Puwar and Parvati Raghuram, 87–98. New York: Berg, 2003.

Prashad, Vijay. *The Karma of Brown Folk*. Minneapolis: University of Minnesota Press, 2000.

Present in All That We Do. Film. Seattle Civil Rights and Labor History Project, University of Washington. http://depts.washington.edu/civilr/bham_history.htm.

Purkayastha, Bandana. *Negotiating Ethnicity: Second-Generation South Asian Americans Traverse a Transnational World*. New Brunswick, NJ: Rutgers University Press, 2005.

Puwar, Nirmal, and Parvati Raghuram, eds. *South Asian Women in the Diaspora*. New York: Berg, 2003.

Ramnath, Maia. "Two Revolutions: The Ghadar Movement and India's Radical Diaspora, 1913–1918." *Radical History Review* 92 (Spring 2005): 7–30.

Ray, Krishnendu. *The Migrant's Table: Meals and Memories in Bengali-American Households*. Philadelphia: Temple University Press, 2004.

Rayaprol, Aparna. *Negotiating Identities: Women in the Indian Diaspora*. New York: Oxford University Press, 1997.

Reddy, Chandan. "Asian Diasporas, Neoliberalism, and Family: Reviewing the Case for Homosexual Asylum in the Context of Family Rights." *Social Text* 23, no. 2 (2005): 101–20.

Reeves, Terrance, and Claudette Bennett. *We the People: Asians in the United States*. U.S. Bureau of the Census: Washington, D.C., 2000.

Rudrappa, Sharmila. "Braceros and Techno-Braceros: Guest Workers in the United States and the Commodification of Low-Wage and High-Wage Labour." In *Transnational South Asians: The Making of a Neo-Diaspora*, edited by Susan Koshy and R. Radhakrishnan, 291–324. New York: Oxford University Press, 2008.

Rushdie, Salman. "Imaginary Homelands." In *Imaginary Homelands: Essays and Criticism 1981–1991*, 9–21. London: Granta Books, 1991.

———. *Midnight's Children*. New York: Knopf, 1981.

———. *The Satanic Verses*. New York: Viking, 1988.

Rydell, Robert. "The Expositions in Portland and Seattle." In Rydell, *All the World's a Fair: Visions of Empire at American International Expositions, 1876–1916*, 184–207. Chicago: University of Chicago Press, 1984.

Rydell, Robert W., John E. Findling, and Kimberly Pelle. *Fair America: World's Fairs in the United States*. Washington, D.C.: Smithsonian Institution Press, 2000.

Satyadeva Parivrajak. "A Glimpse of America." Translated by Raj Joshi. Manuscript.

Scanlon, Jennifer. "Challenging the Imbalances of Power in Feminist Oral History: Developing a Take-and-Give Methodology." *Women Studies International Forum* 16, no. 6 (1993): 639–45.

Scott, Joan W. "The Evidence of Experience." *Critical Inquiry* 17, no. 4 (1991): 773–97.

Shamim, Fauzia. "Trends, Issues and Challenges in English Language Education in Pakistan." *Asia Pacific Journal of Education* 28, no. 3 (2008): 235–49.

Shukla, Sandhya Rajendra. *India Abroad: Diasporic Cultures of Postwar America and England*. Princeton, NJ: Princeton University Press, 2002.

Srikanth, Rajini. *The World Next Door: South Asian Literature and the Idea of America*. Philadelphia: Temple University Press, 2005.

South Asia Center, University of Washington. "Development, Diaspora and the Next Generation," South Asia Center. http://www.uwsouthasiadev.org.

Stuteville, Sarah. "Pakistani Immigrants in Seattle Confront a Huge Challenge at Home." *Seattle Times*, August 17, 2009.

Takaki, Ronald. *Strangers from a Different Shore: A History of Asian Americans*. New York: Penguin, 1989.

Takemoto, Kenneth Kaname, Paul Howard Takemoto, and Alice Takemoto. *Nisei Memories: My Parents Talk about the War Years*. Seattle: University of Washington Press, 2006.

Turino, Thomas, and James Lea. *Identity and the Arts in Diaspora Communities*. Detroit Monographs in Musicology/Studies in Music, no. 40. Warren, MI: Harmonie Park Press, 2004.

U.S. Citizenship and Immigration Services. Department of Homeland Security. "H1-B Specialty Occupations, DOD Cooperative Research and Development Project Workers, and Fashion Models." http://www.uscis.gov/portal/site/uscis/menuitem.eb1d4c2a3e5b9ac89243c6a7543f6d1a/?vgnextoid=73566811264a3210VgnVCM1000oob92ca60aRCRD&vgnextchannel=73566811264a3210VgnVCM100000b92ca60aRCRD.

Usdansky, Margaret L., and Thomas J. Espenshade. *The H-1B Visa Debate in Historical Perspective: The Evolution of U.S. Policy toward Foreign-Born Workers*. San Diego, CA: Center for Comparative Immigration Studies, 2000.

Vaish, Viniti. *Biliteracy and Globalization: English Language Education in India*. Clevedon, UK: Multilingual Matters, 2008.

Vassanji, M. G. *The In-Between World of Vikram Lall*. New York: Knopf, 2004.

Vatuk, Ved Prakash, and Sylvia Vatuk. "Protest Songs of East Indians on the West Coast, U.S.A." In *Thieves in My House: Four Studies in Indian Folklore of Protest and Change*, 63–80. Varanasi, India: Vishwavidyalaya Prakashan, 1969.

Wat, Eric C. *The Making of a Gay Asian Community: An Oral History of Pre-AIDS Los Angeles*. Lanham, MD: Rowman and Littlefield Publishers, 2002.

Weidman, Amanda. *Singing the Classical, Voicing the Modern: The Postcolonial Politics of Music in South India*. Durham, NC: Duke University Press, 2006.

"Who or What Is the Middle Class?" "Gut Check," msnbc.com. http://www.msnbc. msn.com/id/21272238/ns/us_news-gut_check/page/2.

Xiang, Biao. Global "Body Shopping": An Indian Labor System in the Information Technology Industry. In-Formation Series. Princeton, NJ: Princeton University Press, 2007.

Yow, Valerie Raleigh. Recording Oral History: A Guide for the Humanities and Social Sciences. Walnut Creek, CA: AltaMira Press, 2005.

Zakaria, Fareed. "India Rising." Newsweek, March 6, 2006, 32–42.

Zare, Bonnie S., and Nalini Iyer. "Introduction: Problematizing Indian Literary Canons." In Other Tongues: Rethinking the Language Debates in India, edited by Nalini Iyer and Bonnie Zare, ix–xxxvii. Amsterdam: Rodopi, 2009.

INDEX

A

Abraham, Margaret, 155, 249*n*8

acculturation processes. *See specific topics, e.g.,* community-building activity; gender roles; transition challenges

acknowledgments, xv–xvi, xxiv–xxvi

Aditi, in Nair's *Monsoon Wedding,* 248*n*5

aeronautics/aerospace industry, 63, 104–5, 116–17, 128–30

Agee, Joyce, xiv

Ahmed, Sara, 250*n*3

Ahmedi, Asgar: biography of, 221; college experiences, 57, 181–82; community-building activity, 190*f*; departure/arrival experience, 59–60; diet challenges, 72–73; with friends, 178*f*; homeland experiences, 50–51; marriages, 143, 145*f*, 146; migration incentives, 51–52, 56–57; with natal family, 52*f*; in Oral History Project, 4; work experiences, 110–11

Ahmedi, Norma, 145*f*

Air India, 129

airline attendant job, Samarawickrama's, 68

air travel, 59–60, 64–65, 69

Alaska Yukon Pacific Exposition (AYPE), 31–35

Albers, Heike, 245*n*24

Alpha Kappa Psi, 181

American Field Service program, 85–86

Ananda College, 85

Andersen, Erika Surat, 42–45

Anderson, Benedict, 199

Andhra Pradesh, India, 82, 87, 124, 252*n*21

anti-apartheid protests, 185*f*

anti-immigrant activity, U.S.: labor-based violence, 18–20, 23, 25–29; legislation, 16, 20, 21, 240*n*63; quotas/policy arguments, 21, 40. *See also* discrimination experiences

anti-immigrant policies, Britain, 63

Anusilan Samiti movement, 35, 239*n*44

Apna Bazaar, 175

Apollo space program, 116–17

Appadurai, Arjun, 242*n*9

Armstrong, Neil, 129

Army, U.S., 110, 154–55

Artist's Trust, 194

arts/cultural organizations/activities, 98, 189–95, 251*nn*11–13

Aryan identity, South Asian claims, 25, 28, 36, 237*n*15, 239*n*49

Aseshanda, Swami, 196*f*

Asha Seattle, 202

Ashima, in Lahiri's *The Namesake,* 10

Ashok, in Lahiri's *The Namesake,* 10

Asian and Pacific Islander Women and Family Safety Center, 157, 249*n*11, 250*n*5

"Asian Diasporas, Neoliberalism, and Family" (Reddy), 246*n*6

Asian Exclusion Acts, 16, 105

Asiatic Barred Zone, 21

Asiatic Exclusion League, 23

Michigan State University, 91, 99f
Microsoft: Badshah's experience, 127; charity policies, 186, 202–3; community-building role, 175; demographic changes, 74, 126–27; Remala's experience, 125–27; Vashee's experience, 127
middle class, defining, 108, 246n7
"midnight's children," 14, 235n9
The Migrant's Table (Ray), 242n9
migration incentives. *See* education *entries;* political conflicts; work opportunities
The Migration of Knowledge Workers (Khadra), 242n5
military service, 43, 110, 154–55
miners, Chinese, 29
miscegenation laws, 44, 143–44
Misrow, Jogesh, 30, 35, 37f, 40–41
mission schools, 78–79, 88
MOHAI (Museum of History and Industry), xiii
Monsoon Wedding (Nair), 248n5
Morgan, Norma, 143
Motiba's Tattoos (Kamdar), 157–58, 242n8
Mularky, Dr., 177–78
multilingualism: children of immigrants, 166–67, 183; political conflicts, 15, 235n13; South Asian schools, 79–82, 84–85, 87–88. *See also* English language
Mumbai: education experiences, 78–79, 108; Kode's family, 107–8, 161–62; Laly's experience, 61–62
Munshiram, 32–33
Murray, Alice Yang, 209–10, 252n5
Museum of History and Industry (MOHAI), xiii
music organizations, 191–92, 251n12
Muslim South Asians: religious activity, 197–99; September 11 impact, 187–88, 250n7. *See also* Ahmedi, Asgar; Nasar, Rizwan; Parpia, Zakir; Rahman, Jamal

N

Nagar, Richa, xvii
Nair, Mira, 248n5
The Namesake (Lahiri), 10–11
narrators, as knowledge producers, 11–12, 212, 234n3. *See also* oral histories; South Asian Oral History Project
NASA, 105, 116–17, 129
Nasar, Rizwan: biography of, 228; college experiences, 14, 91, 93f, 99f; on community, 172, 173; friendship network, 160; homeland experiences, 68–69, 87–88; homeland relief projects, 208; religious activity, 198–99; sister's sponsorship, 69, 106, 158
Nassar, Rizwan, 5
Natarajan, Nalini, 233n2
Nehru, Jawaharhal, 81–82, 86
Nepal, 241n2, 245n27
"New, Thinking, Agile, and Patriotic" (Di Biase), xii
New Jersey, 174–75, 250n2
New York City, 59, 211
New York Times, 211
nuclear industries, 116

O

Obama, Barack, 186–87
Olcott, Henry Steel, 85
One America, 122, 186–87, 208
"Open Doors" report, 90, 245n27
oral histories: collaboration approach, xvii–xviii, xxiii–xxiv; insight functions, 5–6, 9–12, 207–10, 217–18; limitations of, 11, 210–15, 252n5; terminology purposes, 212, 234n3
Oral History Project, South Asian (SAOHP), overview, xi–xv, xx–xxi, 4–5, 7–8, 207, 214–16, 219–20
Oregon: Dhillon family experience, 42–45; Gadar party formation, 29–30; Samarawickrama's experience, 14, 68, 85. *See also* Laly, Amy